M000217065

The son of a very wealthy and highly assimilated Jewish woman from Central Europe and a famous English literary intellectual whose homosexuality his wife never allowed herself to admit, David Pryce-Jones, now grown into a distinguished literary intellectual in his own right, has an extraordinary story to tell, and he tells it in endlessly fascinating detail.

NORMAN PODHORETZ
former longtime editor of *Commentary*
and author of several memoirs,
including *Making It* and *Ex-Friends*

One of the most passionate and beguiling books on inheritance since Gosse's *Father and Son*. This is a story of a family of almost unimaginable wealth and privilege, of an extraordinary life lived across literary and political worlds, and of a century backlit by war and trauma. It has a candour, a humour and a fierce intelligence that make it a powerful and remarkable book.

EDMUND DE WAAL
author of *The Hare With Amber Eyes*

David Pryce-Jones

Fault Lines

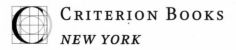
CRITERION BOOKS
NEW YORK

First American edition published in 2015 by Criterion Books, an activity of the Foundation for Cultural Review, Inc., a nonprofit, tax exempt corporation.
Criterion Books website: *www.newcriterion.com/books*

LIBRARY OF CONGRESS CATALOGING-IN-PUBLICATION DATA

Pryce-Jones, David, 1936–
Fault lines / David Pryce-Jones.
    pages ;   cm
Summary: "Born in Vienna in 1936, David Pryce-Jones is the son of the well-known writer and editor of the Times Literary Supplement Alan Pryce-Jones and Therese "Poppy" Fould-Springer. He grew up in a cosmopolitan mix of industrialists, bankers, soldiers, and playboys on both sides of a family, embodying the fault lines of the title: "not quite Jewish and not quite Christian, not quite Austrian and not quite French or English, not quite heterosexual and not quite homosexual, socially conventional but not quite secure." Graduating from Magdalen College, Oxford, David Pryce-Jones served as Literary Editor of the Financial Times and the Spectator, a war correspondent for the Daily Telegraph, and Senior Editor of National Review. Fault Lines – a memoir that spans Europe, America, and the Middle East and encompasses figures ranging from Somerset Maugham to Svetlana Stalin to Elie de Rothschild -- has the storytelling power of Pryce-Jones's numerous novels and non-fiction books, and is perceptive and poignant testimony to the fortunes and misfortunes of the present age" – Provided by publisher.
ISBN 978-0-9859052-3-1 (softcover : acid-free paper)
1. Pryce-Jones, David, 1936– 2. Authors, English—20th century—
Biography. I. Title.
PR6066.R88Z46 2015
823'.914—dc23
[B]
2015034142

Contents

For Jessica, Candida and Adam, and in memory of Sonia

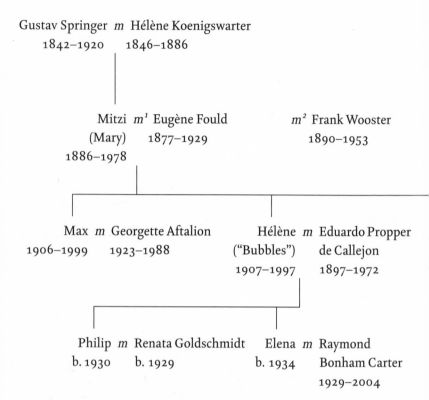

Gustav Springer *m* Hélène Koenigswarter
1842–1920   1846–1886

Mitzi *m¹* Eugène Fould   *m²* Frank Wooster
(Mary)   1877–1929   1890–1953
1886–1978

Max *m* Georgette Aftalion   Hélène *m* Eduardo Propper
1906–1999   1923–1988   ("Bubbles")   de Callejon
                                  1907–1997   1897–1972

Philip *m* Renata Goldschmidt   Elena *m* Raymond
b. 1930   b. 1929   b. 1934   Bonham Carter
                                          1929–2004

The Fould-Springer Family Tree

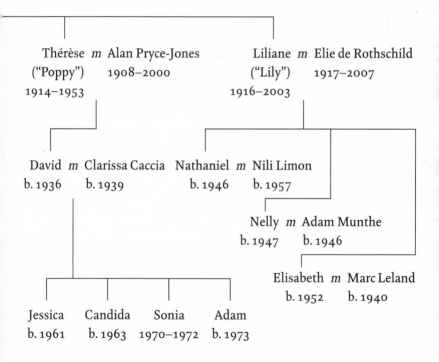

Thérèse *m* Alan Pryce-Jones
("Poppy")   1908–2000
1914–1953

Liliane *m* Elie de Rothschild
("Lily")   1917–2007
1916–2003

David *m* Clarissa Caccia
b. 1936   b. 1939

Nathaniel *m* Nili Limon
b. 1946   b. 1957

Nelly *m* Adam Munthe
b. 1947   b. 1946

Elisabeth *m* Marc Leland
b. 1952   b. 1940

Jessica   Candida   Sonia   Adam
b. 1961   b. 1963   1970–1972   b. 1973

ONE

A Moment in Austria

IN THE FIRST DAYS of January 1953 my mother and I arrived in what was then the isolated village of Seefeld in the Tyrol. Aged thirty-seven, she was returning for the first time since before the war to the country in which she had been born and to which she had a sentimental attachment, perhaps deteriorating into some sort of love-hate relationship. Originally called Thérèse Fould-Springer, she was Poppy to almost everyone who knew her before and after she made her life in England with Alan, my father. Here we were to stay in the Pension Philipp, newly built, and taking its name from the couple who owned and ran this rather modest venture in a post-war Austria still under Allied occupation and unsure of the future. My mother liked the hard-working Frau Philipp. We were there to have a holiday, and especially to ski, before I went back to Eton. An only child, I was sixteen.

My mother's younger sister Liliane had brought us to Seefeld. She had become familiar with this part of the world because her husband Elie de Rothschild had taken a lease on a shoot belonging to the Saxe-Coburgs. The lodge, a wooden chalet, was at the end of a long and twisty track that reached from the next village of Scharnitz high up into the Karwendel mountains, impassable in winter. Herr Ragg, the head keeper, a stout Father Christmas figure with red cheeks and a white beard, seemed to have survived from Habsburg days. He once corrected Elie for speaking loosely about the Austrian provinces Italy had acquired as spoils after the First War, "*Sud Tirol, Herr Baron.*" His younger son, Hubert Ragg, was our guide on the slopes, and slightly too insistent about it. A possible champion, he had lost his nerve in a bad fall while racing, and he wanted to hide it.

Aunty Lily, as she was to me, came with her two small children, my cousins Nathaniel and Nelly, and their nanny Miss Sargent from Norfolk. In Paris they lived in the Avenue Marigny, a house inherited from Elie's father and one of the largest in the entire city, round the corner from the President of France in the Elysée. Thanks to Liliane, they also had a house called La Faisanderie on the Fould-Springer family's estate at Royaumont near Chantilly. The ensemble of buildings there is one of the showplaces of France. In the thirteenth century, the abbey had been built for the Cistercians by Saint Louis; the church and much else was pulled down during the French revolution, to leave a refectory, halls, and imposing monastic quarters around a cloister. This was the property of our neighbors, the Gouins, whose daughter Marie-Christine was twenty when she too was with our party in the Pension Philipp, so to speak a lifelong honorary member of our family.

On January 12 Poppy wrote to her mother, Mitzi or Mitz to those who had known her in the first part of her life, and Mary to those who had known her afterwards. My grandmother was then in her flat in Paris just behind the Madeleine within walking distance of the Rothschilds in the Avenue Marigny. French was the language in which these two corresponded, with bits of German and English as decoration. Poppy's excuse for not writing sooner was that she had spent two very bad days, feeling sick with pains in her liver and kidneys. "Naturally my morale responds, each time I feel better I am filled with hope but I must say that I'm beginning to have more than enough of it. If I don't feel much better I may come back sooner to Paris." She proposes more consultations with her Paris specialists whom she names, Drs d'Allaines, Mayer, and Camille Dreyfus. The rest of this letter is in quite another mode, cheerfully social, describing the New Year's Eve she and Alan had just spent with Harry and Rosie d'Avigdor-Goldsmid at Somerhill, their house on the edge of Tonbridge. It was a home from home. Until that year, we had lived in Castle Hill Farm, tenants on their estate. At Fairlawne, a country house a few miles away, lived the race-horse trainer Peter Cazalet, his wife Zara and his son Edward, exactly my age. We visited them. Staying there were Lady Margaret Douglas-Home and two of her children, Fiona and Charlie, two more friends for me. "*C'était très gemütlich*" Poppy writes in the familiar linguistic mix. She and Alan had completed the upheaval of moving to London and she closes this letter to her mother, "what worries me most in all this is Alan's agony and exhaustion and I wonder if a radical change and a simpler life might be envisaged."

3

The very next day, the 13th, she was writing to Alan. "I know I am more than impossible to live with, but you do know, I hope, how much I appreciate and am grateful to you for all you have always done for me in the past, and alas now I need your unending understanding and thoughtfulness more than ever and I have so little to give in exchange." This suggests that she was confronting her own mortality quite clearly. Yet she goes on as though in some part of herself plans for the future were still believable, "I must come back to Austria with you, it gives me too much heimweh [home-sickness] for the past and all it means to us. Your Pigling [a habitual and mutual borrowing from Beatrix Potter's *Pigling Bland*] who is getting stronger again."

I knew that Poppy in the previous August had under-gone an operation in the American Hospital in Paris but when I went there I was not allowed to enter her room. "You have seen enough doctors," I wrote to her, adding in school-boy language that I hoped she "may never again need to see another." Home again, she was evidently having some unspecified treatment for some unspecified illness. I had observed that often she did not get out of bed in the morning or went back to bed in the afternoon. She and everyone else were studiously silent about the reason for all this, and I was too engrossed in my own life to probe into her health. There were things women kept to themselves out of delicacy, I imagined. Perhaps she was playing up to get sympathy. Poppy was on the best of terms with Camille Dreyfus, a relation of the persecuted Captain Dreyfus. Alarmed because I was a slow grower and nicknamed Little Man at Eton, she had dragged me to see him. I couldn't take him seriously. Counting my vertebrae, he thought I had one too few – "*Mais mon petit, tu es déformé.*" Further inspecting my private parts, he said, "*Mais mon petit, il faut s'en servir.*" Like the others around me, he meant well, but even he held back from telling me that Poppy had cancer. If he also gave her morphine in quantities to put an end to her life, that too was well meant.

Blithely ignorant, I wrote to Alan from the Pension Philipp, "Mummy who has felt ill on and off up to now, has suddenly and completely recovered today, so much so that she went out on Marie-Christine's skis, just to see what it felt like. We are all naturally very relieved, because it was pointless that she should come to the mountains to be ill." In her small hasty handwriting Poppy had added in the margin, "I am so happy to be able to tell you that Thank God today I feel quite alright again. It has been so fine and I have been on skis! Not skiing and only five minutes. Your Baba is in grand form and all the others too. We go to watch the stags tomorrow and Elie comes after tomorrow for the week-end." Lily had a mania for photography, and in that moment out of doors she recorded Poppy wearing an anorak and a woolly pixie bonnet and looking fixedly at the camera as though to stare right through it.

From Seefeld we took a taxi to Innsbruck. We visited the church there and Poppy told me about the great Emperor Maximilian painted in a memorable portrait of majesty by Dürer. At the station, she helped me board the train. A smartly dressed lady in a fur coat emerged from a couchette in the same Pullman carriage, with a companion just behind her. Speaking French, Poppy greeted this lady by name, and was very amused to have caught her out: "The man she's travelling with isn't her husband." She was all laughter as the train pulled away and I had my last sight of her.

In the Pension Philipp after saying goodbye to me, she wrote once more to her mother. This letter is dated January 21. It was high time for her to return to England, she says, but "alas, I feel on the whole not at all well, feeling nauseous above all and when all this started up positively ill." Abruptly she changes subject. Elie had arrived to fetch Liliane and the children. Having just stayed at the palace of Laeken with the King of the Belgians, he had entertaining stories to tell about that royally dysfunctional family. Poppy also boasts on my behalf that I spoke German not too badly and was a remarkable skier who had gone on a cross-country "Ausflug," or expedition, with Hubert Ragg. Finally a passage about Alan shows how well aware she was of what was coming: "He is rather agitated at this moment about our future etc. and as for me my one idea is to simplify his life so that he has less work and fewer worries."

The Eton schedule of lessons and games left very little time for anything else. Several days passed, whereupon I received a letter from Alan to say that Poppy was hurt not to have heard from me, and I was to write to her at once. It was not his style to be brusque and to issue peremptory commands. Rather shocked, I did manage to fill up four sheets of paper which survived in the bundle of correspondence carefully kept with a rubber band on Poppy's bedside table.

Oliver Van Oss, my housemaster, was imposing in every way, in knowledge, taste, and not least physical bulk. He also had a natural humour. In the course of the morning he came to find me to say that Poppy had just died. I was to go to Paris as soon as possible, and he would drive me to Heathrow. On the way in his car he made a point of advising me that grief ought to be expressed and there's nothing wrong or unmanly about crying. Kenneth Rae was already at Heathrow with tickets for us both. In old days before the war he had been a friend of Poppy and Alan in Vienna. The family albums have photographs of him dressed like Alan at the time in lederhosen and white knee stockings, and depending on the season in ski clothes or a bathing costume. At the firm of Cobden-Sanderson, he had been Alan's first publisher and now he was devoting himself and his private fortune to founding what in due course became the National Theatre. From Castle Hill Farm we used to walk through the woods in about a quarter of an hour to his house, Knowles Bank. To me, he was Uncle Kenneth. He wept openly.

Elie shared the Avenue Marigny house with his elder brother Alain. You entered a courtyard where the concierge was in a lodge to the right. The main door to the house was on the left, and you seemed to step into a cavern, somewhere not intended for human habitation. Glass roofing at the top of the vast staircase threw a ghostly light. In reception rooms that nobody went into were pictures by the greatest artists, magnificent Boulle furniture, museum pieces of every sort. Good manners inhibited talking in a normal voice in this forbidding setting. At the end of a dark corridor was a small-ish rather dingy room with a bed jammed in one corner against the wall. I had never seen a dead person.

More than a cemetery, Père Lachaise is a city of the dead. The Fould family possesses a gloomily ornate mausoleum there with plenty of space. Two days after her death, Poppy's coffin was placed alongside unknown ancestors. Hebrew prayers were said. Alan wanted to have Poppy reburied in the local parish churchyard in Kent. Dr Chavasse, then the Bishop of Rochester, refused to grant permission because Poppy had been Jewish. Her final grave is in the Catholic cemetery of Viarmes, the slightly ramshackle village a mile or two from Royaumont.

Alan took me back to Eton. The approach to my house was through an archway, past a row of cottages, rather picturesque. Standing there was someone wearing an old mackintosh and a shabby felt hat. John Betjeman, the poet in his disguise. He had been shuffling about in the doorway for hours. Years later he told me, "I knew the Captain would be sad so I wanted to meet him on his return." In keeping with his view of the human comedy, Betjeman had mythologised Alan's one-time military rank, elaborating it to Captain Bog, a mistyping for Big Nose. There had been an evening when he addressed the school's literary society, caught sight of me in the audience, and called out, "Oooh Baby Bog!" – his face alive with delight in the private joke. Years later too, I wanted my daughters Jessica and Candida to have a memory of someone who had had more influence on Alan than any other contemporary. By then Betjeman was in a wheelchair. "The Captain is like an onion," he said to the three of us. "You peel off the skin and always there's another skin. Those who don't love him think that after the last skin there'll be nothing. We who love him know there is something but what it is we shall never find out."

Back at Eton I was straightaway caught up in a compulsory game of football on one of the far pitches known to the school as Dutchman's. In the middle of the game I stopped, I stood still, struck by the realization that I was being compelled to behave as though nothing in my life had changed.

Two

8 *Le Palais Abbatial*

ROYAUMONT! The accumulation of vowels following that throaty initial *r* is a test of correct pronunciation. Poppy would make me repeat the word, and also practise saying the equally tricky noun *grenouille*, a frog, until she was satisfied that my English accent was ironed out and I could pass for being French and imagine myself a Special Operations agent deceiving German sentries at a check-point. Royaumont! The name alone has an almost enchanted power to bring back the past as though everything was still as it once had been. My grandparents Eugène Fould from Paris and Mitzi Springer from Vienna had acquired the house in 1923. He wanted to make the kind of splash in high society that the French are famous for, but he did not have the means for it. One of the richest women in Europe, she paid.

In those days you drove from Paris for about an hour on the narrow roads of what was then the department of Seine-et-Oise. Through Viarmes, past the garage of Monsieur Fauvarque with its hand-operated petrol pump, and next to it the iron gate leading to the cemetery, you would come down the hill and over a crossing known as the Croix Verte, to enter what seemed like the kingdom of our family, a beautiful and romantic place. An immense stone wall closes off the field to your right. On the far side of it are huge trees, and over their tops pokes up a mysterious piece of masonry, something like the point of a gigantic pencil. In the 1789 revolution teams of oxen had been harnessed to pull down the great thirteenth-century abbey church that had stood here, one of the largest in the country. This huge Gothic spike is a monument to lost scale.

The trees are felled to provide a sudden vista of water and the house, known to us as the château, but more correctly the *palais abbatial*. The abbot of the day had built himself a classic Palladian house that the revolution almost immediately prevented him from enjoying. Standing back a little from the road is a perfect symmetrical cube with terraced steps on three sides that seem to anchor it into the setting. Further round the enclosing wall is another vista, this time of a canal at the end of which is the first full view of the front façade. The stonework is so pale a yellow that it is almost white. Opposite the house on the left of the road is a wide lake and a path screened by poplars leading to a second lake with a pair of swans, and beyond that a third lake where the wild duck flight. And there stands the Gros Chêne, an oak many hundreds of years old, its majestic branches so extended and heavy that iron props and bands and cables have to support them. This tree is the unspoken symbol of continuity, and to walk to it is a pilgrimage of sorts.

Along the edge of the first lake runs a lane, at the head of which is Franto's cottage. Originally a Slovak, Franto was invited by Mitzi to some celebration here and nobody remembered to send him home. A gap-tooth smile in his round weather-beaten face and his rolling gait were definitely foreign, and his French came out as unrecognizable grunts. A keeper, he had a way with animals; his home had the raw smell of a zoo. It was said that he used to beat his wife. In the war the Germans never troubled him. At the end of that lane is the Faisanderie, in old days several separate cottages, all of them now done up in perfect taste for Liliane and Elie de Rothschild, and a long row of cages for rearing pheasants. In the war, Rimbert the head keeper lived there. To summon him, his wife would blow a trumpet and once said to Max, Mitzi and Eugène's son and heir, "*Monsieur le Baron veut-il que je trempe mon mari*," an untranslatable pun as the verb for blowing the trumpet differs only in its initial vowel from the verb for deceiving. Max's story is that he gave the Faisanderie as a wedding present when Liliane married Elie de Rothschild. Elie's story is that he had to buy the house.

The wrought-iron gates in front of the château are kept shut. Whoever is driving will hoot and someone, probably Madame Marius the gardener's wife, hurries from the lodge to open. Ahead is an ornamental avenue of trees planted with geometric spacing between them, and you can glimpse to your left the long low building of Les Pères, so-called presumably because monks or novices were housed here – the two-storey eighteenth-century building has long since been converted into stables. In the park is also the house of Marcel Vernois and his wife Renée, he the bailiff of the estate with its farm and its forests, she the housekeeper, and both of them jolly gnomes of unstoppable energy. Like a French infantryman in the First War, Marcel wears breeches and leather gaiters. We'd walk up partridges or in the evening have a shot at the wild duck on the furthest lake. At the right season he's after eels or crayfish, and fills buckets with white-shelled snails, a feast for everyone from the château and the farm that Renée serves at a trestle table set up in the open. He taught me how to drive. In the middle of the level crossing at Beaumont-sur-Oise, I was at the wheel when the bell began to warn that a train was about to arrive. As the barrier was coming down, I stalled and panicked. Marcel pushed me out of the seat and drove off the rails just in time.

You go from the château through a wire gate, always unlocked, past the column bases that are all that remains of the abbey church, and so to the Laiterie. This is Max's dower house. The entrance is glassed in, and in the middle is a rectangular basin with running water. Max has placed a ceramic eel in it, and small children invariably think it is alive. The Laiterie gives on to the wide cobbled farmyard. You need strength to open and close the huge wooden gate in the high enclosing wall at the far end. The immense storage barn is centuries old. Hens scratch about under fruit trees. Marcel puts on a uniform to take honey from the beehives, and he is also responsible for distilling the cassis served every day after meals. Janine lives in a corner house, she's Polish, a housemaid, and so gentle that she becomes almost invisible.

In front of the château is an expanse of sandy gravel that Albert has the job of raking every morning. A huge man wearing a peaked cap for extra authority, he seems to be keeping an eye out for all comings and goings. The flight of steps up the terrace to the front door has columns framing the entrance and statues set into the wall. Sometimes I still dream of the test I used to impose on myself as a boy, to jump off those steps each time higher, to land sideways on to the patch of grass below. I never dared jump down from the balustrade at the very top.

As the front door opens you would at once be aware of scale and proportion and light. If such a thing is possible, here is intimate grandeur. The hall rises high to a barrel ceiling. At its centre stands a table attributed to the eighteenth-century master Thomire, with a pink granite top over gilded bronze resting on winged sphinxes. Furniture like that conveys a lot of information about the owners and their freedom to indulge their taste. To the right is the drawing room, imposingly circular, with huge windows and a door out to a side terrace. Here the pillars round the wall are purely decorative. Beyond is the *fumoir*, the room no longer used just for smoking, but also where we would gather informally before or after a meal. To the left is the dining room, a matching circle except that it has ornamental painted panels of flowers and birds. The huge round table seats twenty-four. At the far end of the hall the spiral staircase repeats the motif of a circle. The steps are so shallow that you feel like racing up, past the half-landing with Max's bedroom and the schoolroom where we had lessons and played with the electrified set of toy Märklin trains belonging to my cousin Philip and which he had laid out in a mock-Swiss landscape.

Max, the second and last Baron Fould-Springer, is nominally the head of the family. Dark on account of its low ceiling, his room halfway up the stairs is an accumulation of family portraits, an Empire bed, cashmere shawls, piles of newspapers and letters, mementos, and a vast collection of his lucky charm, owls of every size in stones, materials, and styles of every sort. He throws nothing away, not even worn envelopes. He is absorbed in the pages of newspapers that print puzzles and spends lots of time writing notes to himself in a pocket-book in a handwriting of tiny hieroglyphics that nobody but him could make sense of. After *David Copperfield*, he has a long-standing joke with me that he is Murdstone, and he leers, "Boy, I'm going to cane you."

From the moment he was born in 1906, Jessie took charge of him until she died in 1959. She used to subscribe to the *Sunday Express*, and would cut out Ripley's "Believe it or Not," its regular feature illustrating far-fetched facts, and paste these rectangles like wallpaper in the corridor leading to his bathroom.

Every morning, she ran his bath for him and carried a breakfast tray into his room. He had been sent away to a Jesuit boarding school in the north of France and eventually to Magdalen College, Oxford, remaining uncertain which of these establishments was the most unsatisfactory. He must have been the only undergraduate at Oxford accompanied by his nanny.

Handsome, he had cut quite a dash in the 1930s, entertaining at Royaumont and the host of shooting parties at Kapuvár, an estate inherited in Hungary. His game book records a red-letter day there in August 1935 when he and his guests, the Duc d'Ayen, Comte de Beaumont, Comte de Maillé, Comte de Montsaulnier, Prince Achille Murat, and Jean de Vaugelas, shot an astonishing 6,009 partridges. Once past middle age the thin off-colour face, and especially the questioning look in his eyes, conveyed that he no longer found life easy. His usual comment to the news on television was "*On n'a encore rien vu,*" we haven't seen anything yet.

His father's son, he wore a small Star of David on a gold chain around his neck. Also like Eugène, he had a repertoire of stories and jokes, some of them Jewish. Mocking his education, he'd stress the wrong syllables in names such as Aristophanes and Euripides. One of his favourite quotations was "*Quod licet Jovi non licet bovi*"(What is permitted to Jupiter is not permitted to the ox), and another, uttered in a stagey falsetto, was: "*Ach aber ach, das Mädchen kam, und nicht in Acht das Veilchen nahm*" (Oh dear, the maiden came and paid no attention to the violet). Yet another derived from an elderly aunt who had tried to attract rabbits in the park in Vienna by holding out her hand as though offering food and saying, "*Komm, Kaninchen, komm*" (Come here, little rabbit, come here).

Playing the invalid, he chewed every mouthful of his food twenty or thirty times, finishing the meal long after everyone else. Liliane quipped, "*Il a une très mauvaise santé de fer,*" (He has really good ill health.) Actually he was athletic, diving off the high cliffs at Eden Roc in the south of France, flying gliders, riding his horse and most remarkably crossing the ornamental canal in front of the château forwards and backwards on a tightrope. His interests were architecture and art, about which he wrote occasional pieces for the magazine *Paris Match* under the pseudonym Max

Viar, short for Viarmes. When the car fetched him for a day of office routine as chairman of Maisons-Alfort, the family-owned factory that carried us all, he looked resigned to the boredom of it. One woman in his life was Paulette Helleu, daughter of the artist, and another was Cécile de Rothschild, Elie's sister. Asked what sort of a lover Max had been, she replied, "*pas plus mal qu'un autre*" (no worse than anyone else). Solitary after his nanny's death, he married Georgette Aftalion. Already middle-aged, she passed the time of day in an armchair, her bony face and staring eyes evidence of psychic disturbances too deep to fathom. To Mitzi, Max was "my adored Sonny," yet on page after page in her diaries she pulls him to pieces with no apparent understanding that her domination and his dependency might explain the beaten-dog look in his eyes. His homosexual adventures in Paris were an open secret. In his Paris house in the rue Saint-Didier, he holed himself up in the care of Louise Chavanel, more like another elderly nanny than a housekeeper. Every morning there, Dr Vacher, a well-known psychotherapist, came to take breakfast and give professional advice.

White-haired and imperturbable, Jessie and Marion Stainer, the other nanny, were referred to as the duchesses. Throwbacks to the England of Queen Victoria, they were never in a hurry and rarely raised their voices. An unspoken agreement divided responsibility for the children: Max and Poppy (and so ultimately me) going to Jessie, Bubbles and Lily to Nanny Stainer. Rivals as much as colleagues, these two tended to oppose one another, only to unite in the face of criticism or interference. Nanny Stainer came from a large family in Godalming. One of the seven children of a carpenter, Jessie was born in 1872 in Horspath, a village near Oxford. When she was still small, they all moved into Rose Lane, Oxford, a street whose cottages have long since been demolished to make way for university buildings. She and her brothers and sisters had three pairs of shoes to share between them, and only those whose feet happened to be the same size as the available shoes could go to school. A boy had been sent home because he was dirty, and Jessie put on an Oxfordshire accent to relate how the mother had come to rebuke the teacher, "My boy ain't no rose, you larn him not smell him." Poverty and lack of opportunity were part of the natural order of things. A lifetime of hard work had deformed Jessie's feet and ankles so that she had to have specially made orthopædic shoes that she called "beetle-crushers." In her private vocabulary, an umbrella was an umbershoot, manipulative behavior was inkle-weaving, and those she took against were arsehole-creepers. Playing with nicknames, she wrote to Poppy as Kate, and might sign her own letters as Martha. Her philosophy was summed up by an incident at a tennis tournament to which she liked to refer. Jean Borotra had been losing badly until someone in the crowd shouted, "Courage, Pépé!" and he went on to win.

Making their lives in France, she and Nanny Stainer spoke a phonetic anglicised French: rubdisham for dressing-gown, culleryfere for radiator, saldiban for bathroom. Nanny Stainer in fact read *Les Liaisons dangereuses* round and round. Jessie had memorized whole chunks of Shakespeare, as well as a variety of poems and songs, some serious and some comic. She had an excuse for the neuroses and tantrums in the house: you can't expect thoroughbreds to be cart-horses.

You could race up the great stone staircase, three or four steps at a time, to finish at the top in an open space like a gallery, with a shiny floor of black and white marble flag-stones. Busts of Roman emperors were set in sockets at the top of columns. In front of the window at the far end of this open space was a statue in black plaster by the nineteenth-century sculptor Bosio. I always thought this eye-catching figure balanced on one foot was Hermes, but the experts say it is a representation of love, a Cupid.

16 And on that floor is the bedroom I shared with my cousin Elly, daughter of Bubbles, my eldest aunt. In it hangs a life-size portrait of Poppy aged about eleven in a costume copied for a children's fancy-dress party from the Velázquez portrait of the Infanta, a study in reds and orange. Philip, four years older than his sister Elly, has a room to one side and the nannies are on the other side. Before the war Alan and Poppy had a bedroom and dressing-room on this floor. When I was two, I put my hands into the butter on their breakfast tray and then onto the silk bed-head. The fingerprints were permanent.

We children – Philip and Elly and myself – were left to our own devices. On the lower ground floor was the library, built round a single vast weight-bearing pillar. We had this room to ourselves. The windows let in little light and the air was musty. Eugène had collected the books, and they reflected his knowledge and taste in art, literature and politics. Among the several languages he knew was Russian, taught at his mother's knee, and after his marriage he had learnt Hungarian in order to keep up with the management of the properties. In October 1906, for instance, he visited Szabolcz, near Budapest, and could judge in conversation that the bailiff was very professional whereas the bailiff's wife was a Hungarian peasant. Two volumes of Petőfi's poems annotated in pencil in his hand have survived (and so has his complete edition of Heine.) On the shelves of books concerning Jews was Édouard Drumont's *La France juive*, an anti-Semitic diatribe so popular that this copy is from the 200th edition. Drumont's poisonous caricature of the Jew who becomes a Baron "and presents himself boldly in society" was aimed at the handful like Eugène whose every encounter was a test of their social standing.

The books had been catalogued with a card index, many of them had been rebound uniformly, and all of them had a bookplate with an engraving of the house. The table for Russian billiards was one distraction in the library and the gramophone another. The playing needle of this antique had to be changed frequently and the records were 78s of singers like Lotte Lehmann and Richard Tauber. "Mein Herr Marquis" from *Die Fledermaus* and "Di quell'amor" from *La Traviata* were never stale. Over a sofa covered with brown velvet was a stuffed and mounted bird, a bustard with a huge wingspan shot by Max on the Hungarian puszta. Alone most mornings at the desk in that atmospheric room, I began to teach myself to write. Starting with book-length imitations of Agatha Christie, I moved on to sentimental pastiches of Hans Christian Andersen and Alain-Fournier's *Le Grand Meaulnes*, a novel that cast a spell almost as embracing as Royaumont.

Beautiful Mitzi can never have been, gawky as a girl, dumpy as a married woman. Her expressive brown eyes had black rings round them, *zwetschenknödel* or plum dumplings as her eldest daughter Bubbles called them. Up on the top floor, Mitzi reserved for herself a corner room, smaller than others and out of the way. Everyone was expected to start the day by paying respects. You approached on tiptoe, you exchanged whispers with her maid Paulette to find out how well Mitzi had slept in the night. The emotional atmosphere in the house, family relationships, interpretation of the news, were in Mitzi's gift. Still in bed with a breakfast tray, the mail and the newspapers, she might wave a hand or give you a possessive kiss, receiving you with the formal informality of a reigning monarch. The quivering of her thin lips indicated what you were in for, what you had to expect in the afternoon session with her. Notes hand-delivered by one of the servants were storm signals. One that survives reads,

"May you daily have more of the Essential, realizing that no man or woman can give it you." Another missive in the archive is just as typical: "Your injustice and ingratitude towards me have wounded and embittered me. Your words are not those of a happy or sad, good or bad child but those of a cruel woman. Your impressions are evidently almost always false but you remain amused and proud of them."

On the same landing as her bedroom was her boudoir, a low and dark den because the immense wing of the abbey loomed close enough to shutter out daylight. Here were enacted scenes of Grand Inquisition. The future of everyone in the house depended on keeping in her good books. Where she came from, *Kuss die Hand*, a hand kiss, made plain who was giving, and who was receiving, favours. She never used the stairs. The lift had a cabin of some scented wood. When Mitzi stepped out of it into the hall to take possession of her realm, it was as well to be there, ready for whatever it might be. Everything seemed ordered, everything seemed protected and privileged, but all the time under the surface and unacknowledged, the fault lines that Mitzi had put in place were in operation: Not quite Jewish and not quite Christian, not quite Austrian and not quite French or English, not quite heterosexual and not quite homosexual, socially conventional but not quite secure, here were people not quite sure what their inheritance required of them.

THREE

Tivoligasse 71

ACCORDING TO THE Museum of the Diaspora in Tel Aviv, which keeps the record of these things, all Springers had acquired their surname because they had been acrobats at some royal court in Germany, a role apparently reserved for Jews. They came to Vienna either from Ansbach or from Furth in Bavaria. Like the Foulds in France, Max Springer (1807–1885) belonged to a generation of Jews increasingly free to meet everyone else on equal terms and so make what they could of their talents. Max Springer's interests extended from finance to railways and coal mining. His wife Amalia Todesco belonged to one of the most successful Jewish families. Eduard Todesco, Amalia's father, had built a palace facing the side of the Opera, and Max Springer built the smaller but still stately house round the corner at number 14 Kaerntnerring. The latter also founded an orphanage, the Springer Waisenhaus, for Jewish boys up to the age of fourteen. In 1872 Kaiser Franz Josef gave Max Springer and therefore his descendants the title of Freiherr, or Baron. Axel Springer, the German press tycoon, used to write to Mitzi claiming that they were relations, but she believed not.

Expropriated by the Nazis, long since bought and sold by non-Jews as investments in prime property, these great monuments in stone to past wealth have something empty and haunting about them, as though to reproach what happened to those who once lived in them. To brush up my German, I used to stay in an apartment in the Kaerntnerring that still belonged to Mitzi. Dr Hans Mailath-Pokorny, all his life her man of business for Central Europe, lived in it.

He had the challenging features, the moustache, the corpulent figure, and overbearing manner of a Grosz caricature. He had known the German conservative politician Franz von Papen and liked to argue that everything would have come out all right if von Papen had chucked out Hitler instead of Hitler chucking von Papen out. Upstairs in tiny rooms under the roof was Tante Bébé, otherwise Elizabeth d'Italia, lonely and wizened but still quick with repartees. Interrogating her, a Gestapo officer had said, "You are very sarcastic," to which she replied, "All Jews are sarcastic." To survive the war she had gone into hiding in Abbasia near Fiume.

At my request, Lore Mayer, a Viennese historian, undertook a study of the Springers. In the wars and revolutions of Europe, currencies and values have changed or collapsed to the point of worthlessness, so that equivalents to more recent currencies and values are tentative. Figures have to speak for themselves. When Max Springer died, he was worth almost one and a half million florins. At more or less the same time, comparable all-round businessmen Ignaz Ephrussi and Moriz Koenigswarter, Lore Mayer notes, had 3.3 million and just under 21 million florins respectively.

Max's son Gustav (1842–1920) enters the history books as one of the most prominent entrepreneurs in the Austro-Hungarian Empire of his day. Extending his father's interests, he obtained concessions to build railways in Russia, Romania, and the Ottoman Empire. After the Franco-Prussian War, he started the yeast factory at Maisons-Alfort on the outskirts of Paris. His product, Levure Springer, dominated the market. The Vienna stock exchange crashed in 1873, ruining a great many people. In the crisis Gustav picked up shares at rock bottom prices that recovered within a year. His investment advice, "Buy to the sound of cannons and sell to the sound of violins," is sometimes wrongly attributed to the Rothschilds. Roman Sandgruber is a professor of economic history at Linz University. His book, *Traumzeit für Million-äre*, analyses the tax returns of the 929 individuals who in 1910 declared an annual income over 100,000 crowns. With an income of 4.1 million crowns, Gustav is the country's fourth highest taxpayer. He died worth 346 million crowns. Lore Mayer estimates his fortune in Austria to have been in the broad range of 170 to 350 million in the Euros of today. To this must be added what he owned in France, Hungary, and Czechoslovakia, which she puts in an equally broad range of a further 200 to 380 million Euros.

Gustav's extravagance was legendary. Mitzi would remember the luxury of their private train, and his habit of sending his shirts to be laundered in Paris.

Every summer he stayed at his favourite house, Kapuvár, near Győr in western Hungary. Built in the early eighteenth century, this house is on a slight rise dominating the small town. Decorated with a yellow wash, it is in the classical Habsburg style, with a regular façade at the front and an even more regular façade at the rear. The interior was a mass of heavy mahogany furniture and tiled stoves, with stags' antlers as trophies on the walls even of bedrooms. In the same county was Pokvár, taken for its shoot. Puszta Bucsa near Debrecen, Rakoncás, Jenő Major, Zodony, Alag, Csongrád, Szabolcs, Nándor, were among Gustav's Hungarian possessions. "*Grund fliegt nimmer weg,*" land never flies away, had been Gustav's justification for these investments. It was unimaginable that financial and political security would soon dissipate forever. The names of his forests in Slovakia convey a similar elegiac poetry – Vrbové, Šípkové, Čachtice, Lubina, Bohuslavice, and Bošáca. A surviving report to Mitzi from Rimler Pal, her head forester, lists those that he considered could be sold to raise funds for her in 1936 as war was approaching.

A knowing writer, evidently an insider, who published a

sketch of Gustav in a book *La Société de Vienne*, 1885, went under the pseudonym of Comte Vasili, suggesting a Tsarist aristocrat, which almost certainly he was not. Baron Gustav, he writes, was "small and stout, very affable and not lacking wit, with the attractions of a playboy." His head was large and conspicuously bald. Any servant was tipped a crown if he said that the Herr Baron had just come from the barber and was right, but fined a crown if he was wrong. Aged twenty-nine in 1871, he married Hélène Koenigswarter, thus putting himself on a footing with the most socially acceptable Jews. Comte Vasili praises her taste and skill as a hostess.

Fifteen years later, on 23 May 1886, Hélène died giving birth to Mitzi, the only child of the marriage. In the view of some of her descendants, for instance my cousin Elly, the fact that Mitzi never knew her mother is a complete psychological explanation of her desperate lifelong appeal for love. Even as a child, she saw herself giving but not receiving, and the one person who might have paid off this emotional debit unhesitatingly was not there.

On the grounds of protecting Mitzi's health, her father bought an estate of fifty acres some way from the city centre, and there he built Meidling, the house known nowadays as the Springerschloss though it still has the old address of Tivoligasse 71. The property marched with the park of the great Habsburg palace of Schönbrunn. Mitzi used to tell stories about talking over the fence to the Empress Elisabeth or Frau Schratt, the Emperor Franz Josef's mistress. When she had been out pushing the infant Max in his pram, Nanny Stainer liked to recollect, she had often seen the Emperor himself walking quite close and raising his hat to them. Gustav had several illegitimate children, and Mitzi was in touch with one called Helen Lavalle, taking pleasure in acknowledging a half-sister who was about her own age and had settled in Canada.

Meidling is a nineteenth-century pile with irregular and sometimes fantastic features, the roofs sloping steeply, half-timbering, ornamental towers silhouetted against the sky, the whole fascinatingly and even endearingly ugly. Baron Gustav had commissioned the architects of the Burgtheater, and the interior is like a stage-set around a horseshoe stair-case rising from the ground floor up to the roof. Entering, you wait for the lights to go up. A child growing up in such a setting was bound to expect the rest of the world to fall in with her. Mitzi never went to school. She had a nurse known as Moumel with whom she stayed in touch all her life. Miss Maclellan, the unsmiling Scottish governess, seems to have been incapable of anything like maternal feelings but at least she brought Mitzi up to speak and write English natu-rally. Amalie Kostiall, her lady's maid, lived at Meidling until after the Second War when she was almost 100 years old. The absence of any formal education was greatly to dis-advantage Mitzi in later life, leaving her unable to reason, to resolve contradictions, to take a step back and see herself objectively. She would describe how her father made her sit on a stool at his side in the office he had on the ground floor in Meidling, obliging her to learn about business and noth-ing else. At the end of the day the coachman drove him to the Hotel Imperial on the Ring, where he preferred to live in the best suite, leaving his great house to Mitzi and the women attending to her.

Gustav's fortune was at the service of his passion for horseracing. Gustav Jantsch, a pre-1918 Austrian cavalry officer, was the author of *Vollblutzucht und Turf*, and this very comprehensive study of the subject devotes a chapter to Gustav's role in it. The Springer racing colours were black with a red cap. Bucsany in Hungary was the first stud he bought. In the same county in Hungary he then acquired Felsojatto where he had seventy-one mares, which Jantsch says was certainly the biggest stud in the Austro-Hungarian Empire as well as Germany, and most likely France too. In the First War he bought Lesvár but reduced the number of mares to seventeen. At yearling auctions he was a steady buyer, or as Jantsch puts it, "nothing was too expensive for a man who could pay whatever he liked." At one point, he had sixty-one horses under training, fifty-five of them winners. Horses of his were several times winners of the German Derby and a number of races in England. When Buccaneer won the Austrian Derby for him in 1913, he was presented with a silver-gilt cup with an ornamental frieze and an inscription, all of which today conveys the death-knell of the Austro-Hungarian Empire. At the time, the press reported incredulously that he made a present of the prize winnings to the English jockey. After his death in 1920 one obituary called him "Ein nobler Sportsmann," not the usual description of Jewish magnates.

Other racehorse owners had the aristocratic names of Kinsky, Esterhazy, Zichy, and Harrach. Could Gustav really have fitted into such company, or did he stand out and attract envy and resentment? He regularly took Mitzi to his box at the Freudenau racecourse where one day she heard an officer in an adjoining box remark to another, "What a pity the little Springer girl looks so Jewish." Comte Vasili, for one, observes, "Anti-Semitism is making progress day by day, in all classes of this society." Dr Karl Lueger, the mayor of Vienna, is remembered for declaring that he decided who was a Jew, and an aphorism of Gustav's seems a practical response to this kind of discrimination, "*Jude muss man sein, aber nicht zum Abattoir*" – one must be Jewish though not going into the slaughter house for it. Max Springer had set up and paid for the Jewish orphanage, the Springerische Waisenhaus in the Goldschlagstrasse in the 14th district. Gustav took on the responsibility. For Jewish high holidays he and Mitzi used to attend the synagogue there. Less fortunate Jews made demands on her father and on her, as though Judaism really was a common identity. At a pinch, she might quote with approval the lament of a friend, the Comtesse FitzJames, née Gutmann, "*Mes nerfs juifs me font mal,*" My Jewish nerves are troubling me. Ibok, a word with no known derivation, was the family code for Jew, used in contexts when that direct and giveaway monosyllable might be better concealed.

A formal photograph was taken in the park of Meidling on Mitzi's eighteenth birthday. She, her nurse Moumel, and her Scottish governess are the only women among a retinue of well over a hundred men: lawyers and accountants in top hats, clerks in bowler hats, a handful of orphans dressed as page-boys – and in this self-contained circle all have Jewish names with the exception of some foresters and keepers from Czechoslovakia and Hungary in folk costumes.

Singular, set apart by her expectations and the Jewish milieu of her upbringing, Mitzi seems to have protected herself by preserving everything that had a personal bearing from childhood to her death. What an archive she amassed of almost fifty volumes of large thick diaries, correspondence in five languages with many of the German letters respectfully addressed to "Euer Hochwohlgeboren Gnädigste Frau Baronin," little drawings, scraps, *billets doux*, telegrams, business dossiers, bank accounts, lawyers' opinions on the regular forays of the dozen or so governments trying to get their hands on Mitzi's money through taxes or political chicanery, postcards from the resorts of Ischl and Baden-Baden and Carlsbad, letters of condolence, official certificates, cadastral surveys, maps, menus. I pick at random a letter from London solicitors itemizing large holdings in British and American shares, mostly in mining and railroads. This was a fortune in itself but only the part held at Hambros Bank in

London of what Mitzi was inheriting from her late father. She must have rated every last detail about herself and her life so important that the multifarious evidence had to be preserved, duly but not necessarily correctly sorted and filed away in envelopes and packets tidily tied up with string. Innumerable photographs of herself are a sort of chronicle from her pre-1914 appearance in long tight-waisted dresses and hats as elaborate as a still life of flowers, until she poses in matronly suits with one or all of her children around her, all the way down to Cecil Beaton portraits conveying the impression of wisdom and age. Still more innumerable photographs, as stiff as boards and dully brown in the technology of the period, are portraits of elderly men usually in a white tie with decorations or else in a morning coat and top hat. A few are wearing the *Kaiser und König* uniform and distinctive forage cap of the Emperor's soldiers, the whole appearance complete with whiskers and monocle. Occasionally she wrote names on the back of these photographs, otherwise the sitters are unidentifiable. The women are posed self-consciously in ballroom dresses, rows of pearls hanging almost to the stomach, aigrettes, parasols, fancy dress costumes, feather boas, and furs. Liliane used to joke that many of the women around her were members of an "Internationale Judeo-lesbienne," and went so far as to speculate whether her mother and two women who were regular guests at Meidling, Marianne Glasyer and "My beloved friend Giesl von Gieslingen," might have belonged to it too.

Nowhere that I can find in this archive is any mention of eligible Austrian Jews she might have married. On the face of it, the engagement between a pampered heiress from Vienna and a worldly fortune-hunter from Paris looks like a fine example of the traditional matchmaking practised among Jews. But Mitzi writes that at seventeen she fell in love with Eugène at first sight. She accuses her father of obliging her to break off the engagement, and a sentence only two short years later covers what must have been a lot of ground, "the fight I put up and the sufferings and sorrows I endured finally ended in Eugène and myself getting married . . . in 1905." In the archive is plenty of evidence that the demands each made of the other kept their relationship at a high emotional pitch. One of several similar notes from Eugène that she kept with a framed photograph of him by her bedside says, "I would give every minute of my existence, every drop of my blood to see you perfectly happy." In her notes she signs herself "Doggie," and after twenty years and more of marriage could still write, "a big hug from the one who adores you and is more in love with you than ever, even if you, old fool! say I am less fond of you." Cocky was her nickname for him.

27

One thick package has the label, "Letters from the perpetual quarrelling (dramas!) between my father Gustav, Eugène and me." All three of them were accustomed to having their own way and did not know how to let well alone. A two-page letter from Mitzi without a heading but undoubtedly addressed to her father opens with the accusation, typically left in the air, that the harm done to her has entered her heart. Two issues could not be resolved: whether Mitzi and Eugène would settle in Vienna rather than Paris and what nationality their children would have and therefore whether baby Max grew up to be an Austrian or a French soldier. Concessions were made to keep Gustav happy: Eugène and Mitzi would perpetuate the Springer descent by hyphenating their surnames, and Eugène would accept a title so that his son Max could eventually be *Monsieur le Baron.*

Here is one round in the contest, as described by Eugène to his father Léon Fould in a letter of 15 March 1909:

Big news – at lunch, the day before yesterday, my father-in-law says to me (only Mitzi and Hélène were there) that he is going to see Lueger the mayor, in order to settle the question of the little boy's nationality. I answered, "I must ask you to do nothing because as you know you have given me mortal offense and I have taken the decision never to hear speak again of this matter which has always been exceedingly painful to me and to my father." He, "But we promised." Me, "Yes, but if the person to whom some-thing has been promised then refuses his part of it, I con-sider that fact makes it quits, as in my case – and I am quite willing, if I have to, to go as far as the Emperor to explain the situation."

Whether before or after this stormy lunch, an undated letter of Eugène's reveals that Gustav could also play the card of going to the top:

We were at the palace this morning for an audience with the Emperor. . . . The Emperor put himself out to be ami-able, spoke to me in French and asked if I liked Vienna. Then he spoke in German and said he had had "ein schweres Jahr." [A bad year] He really couldn't have been friendlier and looked far less broken down than I would have thought.

Gustav's letters were evidently dictated to a secretary and copied out later in exquisite *schrift*, in the old German style. In his own spiky hand he sometimes gave as good as he got, as in this brutally understated brush-off, quoted in full. "If I am grateful for your letter I cannot all the same forget the two lessons you have seen fit to give me, and you cannot hold it against me if I avoid a third. My compliments to you."

Compromising further, Eugène agreed to divide his time

by spending eight months in Paris, four in Vienna. In the first years of their marriage, however, he and Mitzi lived in Berlin, where ostensibly he was a banker. At best desultory about his career, his real interest was acquiring more and more works of art for his collection, and for this he depended on Mitzi's money. In Paris they rented the second floor of 54 Avenue d'Iéna, a house in a monumental style appropriate to the surroundings and the nearby Arc de Triomphe. Its builder was Emile Deutsch de la Meurthe, and his descendants, the Gunzbourgs, lived below on the first floor. Originally from Saint Petersburg, they had a fortune from sugar. The first Jews to be ennobled as Barons by the Czar, they enjoyed much the same exclusive social standing as the Fould-Springers. Financial advisors said that Mitzi's income was large enough for Eugène to spend annually 100,000 francs on works of art. In the end a full-time collector, he spent five or six times that amount every year.

29

On 2 May 1914 Poppy was born in Meidling, taking her pecking-order place after Max and Bubbles as Mitzi and Eugène's third child. For no known reason she was nicknamed Pimoulouche by her parents, and that was how she signed her letters to them. Eugène also called her Dimples, and notes in his hand are full of the affectionate phrases of a loving father. "A difficult child," in the words of Mitzi's diary, Poppy used to slip into her father's bed in need of reassurance. She could sit on her own bed and cry uncontrollably. Her younger sister Liliane left a pen-portrait of her as she was growing up:

> Bizarre and very sensitive character, philosophical by nature evidently but unhappily she sometimes forgets it, she is small, very small but less small than she thinks, hair lies flat, nose and mouth and eyes are round, very pretty hands, lazy and contrary to the marmot she wakes up in winter at the sight of snow, and on reading bad

sentimental verses and interminable dissertations on vague subjects, looking in the mirror she gives herself up to martyrdom, dark matters – musical, a bit of a poet and quite a good sort, that's my sister Thérèse.

The teenage Poppy went to school in Paris at the Cours Hattemer. She used to complain afterwards that she had received no education in what was then an exclusive day-school. Julien Weil, the Grand Rabbi of France, gave religious instruction to the three sisters. To the end of her life Bubbles could recall snatches of Hebrew prayers. Unusually for girls at that period, Poppy and her younger sister Liliane did their *bat mitzvah*, the ceremony whereby they became full members of the Jewish faith. This took place in the synagogue on the Rue Victoire in Paris. With the two of them in the ceremony were Aline de Gunzbourg from downstairs in the Avenue d'Iéna and Lulu Esmond, friends in a little clique seeing each other virtually every day. For this occasion, the four all wore white dresses evidently in imitation of Catholics at a first communion.

After the First World War, Eugène began the search for a country house. One of his friends, the Marquis Boni de Castellane, a dandy surviving from the *Belle Époque*, told him that Royaumont was for sale. All her life Mitzi resented that Castellane had insisted on being paid a commission for introducing buyer and seller. Eugène merely emended the motto of the Order of the Garter to *Boni soit qui mal y pense*. Purchased and then restored in minute detail according to the original drawings, the château was finally a tribute to the fastidiousness and taste on which Eugène's social standing rested. A thin line divides snobbery from the wish to be correct. He criticized one of the most prominent soldiers in the country for signing himself Ph. Pétain on the grounds that the surname is sufficient for a marshal of France.

Poppy was eighteen when she and Alan were married there on 28 December 1934. Photographers recorded the event, and an enormous number of commemorative albums seem to have been made for the guests. For a formal portrait Poppy is standing in the drawing room. Given the immense train of her dress swirling over the floor and her resplendent tiara of flowers, the pose would be regal, except that Poppy looks far too young and unprepared for the adventure on which she was embarking. Three and a half inches above five foot (according to her passport), perhaps she hasn't even finished growing. She had known Alan only since the beginning of that year. And in another photograph taken on the same spot, he is standing next to her. His morning coat has been marvellously tailored, it has no creases, and his appearance is further formalised by stick-ups, a cravat that might have suited Beau Brummell, and the carnation in his buttonhole. He had already published stories in *The Sketch* and *Harper's*, as well as his two travel books, quite enough to attract the attention of everyone trying to spot a new talent. Unexpectedly expressionless, he seems to want to be taken for a Central European aristocrat whom it would be quite wrong to suspect of any unorthodox or bohemian tendencies.

A carpet had been laid down the steps of the terrace. Five years earlier, Eugène had died and Max was to give Poppy away. Aline de Gunzbourg, Lulu Esmond, Liliane, two cousins, were bridesmaids. Bubbles's five-year-old son Philip was the page. These familiars, so to speak, are distinct from the English contingent in language, religion and culture. Next to the two family nannies stand self-conscious outsiders: Frank Wooster, now Mitzi's husband; Alan's parents, Vere and Harry Pryce-Jones (the latter spoken about as Mr Colonel); and his younger brother Adrian. Also the best man, Patrick Balfour, the one person present who knew everything there was to know about Alan and was himself homosexual. At the time he was sharing a house in London with John Betjeman, and earning his living as a gossip columnist for the *Evening Standard*. In the following year he covered the war in Abyssinia, where Evelyn Waugh, also reporting and gathering material for *Scoop*, found him "an old chum [who] makes all the difference in the world." I knew him only much later, when he was Lord Kinross, author of numerous books including a biography of Ataturk. By then, he was slightly seedy, with the ruddy face of a Mister Punch exhausted by cynicism and the disconcerting habit of pushing his false teeth almost out of his mouth with his tongue. Giving parties, he made no effort to hide the collection of canes in his room. The gossip writer in him loved to recall which of his friends had gone to bed with one another and to tell me tales of Alan.

The service was held in the Protestant church of St Peter's in Chantilly, a few short miles from Royaumont. What did Poppy have to say about that? What could the elderly Jewish friends and relations recorded in the photographs have made of Alan? One of them, Madame Jean Stern, used to play on Alan's surname with apparent innocence: "*Percival Johnson, l'ai-je bien dit?*" – have I said that right? – just to quote it was enough to make Max laugh. At any rate, back at the château they all assembled at last on the steps of the terrace. Visible in some of the photographs is Mitzi's Rolls-Royce, reserved for her. A groom led up a pony harnessed to an open carriage with white flowers woven around its body and the spokes of its wheels. In the postillion's seat, a coachman held the reins. Driven away in this carriage, Alan and Poppy were a couple as singular as any to be found.

Four

Ménage à Trois

SOON AFTER they were married, Alan and Poppy were in a London theatre, so seated that they could not help overhearing the couple in the row in front talking about them. Poor Alan, they were saying, he's gone off with this French girl, nobody knows a thing about her, it hasn't a hope of lasting. Tapping them on the shoulder, Alan reassured these friends that all was well, and here was Poppy to speak for herself and her foreign antecedents.

A large literature records the Foulds and their doings. They were Jews from Alsace. The French revolution allowed Jews to leave the ghetto, and Ber Léon Fould was quick to do so, founding the Fould-Oppenheim bank in Paris in 1795. The bank specialized in loans to Egypt, as described in *Bankers and Pashas* by the historian David Landes. The poet Heinrich Heine was a connection, and one of the elderly ladies at the wedding in Royaumont was Tante Bijou Heine. A deputy in the Assemblée Nationale, Ber Léon's brother, Benoit, made speeches on behalf of fellow Jews. In 1840 he particularly distinguished himself by denouncing Count Ratti-Menton, the French consul in Damascus who was accusing local Jews of ritual murder. Under pressure from Ratti-Menton, the Ottoman authorities had arrested a number of Jews and tortured some to death. To this day, the Arab and Muslim media repeat primitive libels about Jews and Judaism, and even appear to believe them.

When I was writing *Paris in the Third Reich*, I attended the trial in Cologne of three S.S. men with a prominent role in the wartime occupation and lumped together as the

"Paris Gestapo." One of them, Ernst Heinrichsohn, had supervised the departure of deportees from the transit camp at Drancy to Auschwitz to be murdered. Among children driven by fear of the unknown, a fantasy grew that they were going to a place called Pitchipoi. On the station platform Heinrichsohn liked to wear riding clothes and carry a stick with which to hit out. Those on their way to death will have seen this man in their final vision of France. Hélène Allatini was a cousin of Mitzi's from Vienna; she and her husband Eric are in the photographs of Poppy and Alan's wedding at Royaumont. They escaped to Paris after the Anschluss in 1938. Published in French in 1940, Hélène's memoir has the title *Mosaïques*, a tragic pun. Too fastidious and other-worldly to get the measure of the Nazism overpowering her, she reminisces about aristocrats and rabbis in her life. Aunty Lily told me that Hélène wore silk underclothes and changed them three times a day. Both of them elderly, she and Eric were deported in Convoy 63 to Auschwitz on 17 December 1943. Locked without food or water in a sealed cattle wagon, in all likelihood they would have died during the journey. Of the 850 on that convoy, 22 survived in 1945, four of them women. Thousands of Jews had come to Cologne to demonstrate outside the court and march through the city in memory of those who had been murdered. As we were assembling, I happened to notice a wall with a tablet set into it, recording that the Fould-Oppenheim bank used to be on that spot.

Achille Fould (1800–1869), Ber Léon's son, was a banker and economist. At different times during the Second Empire, Louis Napoleon Bonaparte appointed him finance minister. Cartoons of the period draw him rapaciously shoveling all available taxes into the Treasury in order to finance the disastrous wars in which Louis Napoleon tried to emulate the first Napoleon Bonaparte, his uncle. Karl Marx, no less, polemicised against the man he dismissed as the Jew Fould, "a stock-exchange Jew," and one of the most notorious members of what he imagined was the conspiracy of high finance. At a moment when Achille Fould was minister, his mistress, an English demi-mondaine known as Skittles, dropped him into a very public scandal by going to live with the much younger Wilfrid Scawen Blunt, then an attaché at the British embassy at the start of a conspicuous career as a lady-killer. A number of Jews converted to Protestantism as a first step on the roundabout way to assimilation, and Achille Fould was one of them.

A cousin of his was Léon Fould (1839–1924), my great-grandfather, known in the family as "Bon Papa" and not to be confused with his uncle Ber Léon. He had lived through the Commune in the revolutionary Paris of 1870. His wife was Thérèse Praskovia Ephrussi from Odessa, the half-sister of Charles and Maurice Ephrussi, cosmopolitan figures to whose financial and intellectual distinction Edmund de Waal, another of their descendants, pays tribute in his book *The Hare with Amber Eyes*. In 1864 when Thérèse was sixteen she sat for a portrait that brings out her prominent brown eyes, a round face as intelligent as it is innocent, a high straight forehead, dark hair that falls with natural tidiness – Poppy took her real name from her and looked so similar that they might have been twins. Bon Papa and Thérèse had three children: Eugène my grandfather born in 1873, Robert who died young, and Elizabeth, otherwise Tante Lizzie, another of the little old ladies on the terrace at Poppy's wedding. She had married Oncle Jo, Vicomte de Nantois, also long dead but for whose sake she had become a Catholic. German race laws held that Jews converted to Christianity still counted as Jews, and in occupied Paris she had to wear the yellow star that singled them out. Her devoted maid, Clothilde Kannengiesser, a born Catholic and a native of Alsace, sewed the yellow star on her own clothes, and never hesitated to accompany Tante Lizzie in the streets and shops. Alsatians had been obliged to have German citizenship, and Clothilde's courage might well have gotten her shot for treason.

Eugène attended the Lycée Janson, reputedly one of the best schools in Paris. In March 1888, when he was a teenager, his report gave a sketch of his character that others, among them Mitzi and his children, were to substantiate in the future. "He will be an excellent pupil the day when he is able to check his frivolity and the arrogance that prevents him achieving the results to be expected of him." The tone of letters to his parents is light, though what is remembered of his humour still offers clues to a remote and idiosyncratic personality. Speaking of a couple, he described the husband as Sunday afternoon in London and the wife as Monday morning in Paris. "Sich vorstellen und wieder weg," he joked at the sight of any ill-favoured couple whose sexual relations might seem improbable – just to imagine them at it is enough to turn you away, in an unidiomatic translation. A Jew who has become a Catholic priest is "a deserter in uniform." Asked by Mitzi how to spell some word he would keep a serious face and spout a row of impossible consonants. To have daughters, he lamented, was like putting sugar on strawberries that someone else would eat. A dog called Toby, he said, was an "or not," a pun from *Hamlet* that might well escape a French owner. Long after his death, his daughter Bubbles summed up: "Word play constituted his sole defense against those who made claims on him. The laughter of others kept his melancholy at bay."

In photographs he appears either as a good-looking and well-groomed man about town or as a satisfied and conventional paterfamilias with his wife and children grouped around him. The first time Mitzi was pregnant, however, he told his mother that this was "unberufen," uncalled for.

Social life evidently preoccupied him. Writing from St
Moritz to his mother, he gives a typical list of the international set he was pleased to be with, café society in today's
vocabulary: "the Lamberts, Bijou Heine, the Casati, little
Madame Deschamps with the Ritters, Madame d'Hautpoul,
Pierre de Segonzac, Constantinovitch, Marino Vagliano, the
Zoghebs, Mrs. Tiffany, Napoléon Murat," and more besides.
Max remembered that in St. Moritz in about 1912 his father
had overheard four Frenchmen at the next table in the hotel
accusing Jews of vulgar manners and nouveau-riche fur-
nishings in their houses. As someone who considered that
connoisseurship and good taste were essential aspects of his
personality, he moved to their table and tackled them then
and there.

In France the names of the company he kept are Löwen-
thal, Helbronner, Weisweiller, Stern, David-Weill, members
of families whose social success led them to hope they were
assimilated though they could not be sure of it. In one letter
to his mother he calls an angry cousin "Meschuggah" (as he
spells the Yiddish word for idiotic, adding a self-conscious
exclamation mark), while in another written from a boat on
the Nile he explains arrangements for their journey in
"Mitzraîm," a complex pun based on Mitzi's name and the
Hebrew word for Egypt. In his twenties at the time of the
Dreyfus affair, he found himself cut by the upper classes
among whom he so badly wanted a place. Exceptionally, the
Marquis de Jaucourt crossed the Place Vendôme to shake
Eugène's hand in full view of other people. Right up to the
present the members of the family have kept alive the memory of this public gesture – his daughter Lorette was yet
another guest on the terrace at Royaumont when Poppy
married. "*Je ne nous aime pas*" – I don't like us – Eugène used
to say of his French compatriots.

Once when I must have been in my twenties, Mitzi took

me to lunch in Paris at Maxim's. They made a fuss of her there. She'd invited someone who had known Marcel Proust, and they could exchange memories. In a sort of glory by association, for instance, the family had their teeth seen to by Docteur Darcissac, Proust's dentist whose technique by then was half a century out of date. (His even older colleague once drilled my tongue by accident, and then said, "*Mais mon petit, tu renifles comme un petit cochon de Yorkshire*" – you are sniveling like a Yorkshire piglet.) Connection to Proust came through Mitzi's mother-in-law Thérèse who had a salon where he was a regular and watchful visitor. In the library at Royaumont was a copy of his first published work, the translation in 1904 of Ruskin's *The Bible of Amiens*. The flyleaf carries a dedication in his slightly disjointed hand to "Madame Leon Fould. Respectueux hommage d'un ami," followed by his signature.

Mitzi was in touch with Professor Philip Kolb of the University of Illinois at Urbana-Champaign, the outstanding Proust scholar of the day. His edition in twenty volumes of Proust's letters has a good many references to one or another Fould. In the fifth volume of this series Kolb publishes a remarkable letter to Eugène that he dates, no doubt correctly, to 19 March 1905. Eugène was then twenty-nine and Proust had come to a dinner celebrating his engagement to Mitzi. He praises "the ravishing beauty of Mademoiselle Springer" and her air of intelligence although he had not had the chance to speak to her. Insisting that he is writing as Eugène's friend, he appears ostensibly to be congratulating him. It is a solemn moment for Eugène, his life and his friends are about to change, and Proust concludes with resonance: "The task of your wife will be very delicate and very lofty and all your friends place the greatest hope in her that she will be able to fulfill it." Unexpectedly he lets drop that Eugène is a "humouriste," that is someone caught

up in his own comic view of things. Under the circumlocu-
tion and the tact is the unmistakable warning that a homosexual could not expect to have a successful marriage. Had
Eugène read it that way and taken umbrage, the skillfully
drafted ambiguity of this letter would have allowed Proust to
answer that he had no idea what Eugène was talking about.
The fictional Swann is modelled on several of Proust's friends
and acquaintances, and Eugène is one of them.

In the First World War, Eugène made use of his English
and the Russian picked up from his mother to become an
interpreter. Another interpreter, Robert de Rothschild, his
counterpart as a Jewish baron, was senior to him in rank, and
two versions exist of the long-lasting quarrel that affected
both their families. According to Mitzi, Robert de Rothschild heard Eugène saying that his father-in-law in the
enemy city of Vienna believed himself to be ruined. "You
can at last say that you made a love match," Robert de Rothschild is supposed to have interjected, rubbing in the fact
that Mitzi's fortune was the basis of Eugène's lifestyle. But
Robert's son Elie used to suggest that the bitterness between
the two men was some issue of homosexuality.

Frank Wooster had entered Eugène's life before the war.
The illegitimate son of the Birmingham industrialist Sir
Frank Leyland, he was a spendthrift who had run through
such money as his father had given him. Educated at
Uppingham, he had neither the skill nor the intention to
earn his living, preferring to gravitate towards rich people
willing to pay for him. One such was Paul Goldschmidt,
himself raw material for Proust as a well-connected Jewish
homosexual, and Frank moved to Paris to live with him. In
those early days he had played golf at Le Touquet with P. G.
Wodehouse, and it seemed plausible that Bertie Wooster
had immortalized Frank's surname with its unusual spelling. Frankie Donaldson, the first biographer of Wodehouse,

was in some doubt that the dates fitted, so depriving Frank Wooster of what would have been his major contribution to the gaiety of nations.

Frank had undoubted social gifts and a certain stagey presence. By the time I knew him, he had aged very well, and was still handsome and his manner debonair. His hair was white with a slight blue rinse to it. The drawl in his voice left the impression that nothing in life needs to be taken too seriously. A little vain, a little condescending, he was immensely careful about his appearance, dressy in a Noël Coward mode with silk shirts from Sulka and ties from Charvet. At informal moments he liked to sport a foulard round the neck and what used to be called co-respondent shoes, their white leather uppers contrasting with brown toe-caps. Asked what Frank was like, Harold Acton, someone more likely to sympathise than criticise, replied in the words of the music-hall song about a dandy of the period, "He was Gilbert the Filbert." Commissioned in the First War in the King's Own Yorkshire Light Infantry, he had been on the Dardanelles expedition and remained in touch with General Sir Ian Hamilton, its commander. Serving later in France, he had been taken prisoner at Ypres, and his health was said to be delicate ever afterwards. Virtually his sole possession was a regimental drum turned into an unlikely coffee table in the drawing room of Mitzi's rue de Surène flat.

In her diaries Mitzi describes how in 1922 Eugène took her to Florence and brought Frank with him. Her *coup de foudre* on meeting Eugène's friend was to determine their lives. The two of them went out sightseeing by themselves. Here was the first of numerous future occasions when something external, a gesture of Frank's, a conversation by a particular tree, the sight of a cloud or a sunset, the gift of a piece of jewelry, the plucking of a flower, was enough to convince her that she was the chosen beneficiary of a higher order of things. During the outing that day in Florence they visited what she calls the cloisters at Montefalco, and there Frank's "beautiful profile" was consecrated, so to speak. (These cloisters cannot be identified; there seems to be more than one Montefalco.) Whenever Frank was to do or say something that confirmed her idealisation, she attributed "a Donatello look" to him. "Somehow I realized that he would be my comforter," she writes of that Florence outing – cleverly evasive wording in the circumstances. What's more, Gustav had died two years previously, she had inherited Meidling from him, and she lost no time taking Frank there, in other words showing him who and what she was.

Mitzi by then was the mother of four children; a fifth had been stillborn. Seemingly a conventional wife always disposed to indulge her husband, in her diaries she is in the habit of referring to Eugène either as Cocky or more usually as "my darling" or "my old darling." Her obvious impatience with him nonetheless unbalances their relationship. Straightaway after her Florentine epiphany with Frank, she lets Eugène slip out of her daily narrative to the extent that he seems eclipsed. Replacing him as the target of her passions and plans, Frank becomes "my angel." Repeating herself, she credits him with making her more and more ecstatically happy, linking this to a novel and unexpected note of religiosity. Throughout the 1920s many a day in the diary is opened or else closed with the refrain, "God bless us all three."

Here she is writing on 2 May 1928 (which happened to be Poppy's fourteenth birthday but this she does not mention.) "I knew it, angel, I knew you would call me up ... he woke me up at nine, oh! How sweet, asking a hundred times how I was. . . . Oh! the lovely hope in me all day of a sight of my necessary blessing." [Frank arrives that evening at her flat in the Rue de Surène] "My angel! He looks a little tired, has surely got to look much older since two months, but he is bright, radiant. Each word, each look was a blessing kiss [*sic*] . . . It struck me more than ever that we had two bodies. We are so perfectly one soul that I can never quite realize we are two." In subsequent entries she describes herself kneeling before him, kissing his hands and repeating, "I felt our souls were one, one for ever."

At one point a friend, Lucie de Langlade, asked in a knowing whisper how Frank was. Mitzi was infuriated that anyone could mistake her angel for her lover – this relationship had to be on a plane elevated far above the physical. My father was adamant that Frank had confessed to him on the subject of sex, "There is one thing I can't do for my Mary." At another point she quotes Frank's prediction of disaster in the event that she gave herself to him: "You always say if I deceived Cocky I would be quite lost." Yet there are plenty of other intimations: "When he lay in my arms, looking up at me and saying so often, you sweetest one, I could but press him to my heart and long that all the prayer that was in me could pass through my hands and eyes over to him." The tone of exaltation and wish fulfillment leaves open the reality of their relationship.

On a journey before the First World War in the north of France, Eugène and Frank had seen an eighteenth-century house in Montreuil-sur-mer, once a garrison town with historic fortifications by Vauban, and half an hour from Le Touquet and the seaside. Built for a senior officer, the house is an architectural triumph of classical symmetry and ornamental detail, with large rooms on the ground floor for entertaining and half a dozen bedrooms upstairs. Imagining themselves living there in a kind of provincial retreat, the two men had never forgotten it and early in 1928 paid a visit there.

The house is well within motoring distance of Royaumont and it was a caprice to hanker after it. Mitzi alone had the means to make the purchase and soon she incorporates it into her scheme of things as "our dream house." The wife of the owner had the throwaway line, "When one of us dies, *I* shall retire to the country." During negotiations, Mitzi comments that Frank "adores the Montreuil house we love. May we get it so that he can enjoy peaceful days there." A visit to the house at that moment with Frank and Eugène led her to exclaim in her diary that she was "happy, more than one can think or know. I looked from one to the other of my dearest ones and prayed my gratitude." That June she fires off another exclamation, "Montreuil is ours!"

Was she facilitating the homosexual relationship between the two men or on the contrary breaking it up, and was this done consciously or unconsciously? For Frank, the acquisition of Montreuil was a security for the future and a tribute to his powers of manipulation. Was she hoping thereby to claim Frank for herself or to punish Eugène for being unfaithful to her? Impulses of revenge and possessiveness merge inseparably with illusion. Eugène's surviving letters and little messages on single sheets of paper express rather pathetic distress that what was happiness to her was unhappiness to him. The apologetic tone is sometimes plangent, sometimes abject. Evidently he realised what was happening, but felt helpless to do anything about it.

In November 1928, while the colour schemes and interior decoration at Montreuil were still under discussion, Mitzi and Eugène set off on a journey to Asia that was intended to take six months. Bubbles, their eldest daughter, accompanied them. This was an act of reparation for a crisis that strained family relationships. On the lookout for experts to manage her finances, Mitzi had found one called Toto Morange, and she thought to cement his loyalty by pushing Bubbles to become engaged to him. At the last moment, Bubbles refused to go through with this arranged marriage, the wedding presents had to be returned, and mother and daughter reconciled. Mitzi regretted leaving Max, "my adored Sonny," but spared no thought for the two abandoned youngest daughters except to observe that Poppy cried bitterly when her parents left Royaumont. With Miss Purdue, a lady's maid for Mitzi, and twenty pieces of luggage, they embarked on a liner at Marseilles.

They were to visit places in Ceylon and Indonesia; they liked Singapore and Kuala Lumpur; for Mitzi Penang and Angkor Wat were special highlights. In the manner of travellers, they enjoyed sunsets, animals, museums, choosing batik in the market and buying a picture from Walter Spies, the artist who was to become famous for his landscapes of the Dutch East Indies. But underneath the leisure and the luxury, the drama of this triangle was playing out. In the process Mitzi brought to a head the tactic of divide and rule that she applied in matters great and small for the rest of her life.

The dominant character, Mitzi perhaps recognized where her feelings must lead her and sought to justify herself. At the outset, at any rate, she found Eugène "like a baby.... I can't say how adorable and perfect he is these days in every way. And so sweet to me." This mood did not last. Frank was trailing them on another liner on much the same course around Asia, sometimes ahead, sometimes behind. Through him "my soul feels as if it has found its harbour." A ship's concert sent her hurrying to her cabin to be alone with her thoughts: "I longed for the sight of you." Eugène had become "quite stiff," upsetting her. Seasonal shipboard parties were a strain, "He is awful at Christmas and New Year ... what bliss that I can stand this now without the pain and sadness it used to give me." She goes on as if addressing him, "How terrible you can be, how you take it out of me and for such nothings. A naughty spoilt child. When I think of the old age you are going to have I tremble." In Vietnam one night towards the end of January 1929 Eugène went out by himself to Cholon, a part of Saigon, and did not return until almost dawn. "If I died you could go on living," he then told her as recrimination got underway next morning, "not so if anything happened to Frank, he's the air you breathe."

After Mitzi's death, my Aunt Bubbles and I sorted some of her papers. In a folder was Eugène's account of this voyage. Humidity had so affected the paper that the ink had run and there could be no discovering his side of the story. But Mitzi had preserved in a separate packet every one of the letters and telegrams from Frank that had been waiting for her in hotels and agents' offices on shore. Surprisingly anodyne, even banal, they are full of the kind of advice one tourist might give another about where to stay and what to see. Rapture about souls is conspicuously absent. At most, he regretted their separation; he spoke of Eugène as "a funny old man" whom he hoped was helping and not hindering. Moreover he had with him someone he describes as "my little friend," who bought things for himself rather too expensively in the market.

"One doesn't introduce someone like that into one's family," Eugène regretted. But that is what he had done. When they were on a ship sailing from Hong Kong to Shanghai this tangle of sexual competition and deception took a sudden unexpected turn. Eugène fell ill with pneumonia. In a privately printed memoir with the title *I Loved My Stay*, Bubbles records how her round-the-world adventure came to an end in the Astor House Hotel in Shanghai. "Everything began to crumble about me." Nursing him, Miss Purdue reported to Mitzi that he seemed to be very upset, "He fears that he is not the only one in your heart." Mitzi immediately lost her temper and went to talk to him "with a look of sheer fury on her face," and a parting shot to Bubbles and Miss Purdue, "Don't worry! I'm not going to hurt your patient." Not quite fifty-three, Eugène died in the hotel on 1 March. A fortnight later the women sailed across the Pacific, with Eugène's body on board. At Honolulu Frank joined them, and Bubbles confined herself to saying that at that sad time he was "a great help and comfort."

In the eyes of his children their father had been a victim, and victimhood did not suit him. Mitzi did not ask herself if he had died an unhappy man on her account. From the moment Eugène fell ill Mitzi stopped writing her diary. When she resumed four months later in July, she granted herself absolution. Although actually the main actor in the emotional struggle that had come to its unforeseen end in Shanghai, she depicted herself as passive. She was able to repress guilt by denying the way she had manipulated her husband and his lover. As though it was all the doing of these two men, she had been swung on an emotional see-saw of suffering and salvation, and on page after page she repeated herself in the manner of this passage: "God bless those who are left me. I thought I could never write again, but I must note these last days, must put down each detail of these peaceful, sweet, helpful hours. Without you, my angel, I could never have lived on, have stayed alone without my adored one.... Be blessed for the blessing of your sweetness, for each understanding look, for each comprehensive kiss, for those long dear talks about our adored one." In one or two rooms at Royaumont, photographs of Eugène had a tombstone formality. He became something of an unperson, to the point that Alan used to say, "If we had known Eugène we wouldn't have liked him."

That July, she and Frank decided that the strain of events had exhausted them and they had to escape. Just as she had shown him her Vienna so he would retrace for her sake some of his early life in England. The hotel in Eastbourne where they stayed, the rustic cottage they wondered whether to rent, were far removed from anything in her experience. During a walk on Beachy Head he told her that once before on this very spot he had heard an inner voice saying, "Do not despair, someone needs you," whereupon he took her in his arms, "and now I know you were the one." Whether by chance or design, the image he presented of himself corresponded exactly to the image she cultivated of him. At the age of six he had been sent to St. Andrew's, a preparatory school nearby. They went visiting. Whether naively or not, she lets drop that the Brown family running the school "wondered at a lady friend of Frank's." However, Miss Brown was impressed by Mitzi's deep mourning and upgraded her from Baroness to Countess. Mitzi came away satisfied that Frank had been "a delicate sensitive child," and the separation from the mother he loved so tenderly was "the first great sorrow of his youth." It is impossible to decide whether guilt, schizophrenia, or plain absence of self-awareness was impelling her coincidentally and frequently to switch from devotion to Frank straight into this sort of counterpoint about Eugène: "Oh! My Cocky, I cannot think of you without thinking that I can never, never, never stand the terrible cruel crisis. Oh! my darling, how could you die, where are you. In my heart more than ever alive as long as I live."

Mitzi's children could not fail to observe how Frank had supplanted Eugène. That their father's male lover should captivate their mother was the subject of endless speculation. Bubbles was virtually alone in having a good word to say for him. Born in 1907, she was a greater beauty than her younger sisters and made them aware of it too. Back in Austria in the autumn of 1929, Mitzi and Bubbles stayed at Langau, the home of Alphonse and Clarice Rothschild. A suspicious Mitzi asked Bubbles if she was in love, and discovered that she had fallen for Eduardo Propper de Callejon, a Spanish diplomat and supposedly the lover of Clarice Rothschild. A man of the world, he was thirteen years older than Bubbles. Mitzi invited him to lunch at Meidling, "to have a look at him," she wrote. "He upset me terribly. To lunch we also had Alice Townshend, the widow of General Townshend of Kut [where he and his troops surrendered to the Turks in 1917] as she is née Cahen d'Anvers [an eminent Jewish family] of Paris. She is more British than the British. At lunch I heard this Spaniard say, Remember and note my words, in ten years it will be the end of England. Alice after lunch said, Throw that creature out, he is out to marry Bubbles." Frank was in Munich and in October she summoned him to come and to make "his friend Bubbles" understand that she should give up Eduardo. But he concluded otherwise: The couple would be happy, and besides, "You are in business with interests all over the world and a diplomat can come in handy." That was enough to settle it. On December 28 the Abbé Mugnier, a veteran of the Proustian circle, married Bubbles and Eduardo in the church at Asnières, two or three miles from Royaumont. Eduardo was a Catholic through his mother, with Jewish origins through his father. He insisted that Bubbles become Spanish but said he would never put pressure on her to convert to Catholicism. Mitzi had chosen the date for the wedding, but because it fell within the year of Eugène's death as usual she soon convinced herself that others were behaving with the express purpose of causing her to suffer.

In the summer of 1930, Max summoned Frank to his house in Paris, and the fact that he was still in bed when Frank arrived must have spoken volumes. He had an ultimatum to deliver and it would not take long. He was now the head of the family, he said, he had been made unhappy by Frank and he did not want his younger sisters to go through what he had gone through. Frank was asked to leave at once for Royaumont, take away clothes he had left there and never come back. Instead he went to Mitzi's flat in the Rue de Surène, where she found him lying on a chaise-longue looking ill. "It might kill you, the sorrow of it all," he began. Playing on her emotional neediness, he explained that Max adored her and always felt that too much of her love went to him, Frank. Nor could he see how he had made anyone unhappy. Here was a clever appeal to take his side while finding a plausible excuse for the behaviour of the Sonny she claimed to adore. She fell in with it: "Long and silently, I kissed his hands and then very gently I told him, Max has married us."

The indignant Mitzi immediately confronted Max: Did he expect that she was never again going to see Frank? Unconditionally surrendering, he apologized and would make what amends he could. He and his younger sisters a few weeks later accompanied Mitzi to the Bayreuth festival. They then stayed at the Grand Hotel in Nuremburg. As though the scene ordering him to depart had never occurred, Frank came over from Berchtesgaden where he was with friends, and moved into the hotel. "I went to bed at 10," Mitzi noted, "he undressed and in that red and white pyjama that suits him so beautifully he lay on the bed beside mine. I cuddled up in his arms. Utter confidence. Utter pure joy. My heart was beating much faster than his.... I prayed pressing his head to my heart. He stayed there. All at once he jumped up and said, 'Must go now, my darling.' How I longed for him to stay but when he says he wants to go I know it's right towards our pure oneness that he goes [*sic*]."

Max's bid to stand in for Eugène as head of the family had failed. Father and son owed their way of life to Mitzi. Had either of them insisted that the relationship between her and Frank was destructive and intolerable, she had only to resort to the power of her money; she could cut them off at any time, in which case they would have to earn a living. When all was said and done, here was a competition for resources. Frank had nothing to lose, everything to gain. Eugène, and then Max, had everything to lose, nothing to gain. A penitent Max soon went to Montreuil and she gloats that he "begged my pardon so sweetly." Unable to stand up to his mother, for the rest of his life he never quite gained independence and his rightful status.

"My children!" she was expostulating in June 1931 about what she felt was their continued resistance to Frank, "Why are you all so complicated, theatrical, méfiants [mistrustful] and egotistical ... they have it well in their minds that he speaks against them to me." She attributed this to the nannies whose moral code was far too rigid to accommodate Frank. This was a moment for divide and rule. She took Poppy alone of the children to Montreuil and after a happy evening together "ever so tenderly told her the nannies had to be pensioned off. First she turned to stone and said nothing." Just seventeen at the time Poppy then screamed, "We are always alone, nobody loves us but Nanny, she is everything to us," and went on, "You do nothing but laugh since my father's death." Since that death, Mitzi wrote expertly shifting the blame, this was "the most cruel blow I have had. I left her."

Back at Royaumont three days later, with what she considered "a world of tenderness," she told the nannies that they had to leave. Nanny Stainer replied, "You will never manage to part me from the children." Jessie was even more blunt, "I don't know why I listen to your palaver," and banged the door. Whenever this scene was mentioned in years to come, Jessie would emphasise that she could never have left the children. And next morning Poppy returned to the charge,

"For seventeen years you have done nothing but kill me!" To Mitzi, she "was like a lunatic for days." Fault lines were out in the open.

In fashionable places such as Naples, Capri and Venice, offering museums, opera houses and five-star hotels, Mitzi had only to announce her arrival with Frank for them to receive invitations from other rich or prominent local people. At the time Egypt was effectively governed by the British almost as though it were a colony, and some with social aspirations were in the habit of going out there for a winter season. Frank was one such, travelling to Egypt as before with his old lover Paul Goldschmidt. Wherever he was, work proceeded in his absence at Montreuil. The "dream house" proved too small and inconvenient. A footbridge from its garden led over a sunken street to a park and a row of cottages. Mitzi had bought the park and three of the cottages, which were then pulled down. Supposedly an architect, Frank had designed a much larger new house to be built on the site. His original drawings, it is said, omitted a staircase, and Frank had wanted to have shutters and windows that opened outwards. Mitzi told me one day that Frank had gone ahead with the building regardless of expense at the height of the Depression. As the works were nearing completion, a bill of particulars shows that she still owed just over two million francs. She was fretting about paying when a letter arrived from Hungary with a huge payment to compensate for laying a railroad across one of her properties. By the end of 1932 she and Frank had moved into Montreuil, and in January 1933 they had a civil marriage in the town. In the same month that Adolf Hitler became Chancellor of Germany, Mitzi became English; suddenly, thanks to Frank, "my country has ever been England." A short year later, she had accommodated herself to "Our England ... each time you are in London you feel, if possible, prouder to have an English passport."

52

The change of nationality was accompanied by conversion to the Christian faith. She would be free from those Jewish nerves that were always troublesome. In her diaries she persuaded herself that she wasn't escaping but once again was quite right to be doing what she wanted to do. "It's queer how in my heart I never felt driven to the Jewish religion. I only protect the race the moment anyone attacks it, but I don't like them." In June 1933 she asked herself, "A Hitler, who can understand?" In common with many frightened and wishful Jews everywhere, she was interpreting Nazism as the personal aberration of Hitler. She and Frank could visit Bayreuth and drive through Nazi Germany as though it was still the country they had always known and the stormtroopers and swastikas were local colour, not worth a second glance. The danger was apparently unimaginable even to someone so well travelled and cosmopolitan. Yet what the new British and Christian Mary Wooster imagined was the final step in a welcome process of assimilation was only impersonation.

Marriage to Frank drove the somewhat pointed hinting of sexual repression out of her diaries. "I thought that our oneness was something so wonderful that physical union could not better it," she had confided to herself. She told Father Cardew, the priest who received her into the church, that the relationship with Frank had not been physical, and he took it that Frank had displayed the manners of a gentleman, waiting until he had made an honest woman of her. At Montreuil on 17 May 1934 and still confiding to herself as usual, she resorts to explicit language, "The first time I was yours at last was on a 17th. The first time in our new house."

Long after Frank's death, in the *fumoir* at Royaumont, we were gossiping about some contemporary of Mitzi's who was said to have had an affair with her gardener. "*Quand on a eu Frank on n'a pas besoin du jardinier*" (When one has had Frank there's no need for the gardener.) Mitzi's sudden vulgarity seemed altogether out of keeping, the kind of thing she thought people ought to be saying in those liberated days. As though passing off the wisdom of a lifetime's experience, on other occasions, and especially to her grandchildren, she was in the habit of stating as it were ex cathedra: "Homosexuals make the best husbands."

53

FIVE

Reputed Father

Heb dduw heb ddim, ddu a digon – the Pryce-Jones motto

I WAS BORN in Meidling on 15 February 1936, in the corner room on the first floor where Poppy had also been born exactly twenty years earlier. Whether my first name acknowledged Jewish or Welsh antecedents was apparently much discussed in the house. What it might mean socially or culturally for me to have a surname that is identifiably Welsh was never raised either at a personal or an abstract level. I was twenty before national service took me to Wales for the first time and then only to practise platoon attacks at Trawsfynydd, a military training ground with a nuclear power station in the distance. In the village there I wrote a cheque to a man with exactly the same names as myself.

Marriage brought me to the land of my Welsh fathers. Clarissa's parents, Harold and Nancy Caccia, lived at Abernant in the Wye Valley, and we acquired Pentwyn, a cottage nearby but much higher on the edge of Eppynt, the open hill with a view of the Black Mountains fifty miles away. Time was when Clarissa had ridden up on her pony and formed a wish that one day she would live here. One room had a bath that had never been plumbed in. The slates were sliding from the roof of a separate building, once a barn. A long time later, we had made a home, and Clarissa's mother called it Pen-trianon. I was weeding the minute garden when a neighbour telephoned to say that Princess Margaret was staying with her, and she was about to bring her round to show her the barn.

More incongruous still than the royal party in this isolated retreat was the visit of Svetlana Stalin. Cursed by her parentage, tempestuous by nature, she existed in a perpetual storm that might break in any direction. A circle of friends wished her well, and among them were Laurence and Linda Kelly, both historians with experience of the Soviet Union. During a meal in their house I invited Svetlana to Pentwyn, never thinking she'd accept. My nerve failed when we picked her up as arranged in a hotel in nearby Hay, and I apologized for the cottage's lack of amenities. Does it have running water, she asked. Having said point blank that she refused to talk about her father, she would come down from her room and talk exclusively about him, tormented that she couldn't help loving a father whom she knew was a monster. At moments, a tiger gleam in her eyes gave her an uncanny look of Stalin himself. In another mood, she took over the kitchen with a special recipe for chicken. When she had retreated to Wisconsin for her last years, I sent her a novel of mine and got back the title page, torn out without further comment.

Not long before he died, Alan stayed at Pentwyn. He wanted to pay a last visit to Dolerw, the Pryce-Jones house at Newtown where he had spent childhood holidays. It was raining that day and he refused to put on a coat because, "I don't get wet, I'm Welsh." Links had survived. He had been President of the Montgomeryshire Association, and he had promoted R. S. Thomas whose early poems with their angry mourning for a lost Wales had been published locally in Newtown.

Like Meidling, Dolerw is the monument of a self-made man out to show what he can do and expecting to be admired for it. Welsh gentry lived here in the eighteenth century. Briefly the house came into the possession of Charles Hanbury-Tracy, a local grandee and Liberal Member of Parliament. From the 1870s onwards Pryce Jones, as he was originally called, transformed Dolerw into a large Italianate villa complete with a tower. He and his wife, Eleanor Morris, had four daughters and four sons, the youngest of them all being Harry (1878–1952), father of Alan. Another of the four sons, my great-uncle Victor, sold the lease in 1947 and moved to Norfolk where he and his wife spent the rest of their lives riding to hounds. Since then, Dolerw has been successively a Catholic school, a convent, and a Voluntary Sector Resource Centre, four dissociated words that give away public funding.

Born in 1834 in Llanllwchaiarn near Newtown, Pryce was the illegitimate son of Mary Goodwin and, according to the parish record, his "reputed father William Jones." He built a small draper's shop into the Royal Welsh Warehouse or RWW, a concern primarily based on processing wool, the staple product of that countryside, into flannel, blankets, sleeping bags, extending the range gradually into clothing and household goods. Trading internationally, he pioneered marketing by mail order, using his influence to have a railway track laid where it suited him and organising special trains to and from London for his business. Mr Sears and Mr Roebuck are said to have visited, learnt how he operated, and sold him founder shares in their business. The RWW, a huge lump of red brick, still stands today as he left it, with the family name up on the roofline in outsize white lettering. A stone set into the wall by the main door commemorates a gold medal the RWW was awarded in Vienna in 1873, by coincidence the very year in which Comte Vasili observed Gustav doing himself a favour by buying good stock cheaply. By 1880, the RWW was employing 6,000 workers and had about 250,000 customers worldwide. When Queen Victoria knighted him in 1887 he hyphenated and duplicated his name, to become Sir Pryce Pryce-Jones.

He enjoys a nationalist image as a model entrepreneur who proved that the Welsh could succeed through their own endeavors and so dispense with English patronage. His obituary in a local newspaper, the *Montgomery Express*, concluded that his business acumen amounted to genius and had brought worldwide renown to the Principality.

The telephone rang one day at Pentwyn and a friendly stranger informed me that great-uncle Victor had left portraits of these forebears of mine to one of the churches at Newtown. The sanctuary where the portraits were hanging was being converted into a badminton court and unless I retrieved them that very afternoon they would be put on a bonfire. Far from flattering the couple, the artist, Arthur Nowell, depicts stiff and forbidding figures against a dark background, he in a morning coat, she holding a teacup with no suggestion that she might offer a cup to anyone else.

The historical record bears out Arthur Nowell's characterization of his sitters. At a moment when a general election was in the offing I was in the main street of Builth Wells, the small town closest to Pentwyn. For a long time this part of Wales has been politically volatile. An elderly man came out of his shop to ask me, "Why aren't you standing for parliament?" I asked if he thought I should. "You should be like Sir Pryce, he used to give us five shillings to go and break the Liberals' windows." The Liberals were one or another member of the Hanbury-Tracy family, owners of Gregynog, a grand house, and accustomed to treating the position of Lord Lieutenant of the county or election to parliament as member for the constituency of Montgomery Boroughs as tribute rightfully due to their status. Between 1880 and 1895 Sir Pryce, a Conservative, engaged in a political contest with the Hanbury-Tracys. Sir Pryce won the majority of the elections in this period, and went to Westminster with a dozen Welsh MPs in his pocket. Thanks to this parliamentary machine, it is said, he was able to promote his interests, for instance getting the railway track to Newtown laid right up to the Royal Welsh Warehouse.

58   Celebrating victory in the 1892 election, Sir Pryce and Eleanor went by train to Llanidloes, half an hour or so away from Newtown but still in the constituency. This was Liberal territory and a crowd was waiting to greet them with three cheers for Frederick Hanbury-Tracy, the loser, and to boo ("hoot" is the word in the press accounts) the Pryce-Joneses. After taking tea in the one and only hotel, Sir Pryce and his wife retreated to the station, and on the way were jostled and bruised. Losing his temper, he hit out with his stick. When he struck a little girl in the face and drew blood, a police inspector stopped him by taking hold of the stick. By the time that Sir Pryce boarded the train home, he had lost his hat and the angry crowd then burnt it.

The Liberals then accused him of buying votes. The petition was heard by Baron Pollock and Mr. Justice Wills. One charge was that Lady Pryce-Jones had called on the wife of one John Withers, "a somewhat prominent Liberal," and promised to get their daughter into Ashford High School for Welsh girls if Mr Withers voted for Sir Pryce. Another charge was that in pubs in Llanidloes one Abel Goldsworthy, in the employment of Sir Pryce but "a person with no money," offered money or drinks to bribe people to vote Conservative. The local *Montgomery Express* was delighted by the final verdict that Sir Pryce had nothing to answer for, writing that he had gained "one of the greatest victories that has ever been achieved by any Welshman." Years later, however, the considered opinion of the left-wing historian Henry Pelling was that this episode almost unseated Sir Pryce and he and his Conservative colleague indeed formed a corrupt political machine. In the 1895 election, Sir Edward Pryce-Jones, the eldest son (titled because he had been made a baronet), took over the seat, and the Hanbury-Tracy family retreated to Gregynog and abandoned the constituency.

One of Sir Pryce's four daughters had married a Powell and lived at Plas-y-Bryn near Newtown. Commissioned by a magazine to interview Dilys Powell, a relation of theirs and the veteran film critic of *The Sunday Times*, I discovered quite fortuitously that she was a Plas-y-Bryn cousin, and probably the last person alive able to recall visits to Dolerw before the First War. At tea on the lawn one summer day when she was still a child, she recalled, Sir Pryce had sat her on his knee.

My grandfather Harry, the youngest of Sir Pryce's sons, gave me the present of a toy horse and cart in wood that the estate carpenter at Dolerw had made for him. His nanny had taught him some nursery songs in Welsh, as folklore rather than genuine culture. Unlike his brothers, he played no part in the Royal Welsh Warehouse. Eton and Trinity College, Cambridge, thoroughly anglicized him. His social standing changed. Popular, called PJ by his friends, he exemplified the English gentleman of his day. The gaze was firm, the manners polite, the voice reserved. The slope of his shoulders made him appear slight, at a physical disadvantage, but this was misleading. He excelled at all sports with a ball. Decades after the event, he still minded that he had played well all one summer in the Eton cricket eleven only to be dropped to twelfth man for the all-important match against Harrow. Almost every day he wore the tie of a cricket club, either the MCC or I Zingari. If ever he felt socially insecure as the son of a tradesman who furthermore was illegitimate, he gave no sign of it.

A very good shot, he received invitations to grand houses for shooting weekends with grand people. According to his game book, he was regularly invited to shoot with Lord Pembroke at Wilton. Another of the guns there was Guy

Dawnay, who further invited him to shoot at Beningbrough in Yorkshire, the house of his parents Colonel Lewis and Lady Victoria Dawnay. Guy had a younger brother Alan, and a sister Vere. At first sight, Harry fell for Vere though too shy to declare it to her. Lewis Dawnay and both his sons were in the Coldstream Guards and seemingly swept a willing Harry away into the regiment. He and Guy reported to Wellington barracks together in October 1899, two weeks after the outbreak of the Boer war.

A short month later, with no preparation and even less training, and aged only twenty-one, he was in action. "We started at 4 A.M. and met the enemy at 6.30 at Modder River," as he described the battle to his mother at Dolerw, "they were heavily entrenched, in a very strong position, about 5,000.... I personally had a rough day of it, as I swam the river twice with Colonel Codrington and a few others to find we were cut off and the Boers were on us ... when it got dark, they suddenly began, they simply poured shots into us ... we were simply lying in the open. I really gave up all hopes and only prayed that I should be finished off without pain. We were ordered to cease fire and retire, had the enemy advanced we *must* have been annihilated, as they were 800 opposite our 100 and only about 300 yards away." As so often in that war, courage narrowly averted military disaster.

The idiom in which he often writes has since passed into something close to parody, but it served as understatement to those reading his letters. "The line was awfully cut up by Boers.... The Boers gave us a warmish time.... I had a ripping bathe in the dark ... fighting really is an awful game." But already by April 1900 he was complaining, "It is too annoying this war going on as it is. I really don't see how it is going to end. We seem to be losing instead of gaining ground." Ten months later he had had enough: "I feel as though I have been out here all my life." On two pages he lists the novels he has been reading, all long forgotten with the exception of those by Mrs Humphrey Ward and George Meredith. When the Coldstream took up quarters at Graaff Reinet he spent a lot of his time shooting duck and playing polo. 61

Gideon Jacobus Scheepers was a Boer commandant born the same year as Harry. A tribunal sentenced him to death on seven charges of murdering Boer loyalists, aggravated by additional charges of arson and train wrecking. On 17 January 1902 Harry wrote home to say that he had "the doubtful pleasure" of commanding the firing party. In his mind he was certain that the man deserved to be shot. A photograph captures the moment of execution with Harry at the centre of the drama and the regiment lined up at attention on three sides of a square. Next day he noted in his diary that only fifteen of the twenty men had loaded rifles, and jotted down the requisite orders in capital letters, "Firing Party – Volleys – Ready – Present – Fire!" He never mentioned this episode to me. Once in my hearing he said with a certain visible distaste that in South Africa he had witnessed Field Punishment Number One. This involved tying to the wheel of a field gun a soldier who had disobeyed orders in action. The man might end up with his head on the ground when the gun took up a firing position. This was the equivalent of a death sentence. Otherwise all he would say was that he wished he had bought a farm in the Karoo and settled there.

That December, the authorities at Newtown planned a reception to celebrate his return. The local *Montgomery Express* announced that this was cancelled: "Modest to a degree, the gallant Lieutenant would rather that we simply said he did his duty, and having done it, it was his wish to return home without any demonstration." A band nevertheless greeted him at the station, playing "See the Conquering Hero

Comes." The mayor, Mr T. Meredith, presented a silver cup "of exquisite workmanship" and in a speech to "a vast multitude" hoped that in time to come Harry's name "would be as well known in military circles as Sir Pryce's had become throughout the known world (loud cheers)." Some of that vast multitude then dragged him through the town in the Dolerw carriage, and the newspaper describes him rising from his seat to say among other tactful things that, "In South Africa, Montgomeryshire men had served their country very well, and he was always pleased to meet them out there."

Reticent, he glossed over his courtship at Beningbrough. "Delightful evening with Vere. She said goodnight to me," or "My own darling Vere," is about as far as he allows himself to go in his diaries. May 28, 1903 is the date of their engagement, to judge from Vere's inscription to Harry on that day of Elizabeth Barrett Browning's *Sonnets from the Portuguese*:

> I write with ink; thou need'st but look,
> One glance need'st only dart –
> I write my name within thy book,
> Thou thine upon my heart.

Six months after becoming engaged, he felt obliged to postpone marriage for the sake of soldiering abroad again. "I must go to Northern Nigeria for heaps of reasons – still it may prove the turning point in my career (if I have one in store!)" Seconded to the West African Frontier Force, he was to command two companies of the First Battalion of the Northern Nigerian Regiment. His father gave him an allowance of £1,200 a year, which made him rich, though not by the standards of Coldstream officers. He passed on to Vere his mother's assurance that with care they could live a married life on this money, "with five servants, allowing £300 for a house, but can one be got for that?"

Once again he found himself in the thick of things without any training or preparation in a mission for the Empire with only commonsense to rely on. Arriving at Lagos in February 1904 he dined at Government House with Sir Frederick Lugard (later Lord) who for all his reputation struck Harry as "an insignificant little man." In April he set off for Katagum with sixteen Yorubas and eighteen Hausas. These carriers nicknamed him "The White Man with the big nose." On the trek he was soon put to the test. "Some natives attacked us and insisted on a palaver! I tried to pacify them till they came so close and one arrow going through Musa my boy's hat. I fired three shots over their heads and then dropped a man at 80 yards! This apparently settled them, tho' I was very anxious." He acted in self-defence but one wonders what the judgment of the ladies at Beningbrough could have been when they read about this fraught encounter.

At Katagum, he noted that the mere presence of a white man is "such an excitement." When a colleague with the name of Barber turned up, he and Harry sang the Eton Boating Song. On his own and out of touch, responsible for law and order as though judge and district commissioner rolled into one, he was empowered to lash whoever he thought deserved punishment. Finding a private by the name of Andu Kontagora guilty of assault, for instance, he decided that he himself would give the man twenty-four lashes and fine him five shillings. He and his carriers were also covering a wide area on behalf of a boundary commission, reaching remote places whose names he records – Zogo, Zungero, Hadeija, Tubzugna. *The Morning Post* that May carried a report from Zungero: "Cannibalism and human sacrifice were on the wane, and the natives were daily becoming more desirous of co-operating with the Government in the development and welfare of their country." Addressing Lady Victoria Dawnay, his future mother-in-law, as "My dear little Mother," he threw in some local colour, "My house is very uncomfy, being a round mud one about four yards in diameter and full of white ants which eat everything."

I possess a pocket notebook in which he listed the men under his command, the medals he awarded, and the live ammunition he issued to each of them, with brief comments, mostly approving, on their character. He played polo with the Muslim emirs in the north. Nigeria was another country in which he would have liked to live, and he regretted leaving. Gamba, his orderly, cried at their parting and said over and over again, "*Sai Wale Rana*" – Goodbye till another day.

Back in England in April 1905, he lost no time marrying Vere. "We give you our darling child without a misgiving, knowing what she is to you," Lady Victoria had written to him a year previously on hearing of Vere and Harry's engagement. She followed this up: "One line of greeting on his wedding morning to our beloved Harry knowing well that he will prize the great treasure we are giving him today, with God's blessing." The fulsome style of his dear little Mother surely contains something cautionary.

In his autobiography, *The Bonus of Laughter*, Alan shows more affection for Lady Victoria than for his parents. During one Christmas holiday he insisted that he and I invite ourselves to lunch with the current tenant of Beningbrough. During the meal he made sure this lady, herself a dowager Countess, appreciated how glorious the background of the Dawnays had been. Alan's grandmother was a Grey, descending from Prime Minister Grey of the Reform Bill; his grandfather a son of Viscount Downe. Lady Victoria's sisters were Mary, wife of Lord Minto the Viceroy of India, the Countess of Antrim, and Lady Wakehurst, known as Cousin Cuckoo. "I imagine that any intellectual interest I have inherited comes from the Greys," he writes, and the next sentence pins down his emotional ratings, "The Pryce-Joneses certainly had none." What the Greys and Dawnays truly had were titles, connections and standing.

Twenty-one when she married, Vere knew hardly anything of the world. In a portrait painted of her at about that age, she looks demure, but the artist, Ellis Roberts, also catches the wariness of someone who would assume that the experiences of life were likely to prove demanding if not unpleasant and she would wish to be excused from anything like that. Out of affection, and also in the manner of that day, her two brothers, Guy and Alan Dawnay, helped to make sure that she had no chance of moving outside the protective but limited social circle of their family and friends. All her life, they began their letters to her with the proprietary address, "Dear old thing." As a properly brought-up child of the Victorian era, Vere kept albums, she collected autographs and crests, especially those of royal persons; she copied out uplifting poetry and she even played the violin and wrote the six verses and music of a hymn. One unconventional activity was competitive swimming and diving. For several years leading up to her marriage she won gold medals at various London clubs with swimming pools. It was a topic for the more genteel gossip columns. As a "Society Mermaid," in the words of one magazine, *The Lady's Realm* of June 1904, she was "wonderfully pretty and graceful."

Once married, Harry returned to regimental soldiering with the Second Battalion of the Coldstream Guards stationed at Victoria Barracks in Windsor. In the interests of his career, he and Vere set up a London house in Buckingham Palace Road. Promoted captain in 1909, he was appointed ADC to General Sir Charles Douglas, then GOC

Southern Command. When Douglas became Inspector-General of Home Forces, Harry went with him as Private Secretary until April 1914. Peacetime routine was formal, even boring, right up to the scare of war. "Isn't this Austrian Tragedy dreadful?" was Harry's reaction to the assassination in Sarajevo of the Archduke Franz Ferdinand at the end of June 1914. The declaration of war on 5 August happened to coincide with Vere's wedding day. "I feel I am slowly dying by inches," she noted, "one manages to bear up in public, though in private one is absolutely overwhelmed with waves of despair." Six days later, Harry's battalion marched out of Victoria Barracks. The adjutant was Alan Dawnay, his brother-in-law who had been engaged and just had time to find a vicar to rush through a wedding service. After parting, Vere went home, "feeling like a stone, and crept into bed and laid my head in the dent of Harry's pillow where his own dear one had been – all was over! They had no idea where they were going, not even the Colonel had a notion." To his mother Harry wrote, "Take care of yourself and don't worry about me." On 12 August, the day the battalion sailed for France, his stiff-upper-lip tone was hardly modified for Vere:

> I still cannot quite realize what is happening, and feel as if I have been through a succession of awful nightmares. I do realize what a dreadful time it is for all of you who have to go on living the same life from day to day and all the time having this dreadful blackness hanging over you, but I know you will realize it is really for the best and that we must come out alright in the long run.

At the start of this war, Harry was thirty-six. Within days he was sleeping on straw in a farmer's shed, and by the end of the month he was in action, soon confessing to have cut buttons embossed with a crown off the uniform of a dead German and handing one of them to a fellow officer as a souvenir. In France for the entire duration of the war, he kept a diary and wrote letters to Vere that are vividly descriptive yet free from anything like literary effect. With extreme modesty he does not dwell on the occasions when he was mentioned in dispatches. "Found a pair of new boots and 25 cigarettes in each boot from Vere. Boots v. comfy," is a typically restricted entry. He asked her to send fifty cigarettes every other day, and also, "some Brand's meat lozenges and chocolate and acid drops and tobacco each week." Vere quoted another Coldstreamer telling his wife that "H. P-J. comes down here every other night from the Trenches. He is always splendidly cheery about everything." Vere's nerves soon went. "I cannot any longer stand the thought of you remaining in those trenches." She would lobby to get him a safer posting. "You can trust me not to say anything I ought not to say ... you are having a million million harder time than dear old Alan." The latter was soon imploring him to accept the offer of a staff job "in fairness to Vere. When you consider the intense relief it would be to her, I feel that your personal feelings ought not to weigh ... take it, do, old boy." As a staff officer at headquarters of the 38th (Welsh) Division he found himself at Amiens. The Eton College Chronicle published a list of 209 Old Etonian officers from the top ranks downwards who held a dinner at the front in October 1917, and his name appears at Table 7. When the Second Coldstream returned to Victoria Barracks on 25 February 1919 many of the officers including the colonel had been killed and of the thousand or so non-commissioned officers and men who had marched out only fifteen survived and just two had served with the same company throughout the war.

Alan Dawnay made his name as a member of the Arab Bureau, the wartime think-tank in Cairo influencing British policy in the Middle East. He was the liaison officer between the Egyptian Expeditionary Force commanded by Field Marshal Allenby and Faisal, the son of Sherif Hussein and leader of the Arab revolt in the desert against the Ottomans. Faisal's champion was Lawrence of Arabia. *Seven Pillars of Wisdom*, Lawrence's account of this campaign, is a masochistic psychodrama that has established the lasting misperception of Arabs as victims of betrayal and the British as traitorous victimisers. He achieved this effect by describing his British colleagues in language that compacts praise with denigration. Alan Dawnay, for instance, was "Allenby's greatest gift to us – greater than thousands of baggage camels. . . . His was a brilliant mind, understanding to a degree, feeling instinctively the special qualities of rebellion, and developing them." "To a degree" conveys "not at all." Writing from an address in Heliopolis on 10 July 1916 to congratulate Harry on his Military Cross, Alan Dawnay came clean about Egypt as he found it. "This is not a nice country, the people are too loathsome and one gets so tired of the desert."

Guy Dawnay was thirty-seven in 1914. A staff officer with Sir Ian Hamilton at Gallipoli, he reported to London that the expedition was a disaster, and he recommended evacuation. Maurice Hankey, Secretary of the War Council, found Dawnay, "disagreeable and too big for his boots." Lord Kitchener, the Minister responsible, took Dawnay's side and drew the line under this military disaster. Dawnay then joined the Arab Bureau, and in *Seven Pillars* Lawrence heaped his usual destructive praise on him. "Dawnay's cold, shy mind gazed upon our efforts with bleak eye, always thinking, thinking. Beneath this mathematical surface he hid passionate many-sided convictions, a reasoned scholarship in higher warfare, and the brilliant bitterness of a judgment disappointed with us: and with life."

Granny Vere never spoke to me about her brothers. Controller of Programmes at the BBC in the mid-Thirties, Alan committed suicide in 1938. Guy became a successful businessman, founder of the investment bank Dawnay Day and chairman of Armstrong Whitworth. I could well have met him and his descendants but we had all gone our separate ways. One day my father gave me a pair of Arab jars about a foot high, the bronze metal beautifully worked, with holes for sprinkling at the top of elegant elongated necks. They had been the gift of Lawrence of Arabia to Uncle Alan, he said. Take out the stoppers and these jars have a lingering perfume of rosewater.

Six

Here He Is!

"IT WAS NO ACCIDENT, Pryce-Jones, that you have lived near three royal palaces," runs a private joke in *Where Engels Fears to Tread*, Cyril Connolly's unsurpassed satire of the bourgeois writer mimicking a revolutionary proletarian in the heyday of the fellow-travelling Thirties. The first of these three was Buckingham Palace. On 18 November 1908 Alan was born in his parents' house in Buckingham Palace Road. Harry and Vere will have taken it for granted that they had to do for Alan whatever had been done for them. A dutiful couple, they were bound by the conventions to which ladies and gentlemen of their generation subscribed without question. To the end of his life, Alan spoke about the limitations of his parents. He couldn't help patronizing them. The best that parents of this kind could do wasn't good enough.

Vere overdid motherhood. She dealt in superlatives. Things were either uniquely wonderful or uniquely dreadful. A series of miscarriages hadn't helped what Alan summed up as "the nervous tensions that beset my mother." Alan thought himself spoiled "in the sense of being humoured," and at the same time neglected. Photographed as an infant, he had been put into a layered lace dress like a girl's, and for a portrait when he was about ten he wore a pale blue velvet suit with an elaborate lace collar. Delighting in his gifts and precociousness and fearful of the roughness of other boys, Vere felt too protective to send him to school. She preserved the youthful poems that he had no trouble writing; she listened to him playing the piano, her very own Bechstein grand; she considered him a genius.

A Harley Street specialist by the name of Maurice Craig obligingly told her what she wanted to hear, writing to her in April 1917.

> I am certain that at the present moment school would be the worst thing in the world for him and I speak from the experience of constantly seeing school tried. I should let him do no lessons till he is nearly ten. . . . Music lessons ought to be very short and difficult exercises kept down to a minimum. I strongly advise that he should be kept away from parties and entertainments. . . . The main point in bringing him up is to retard mental development and keep the physical if possible a little ahead of the mental, though I am afraid this will be very difficult."

Thirty years later, her opinion hadn't changed. She wrote to Alan, "You, of course, were the most brilliant child who has ever been born into this world, in any country, and in your case I am still sure we were wise never to let you go to a private school at all."

Alan grew up with the sense that he was numbered among those with the means and the standing to be able to live as they pleased. He was ten in September 1918 when his brother Adrian was born and the difference in age guaranteed an unequal relationship. Less was expected of Adrian, he did not write poems or play the piano, he was allowed to go to a prep school. The education of their two sons cost more than the parents could easily afford. Although much decorated and mentioned in dispatches in the war, Harry had not risen above the rank of colonel. Seconded to Field Marshal Haig's staff quartered in Montreuil, of all places, he had lost seniority. Between the wars, he still had a paid job and an office in the Duke of York's Headquarters in Chelsea, dealing with the recruitment and training of the Territorial

Army. "No kinder, quieter man ever lived," is one of many a backhand compliment that Alan pays him. To go straight on to say that he was not a practical man was to cut away the ground under someone engaged in military administration. Perhaps it was Harry's conception of correct behaviour that obliged Vere to keep accounts of her expenditure, which neither of them ever added up. It turned out that he never asked to see Vere's marriage settlement, so its investments remained exactly the same as on the day when they were made, except that some by then no longer existed or were bankrupt.

Long after Harry and Vere had died and Alan had only memory to go on, he sketched their personalities, the detail and the tone calculated to expose their limitations. "My father is very much the colonel, with mouse-coloured hair and moustache, gold watch-chain – he considered wrist-watches, like suede shoes, and heaven knows, pocket-combs marks of the beast (an effeminate beast); my mother ran to strap shoes, mink capes, a regimental brooch in diamonds – the Coldstream of course – and sufficient but not obtrusive pearls ... they were endlessly loving and unselfish, endlessly, also, at odds with reality."

From 1931 onwards, Harry and Vere and Adrian abandoned Buckingham Palace Road to live in a grace and favour house in Windsor Castle, the second of the royal palaces in Cyril Connolly's satire. This consisted of rooms set into the Henry VIII Gateway, the public entrance to the castle and built in Victorian Gothic style. This architecture dictated the strange asymmetrical interior of the house, all angles and niches and window-seats, a corridor poky and dark because so little light of day came in, and a staircase dangerously steep with virtually no light at all. A few feet outside the drawing room wall was a sentry box, and the day and the night were punctuated by the commands of the sergeant changing the guard, the hard smack of the guardsman on duty shouldering his rifle and then the clip of his boots on the cobbles as he marched the regulation number of paces in order to stay awake. In a final promotion that must have been close to his heart, Harry became Harbinger (a title of seniority) of the Gentlemen at Arms, a body of retired officers with ceremonial duties to perform for the royal household in resplendent uniforms complete with a plumed helmet and sword evoking another age.

In the course of the war my grandfather took me with him to Buckingham Palace where he was to receive the Order of the Bath. Many of the men awarded medals that day had been carried on stretchers into what seemed to me then an immense hall. Nurses attended some of those most wounded and bandaged. King George VI moved among them, a slender figure in a naval uniform. His features were sleek, sharp-boned like a whippet's. He patted me on the head and said that there was a lot to see of interest in the big rooms of the palace.

On the day the war ended, Harry showed me the copy of *The Times* with the Six List printed in full. Dr Franz Six was the Gestapo official charged with drawing up the list of Englishmen to be shot out of hand immediately after a victorious German invasion. There was Alan's name, and in brackets after it *Tätig Kreis Petschek*, Active in the Petschek circle. The Petscheks were Czech industrialists and anti-Nazis who had saved their holdings from expropriation by the simple expedient of transferring ownership to trusts in neutral South America. (Sharing the honour to be on the Dr Six list is Clarissa's grandfather, Sir George Barstow, chairman of the Prudential.)

On a Sunday while I was at Eton I would try to finish the compulsory extra work on some scriptural subject in time to have tea with the grandparents in Windsor Castle. A secret entrance led from the High Street to the so-called Hundred

Steps and steeply up an embankment to cloisters and St George's Chapel. Inside is the white marble effigy on the tomb of the Prince Imperial, Napoleon III's son. Corresponding to the blow that had killed him in the Zulu wars, a black stain appeared on its cheek, returning no matter how often it was scrubbed away. My grandfather liked to take me to check on a phenomenon that he was sure had no rational explanation. Sometimes we walked in the Great Park or used a special key that residents of the Castle were allowed for access to Frogmore with its mausoleum. Helplessly undomestic, Granny Vere neither shopped nor cooked. Mrs. Butler, the one and only pair of helping hands, did not come in at the weekend but would have prepared sandwiches and a Fuller's chocolate cake. On one occasion when they had not been expecting me, I caught Harry eating cornflakes with water. They were saving money. One November afternoon with the Thames Valley mist gathering, I was playing football on one of the numerous distant pitches that were not so easy to locate. These insignificant games between junior house teams were compulsory, and nobody ever came to watch them. But there by the sideline was a solitary spectator perching on a shooting stick, my grandfather, wearing a heavy overcoat and his brown felt hat.

Eton in his time, Alan insists in his autobiography, "was not a very lively place." Henry Yorke was his only creative contemporary, he said, except that on the very next page he contradicts himself, naming as friends at the school Peter Watson the future sponsor of *Horizon*, James Lees-Milne, A. J. Ayer, the bibliophile Jake Carter, and others equally successful. In the swim, Alan was free at last from the eccentricity of being kept backward for fear that he was too forward. The school used to publish what was called the Calendar, an alphabetical list of all the boys, and any who had won a prize was rewarded by a footnote recording it. Alan's footnote was many lines longer than anyone else's as year after year he had scooped all the prizes available for literature and music. His self-portrait as someone who couldn't kick a football and wanted to leave the school as soon as could be is the cliché that aesthetes have cultivated to ensure that nobody mistakes them for hearties.

Besides, Alan never raised the possibility that I might go to some other school. My mother was not so sure. We had struggled round the London shops to buy the right clothes, including the Eton jacket, known as bum-freezer, worn by boys below a certain size. She had stayed up late sewing on name-tapes. My parents were due to accompany me on my first day at Eton. At Tonbridge station where we started the journey, Alan caught his hand in the train door, turned white and decided that he had to go home. Poppy called after him that he was the one who'd set his heart on sending me to this English school, she was a foreigner, she didn't know the customs and couldn't manage on her own. But of course she could, and did.

The Fourth of June is an Eton holiday when parents come to watch sporting events on the cricket pitch and the river in an atmosphere similar to Ascot races. On one of these occasions Alan and I were walking through the school when someone came up from behind and put his hands firmly over Alan's eyes. You are a lower boy, this man began to intone in the school idiom, you are late for chapel, you will be punished with a week on tardy book, you have got a rip for your essay, you haven't done your extra work, your tutor Mr Whitworth is extremely put out. This turned out to be Henry Yorke, whose first novel (writing as Henry Green) is set in the anagrammatic school of Note.

Cyril Connolly had more of a story to tell. In some ways he and Alan had much in common. His father was a regular army officer with the rank of major. In the background, relations with aristocratic titles were to be envied and emulated. "Why had my father not got a title?" was one of the questions to which Cyril wanted an answer. *Enemies of Promise*, published in 1938 when he was already thirty-five, is about self-discovery, and Alan acknowledged that he recognized in it "a more intelligent version of my own uncertainties." Cyril was speaking for many in his generation who thought of themselves as writers. The ambition was to write a book that would hold good for ten years. Combining experience and imagination, fiction was self-evidently the highest form of literature. At Eton, Cyril had created a hothouse of romance with other boys in College. Nostalgic submersion in the memory of that past overpowered the practical difficulty of choosing a subject that could support the intended master-piece, and then sitting down to write it. Masters of the false start, Cyril and Alan both amassed in their papers innumer-able notebooks with one or two pages of writing and the rest expressively blank.

When we lived in Kent, Cyril came to the house, and his name is in the visitors' book for the first time in 1943. He published in *Horizon* Alan's account of postwar Vienna and also a short story that reads like another false start. It was in our house that Cyril hid a half-eaten plate of eggs and bacon in a drawer and left a chamber pot in the spare room for Poppy or Jessie to empty. He took no exercise, he let himself go, he waddled rather than walked, his face was fatty and colourless but with a redeeming gleam of humour in his eyes. I must have been at least twenty when I came to know him well, and by then his affections, transferred to women, were as demanding as ever. At the peak of his Eton intoxica-tion with literature and sexuality, he told me several times, a small boy had been fagged to bring him a note. This was Alan, and the note read, "Here he is."

The chances were high that Alan would think his early

life had been a strait-jacket from which he had to escape by whatever means there were. In 1926, he talked his way out of Eton and was allowed to spend that summer and autumn in France. As the train moved out of Victoria Station, he records unconsciously a family tableau in the diary that he now began to keep: "Mummy walks quickly besides, a little tearful and Daddy waves in the background." The impatient departing schoolboy arrived in Paris as the fully-fledged adult he was to be for the rest of his life, just as a caterpillar emerges in the new unexpected form of a butterfly. In the Ritz Bar he met up with Lord Tredegar (writing as Evan Morgan), "dear darling Evan, whom I love more deeply every time I look at him," and Hugh Lygon, the original of Sebastian Flyte in *Brideshead Revisited*, not to mention "a dear little German boy, Gustav. All the Queens were there." Without introductions or preliminaries of any kind, suddenly this escaped schoolboy is in Touraine, the guest of hospitable French dukes and counts and their cosmopolitan neighbors, appreciating châteaux and possessions with the total confidence of a connoisseur.

That November, telegrams from Harry urgently recalled him to sit for his entrance examination to Oxford. Sir Herbert Warren, President of Magdalen College and a renowned snob, interviewed him and noted his testimonials: "I liked what I saw of him." Going up to Oxford in October 1927, Alan wrote regularly to his parents. In Magdalen's New Buildings (elegantly eighteenth-century in fact), he had "charming rooms, both panelled in a rather decadent cream-beige" which he had improved with a few alterations and the hiring of a piano. "I have five tutors but only very few lectures a week, so that I can easily do a few Newdigate poems." He tells them about dinners with Peter Watson and Graham Eyres-Monsell and George Harwood, friends richer than him.

In his second term, he opens one of his letters, "Lest you think too badly of me, I enclose a chronicle of my late doings." And chronicle it is, with names and places. On the back of one envelope is a scribble whose pay-off is in French, "I propose to have the Imperial Coronet stamped on my paper. *Bel effet*?" He has been to parties in houses as grand as West Wycombe and Sezincote. Cecil Beaton "walks like an exhausted pendulum," his orbit getting smaller and smaller until it swings up more violently than ever. A leaving party for Lord Clonmore was followed by "a fancy dress dance for which I wore a ballet skirt and tights and ropes and ropes of Woolworth jewellery and had rather a success."

John Betjeman also had rooms in New Buildings at the time. *Summoned by Bells*, his autobiography in verse, catches similar highlights of camp showing-off. (Kolkhorst was a university lecturer in Spanish, an eccentric, a Colonel in Betjeman's imagination just as Alan was Bignose: "Dear private giggles of a private world," as that poem has it.)

> Alan Pryce-Jones came in a bathing-dress,
> And, seated at your low harmonium,
> Struck up the Kolkhorst Sunday-morning hymn
> "There's a home for Colonel Kolkhorst" – final verse
> ff with all the stops out . . .

> There Bignose plays the organ
> And the pansies all sing flat . . .

In Alan's old age, the university and the college used to appeal to him for donations as though he were the loyal alumnus that he made sure not to be.

He didn't care for anyone or anything that made demands on him. At the end of February 1928 he told his parents, "All is exceedingly well between me and the Dean. The authorities are easily pacified, being by nature loving and utterly obtuse and before long I shall be President of the Junior Common Room and sink into an unparalleled depth of academic superiority. Seriously, don't worry." What he had sunk into was debt. Here was the first instance of an attitude that was to shape his life, that he could be as extravagant as he liked because somebody was bound to turn up and pay the bills. He knew it of himself of course. "If one can't afford something the moment one wants it," he wrote in his diary just three years later, on 24 May 1930, "one must just arrange for someone else to pay for it." This time, Harry came to Magdalen and after a meeting with the college authorities signed the cheques without apparently demurring. Immediately afterwards, by way of imposing discipline, the Dean of the college gated him, meaning that he had to be in by nine o'clock at night. On that very same evening, Alan went in a white tie to a ball, was caught returning, and rusticated, that is sent down for the rest of the term, rather an indulgent punishment in the circumstances.

According to Alan, his father had no idea how to cope with him at this point, and could only say that there could be no question of returning to Magdalen. Alan was unemployable but could no longer live off his father, he could never marry, he had no future. But that same afternoon, Alan continues, fortuitously a friend contrived a meeting with J.C. Squire, editor since its inception in November 1919 of the *The London Mercury*, a monthly for those whose literary taste stopped well short of T.S. Eliot and *The Criterion*. Squire apparently had heard of the prizes Alan had won at Eton and offered him a job as assistant editor, to start the following Monday.

Harry and Vere and friends of theirs had long been sending out Alan's poems in the hope of attracting attention. "Dear darling" Evan Tredegar was a writer whom they knew and they had introduced Alan to him. Writing on *Times* notepaper with the date 5 January 1926, that is to say well before Alan's first term at Oxford, an acquaintance by the name of R. I. H. Shaw says that he has been talking about Alan to Bruce Richmond, editor of the *Times Literary Supplement*, and also to A. P. Herbert. The latter thought that an approach to J. C. Squire was "excellent advise." To meet him, "you have only to drop me a line." Sure enough, ten days later Alan had an appointment at 4:30 in the afternoon with Squire.

Squire and *The London Mercury*, then, had been hovering in the wings for some time before Alan's misadventure. A few weeks after his father had made it clear that rustication meant being sent down from Oxford, Alan returned to France. Cast in exaggerated self-congratulatory mode, a series of letters home begins on 5 June and gives no clue that there might have been family tension about his prospects. On entering France, trouble with the customs over his typewriter had left him "mentally a broken fountain with no drop of water" but this passed soon enough. He rejoiced to be starting his novel. "Harvest And The Ruin" was the title of one of the poems he posted to his parents, jotting on the typescript, "The thing is very fine." On his behalf, a friend had approached J. L. Garvin, influential editor of *The Observer*, and Alan was critical for fear this might be seen as an embarrassing put-up job. Another contact led to Blanche Knopf, an eager talent-spotter and founder with her husband Alfred of the New York firm that still has their name. She asked to see what Alan had done so far, which he thought "impertinent," even "damnable insolence!"

Three weeks later, on June 26, he sent a postcard from Montbazon in Touraine. "As for Sir Herbert Warren, I consider that the privileges of dotage can be carried too far. Boo to him!" Uncle Guy Dawnay had taken sides with Alan because, in Alan's words, "He knows a genius when he sees one. I have just finished the first section of my novel. . . . I have written a very remarkable poem. I *am* a Clever Young Man!" In the margin a caricature of himself thumbing his nose at Sir Herbert illustrated his feeling. By July 5 he was informing them that he had written 1,617 words more of the novel. "Bless you, poppets," he addressed them, ending with spoof signatures, C. B. Cochrane, A. A. Milne, Noël Coward, and Queen Mary.

"For Ever Grey" is the title of another poem sent home on August 11. The opening lines are:

Nothing is sad this morning, nothing grieves,
The earth is slow and sweet, the quick feet of a hare
     go gladly.

Alan patted himself on the back, "Shelley pales before this slight but distinguished piece. Observe the brilliant technique, the clever internal rhymes." Or again in August, "My famous book has already begun – some 2,000 words are written – magnificent stuff." The weather was so hot that month that he bought "a straw hat 70 foot round." Asking him to begin in the office on the 23rd of the month, Squire put paid to the Oxford episode. Unidentifiable, the famous novel remained one among other false starts but the aspiration endured. Reading *War and Peace* a few years later, he noted in his diary, "Such is my vanity that I long to tackle an enormous novel myself." He was capable of analyzing what was holding him back.

Whenever I write about people they are always quite inhuman – far more intelligent than human beings and very eccentric. I don't know what to do about this. Also I can't write "hearty" conversation. All my characters speak in a pert, queenly way because that is the language of the people I have always lived among.... I am so shy of squalor and noisy crowds and I hate the poor so much that I am not sure that I could [just set out at random]. Yet I don't see how otherwise to get in touch with ordinary people. Certainly it is not easy to do it in my usual procession from Ritz to Ritz. How passionately I long to be stupid and a stockbroker.

"Lately," reads an entry in his diary dated January 1932,

the great thing has been my sailor, Tommy, lately a midshipman on the *Devonshire* and now on leave. Sailor and I had planned a weekend in Glastonbury (why?) but he had influenza at the last moment.... I lied to my family that I was going to Windsor, took rooms in Laurier's Hotel and he came. Oh, what furtive pleasure! What laughter!... actually my emotions about the Sailor were piercing: I liked the queer heartiness, the shyness, attempts at intellectuality, violence, childishness.

At the same time he had a vital insight.

The reason no homosexual affair can ever be translated into art is that there is no common ground of homosexual, as of heterosexual, experience. Homosexual affairs are entirely personal; without knowing the actual lover, without *being one of them*, no translation into art could mean anything.

If there is a solution to this impasse, Alan never found it.

In the course of a lunch many years later still, Mitzi suddenly turned on him, saying that she had never believed that he had written a word of the great novel he was always talking about. It was virtually completed, Alan protested, and he summarized there and then a Kafkaesque plot he had devised around the life of Geoffrey Madan, a brilliant eccentric who had devoted himself to writing aphorisms. I was completely convinced that he could not have improvised so circumstantially on the spur of the moment, but Mitzi was right.

Seven

84 ## *Money! Money! Money!*

> *With weekends in the country and holidays in France,*
> *With promiscuous habits, time to sunbathe and dance,*
> *And even to write books that were hardly worth a glance,*
> *Earning neither reputation nor the publisher's advance:*
> *Just like a young writer*
> *Between the wars.*
>
> WILLIAM PLOMER, "Father and Son: 1939"

THE VILE BODIES of the 1920s were pioneers of a contemporary art of attracting fame by being infamous, acquiring social status by appearing to mock it, altogether transforming unconventionality into convention. Like others in this London set, Alan was sure that he could make his way abusing privilege as much as he liked and never have to pay a price. A slim young man, he had good looks and an appealing manner that made friends and got him invited wherever he wanted. A slightly odd feature was that in an age before orthodentistry both his canine teeth stuck out slightly, adding a touch of vulnerability to his smile. At that stage he had no money, and put a great deal of his natural talents into getting in with the right people.

Homosexuality was Alan's early passport to social and literary success, and I used to wonder to what extent, if any, it had been formed by his mother's possessiveness, her wildly over-the-top praise for everything he did, and in contrast his father's withholding of emotion. At a time when homosexuality was criminalized, Vere and Harry had received enough information from Alan himself to know that the way he was behaving was not a matter of style but part of his self-discovery. Poppets indeed! Their second son, Adrian, Din or Gruffy to his parents and to Alan, was brought up almost as though he were an invalid. Sent to preparatory school and then Eton, he wrote letters home almost daily in an unmistakable spirit of dependency. As an adult he was a friend of Lord Montagu of Beaulieu and had been present at parties with boy scouts and RAF servicemen in the beach house at Beaulieu, which led to scandal and prison sentences for Lord Montagu and a friend of his. In the manner of Oscar Wilde, Adrian ran away to France to lie low for a while. Unworldly as Harry and Vere were in some respects, they can hardly have helped drawing obvious conclusions from the conduct of their two sons. It stretches credulity to breaking point to suppose that they never asked themselves whether responsibility for the sexuality of their two sons lay with them or in the genes.

After Evan Morgan in pre-Oxford days, another of Alan's lovers was Harold Nicolson. According to his biographer James Lees-Milne, Nicolson was only attracted by younger intellectual men of his own class, and he furthermore "believed that homosexuality should be a jolly vice, and not taken too seriously." Nicolson is quoted saying of Alan, "I like him more than I care to think." He was the first to put about the word that Alan was the new literary star in London, and a masterpiece, probably in the form of a travel book, could be expected from him. The book should be such, Nicolson suggested, that a suitable title would be "An Exhibitionist in Asia."

In the south of France in the summer of 1929 Somerset Maugham was next to take him up, inviting him to the Villa Mauresque. On boating trips and parties around the swimming pool there were up to a dozen naked young men. On 24 March 1930 Alan was writing with more introspection than jauntiness: "My atmosphere is lunching with John Banting and Brian [Howard] and Eddy Sackville-West in Charlotte Street, or spending the weekend with Maurice Bowra at Oxford, or staying with Hamish [St. Clair Erskine] at Sussex. Other things I hate . . . except that I want success, tremendous success and lots of money." (Then a young Oxford don, Bowra was already well on the way to becoming what might be called the general secretary of the Hominform, collating and spreading gossip to the like-minded.) Alan again:

> When I am with Sandy [Baird] or Brian or Eddy I am a quite different person. Instead of being a young, brilliantly promising poet, a sort of solitary yet kind creature, I become a very shy, rather ineffectual eccentric, a person trying to attract attention by wit and by ballet movements, by light colours and lithe motions. I become rather old, rather silly and inarticulate, a tangle of inferiority. That kind of collapse is only mitigated [by people] who take me *gratis* as a first-rate, scintillating character, a genius, a handsome wit.

Robert Pratt-Barlow, known as Bobby, was the unlikely individual who more than anyone else established Alan. Born in 1885, he was in many ways a representative late Victorian. Outwardly he was correct to the point of stuffiness, as when he once refused to respond to someone in a hotel paging a telephone call for Mr Barlow: "My name is Pratt-Barlow." He looked like Harold Nicolson, that is to say a stocky figure whose cheeks were pink and moustache whitish. Through his family's interest in John Dickinson, the paper manufacturers, he had inherited a fortune. One friend was D. H. Lawrence, and the collection of his letters edited by Aldous Huxley ends with one to Bobby.

No sort of intellectual, he divided his time between living in Taormina in Sicily and going on extended travels. Quite often he seems unobservant. For instance, writing from Hamburg in August 1930, by which time Hitler and the Nazis were only some thirty months from taking power, all he had to say was that Germans "make the best use of the open air [and] know how to dress properly. They are healthy, unhypocritical and constructive. . . . What a difference between now and before the war."

A Coldstreamer in the First War, Bobby had become a family friend through Harry and Guy and Alan Dawnay, brother officers. When the latter committed suicide in 1938, Bobby wrote to Vere: "I loved him more than anyone I have ever known, and for all that time I have always wondered why. . . . When he decided to get married, I thought the bottom of my life had fallen out, so conceited was I, I imagined that no one understood him like I did." He repeated himself to Alan, first saying, "You have certainly done wonders for me," and going on, "As for Uncle Alan why I loved him so I don't know. From the first moment I saw him from another table in Magdalen Hall, I knew something of a most remarkable kind had entered my life."

Bobby was my godfather and in my last year at Eton he told Alan that he wanted to meet me at last. Stromboli was belching fire and smoke as we flew past it, and the pilot took the plane down and circled so that we could all have a good look. It would not have been in Alan's character to provide some preliminary sketch of Bobby; he took life as he found it and expected everyone else to do so as well. His diary entry for 27 January 1930 calls Bobby "kind, supportive and discreet," which was true as far as it went. In his memoirs written long after Bobby was dead, he resorted to particularly arch phrasing to dress up the facts presentably. His father and uncles ragged Bobby affectionately, as Alan puts it, "for was he not musical – a word which around 1910 also served as a euphemism for homosexual." He also tried to close the subject: "At no time did his private life impinge on mine."

Casa Rosa, Bobby's house, was in the centre of Taormina, a compound around a courtyard. Painted outside a soft rose-red shade, the interior walls were embellished with ceramic tiles. The butler was a boy of about twelve. In the kitchen were other boys of that age, all of them in shorts, some without shirts, introduced as the cooks. I spoke Italian too badly to ask them urgent personal questions now in need of an answer. Arriving at Eton, all new boys had to congregate in the school library to listen to Robert Birley, the headmaster, lecture on sexuality. Whatever he had to say was pitched at a level so high-flown that none of us could understand what he was talking about. At about that same time, Alan had given me advice, "Sex is like *salade niçoise*, you should try everything once." I had already gone to bed when Bobby came into the room to give me a book, which he said he wanted me to read. He went out of the room immediately. I was left holding one of Krafft-Ebing's works discussing sexual practices most of which I had never heard of before, and some of which I have never heard of since.

Next morning the whole household, at least ten strong, set off on a train of donkeys for Bobby's country house at Mufarbi, the village higher than all others on Mount Etna. Here was a Sicilian version of the classic English pattern of leaving town to spend the weekend in the country. Aubrey Menen's novel *The Duke of Gallodoro*, published in 1952, is an amusing send-up of Bobby and these boys, leaving open who exactly is exploiting whom. (Scandal and gossip spread far and wide. Letizia Fortini's novel in 1987, *Esilio e morte di Robert Fox Lambert,* has an English upper-class protagonist and a Sicilian boy copied in close detail from original models in Casa Rosa, but by then Bobby was dead.) The donkey ride lasted three hours. The little boys in their shorts constantly laughed and sang. Little had changed in the property at Mufarbi since it had belonged to a contadino. There was a pergola, vines, lemon trees, and drifting up into the sky above our heads the smoke-and-fire eruptions of a volcano outdoing Stromboli. Krafft-Ebing and his book were never mentioned again.

At the beginning of 1930, Bobby and Alan set off on a prolonged journey to the Middle East. Harry and Vere appear to have had no reservations about it, and paid for some of Alan's expenses. *The Spring Journey*, Alan's first book, offers no particular point of view. Alan wrote as a tourist interested in his own reflections rather than a traveler interested in other people in other countries. Attached to the pages like so many credentials are allusions to writers and books, Muntaner, Mallarmé, Julien Benda, Balzac, *The Book of Nonsense*, George Stephens's *Incidents of Travel* (1838), De la Motte Fouqué, Seneca, Trebellius Pollio, and many more. Now and then a phrase testifies to adventure with language: "Like a gong she returned one note, however hard she was hit."

Egypt was then under British rule, and fashionable Europeans spent the winter there. In common with such visitors, Bobby and Alan did the round of Shepheard's Hotel, the Pyramids, camel rides to a Coptic monastery, snake charmers, and boats on the Nile. Cairo, they found, was "appalling," and Tutankhamen's tomb a "disappointment." For the month of February Bobby rented the Villa Bella Donna in Luxor. In control of events and movements, and also the paymaster, Bobby nonetheless does not feature in *Spring Journey*. In letters home and his diary Alan has bright descriptions of other people in Luxor, for instance Robert Hichens, author of *The Green Carnation*, the famous singer Dame Nellie Melba, the Queen of Romania, and Marthe Letellier, once flattered as the most beautiful woman in

France. Personalities of the kind were hardly suitable material for the travel book Alan had in mind. Back in London was Patrick Kinross, a friend then at the outset of a comparable literary and sexual career, and he would have relished Alan's letter of 25 February about goings-on in Luxor: "The most extraordinary thing, however, is the gaiety, the bed-worthiness of every inhabitant. One can't go behind any bush without giving embarrassment to somebody – twice I have found my dragoman in my bed of an evening, and that's not the half." This too did not find its way into the book.

One encounter, though, was destined to have repercussions. Staying in the grand Winter Palace Hotel were Paul Goldschmidt and Frank Wooster, the sort of friends that Bobby made it his business to have. At that point, Alan could not have appreciated the complexities of Frank's emotional life. In the three years since Eugène Fould-Springer had died, the widowed Mitzi had come to the conviction that she could not have betrayed him by falling in love with Frank because what had happened was God's work. Frank had to devise some way of reconciling this absolution of hers with the sexual relationship he had had with Eugène, while also weighing the future security that Mitzi's fortune might bring him. Escaping to Egypt with his long-standing lover Paul Goldschmidt, he was two-timing Mitzi just ten months before he finally gave way and married her. Frank Wooster, Alan observed, after tea in the Winter Palace, "is a kind middle-aged man, with a face which looks as though he might have cancer – pale and with large bright blue eyes which seem added to his face from outside. The shape of his head is good – of his conversation less so, being of that kind of archness which is chiefly about bracelets." And then, "Paul Goldschmidt is an elderly person who pays – a very sweet, rather pathetic figure."

(Bobby of course followed every twist and turn in the Mitzi-

Eugène-Frank triangular relationship. On 14 September 1932 Mitzi and Frank went to the Bayreuth festival and Bobby came over from the hotel in Berchtesgaden where he was staying – a few weeks later Hitler was to seize power in Berlin, and a few weeks later still Mitzi and Frank were to marry in London. In 1935 when they were all three together in Salzburg, Bobby asked Frank what he would have done in Eugène's place when he realized Mitzi's feelings for him. "More energetic," was Frank's answer. Then she asked what Frank meant by this, and heard a skilful put-down: "If you had been mine, you would never have missed tenderness or love or understanding, you would never have needed what I have been to you.")

Before moving on from Luxor to Jerusalem, Bobby put in a preliminary report to Harry and Vere.

> I really think Alan is enjoying himself. I certainly am, and am finding him a most delightful companion, as you said I would. Also he is working quite a lot, scribbles away at something every day.... Yesterday was dispatched a long poem to Brian Howard for some paper or other.... I don't find Alan unmethodical and I am sure he is ambitious ... and although he excels at so many things, he never pushes himself forward in anyway, a good trait this. He is also very nice and considerate to me.

At that moment, the gathering confrontation between Jews and Arabs in the British Mandate of Palestine could still have gone some other way. Colonial officials, High Commissioners, local governors and Palestine policemen have recorded the politics and practices then in place. Among journalists, Vincent Sheean or Arthur Koestler wrote immediate reportage that stands the test of time, but no book captures the human dimension, the atmosphere as the old

Ottoman past was giving way to the fraught present. Alan lacked the experience or the interest for this; he did no interviews and quotes nobody. He spent his time in Jerusalem. Apart from a brief excursion to Nazareth, he saw nothing else of the country, not even Tel Aviv, and so trapped himself in stereotype observations: "This is the most violent country on our globe." Or again: "The Government is accused of favouring Jews, but is actually pro-Arab. In fact, disliking the Jews seems the only common factor." Jerusalem, he held, is always primarily an Arab city, "or perhaps it is true to say that it is never a Jewish city." For the most part, he could see nothing good about any of the inhabitants. He confesses, "I could never prevent myself watching the Arabs as a curiosity." Lack of engagement forces him into phrase-making, for instance speaking of "the iron-tasting miasma which hangs round an Arab," whatever that might mean. Jews were also curiosities: "Sometimes an old Shylock is fine to look at."

Amman was horrible, so violently anti-British that "we were a little afraid of having our noses pulled in the streets." In a letter to his parents he says that he and Bobby were too overwhelmed by the "unpleasantness" of Damascus to want to stay there, but also enclosed in the envelope a photograph of himself in the nude. On April 18 in the Hotel Continentale in Beirut Bobby wrote to Harry and Vere what sounds like a deliberately bland end-of-term summary. Alan "continues to be a most charming, entertaining and considerate companion." Next day in the same hotel Alan adopted the same tone to his parents. A perfect companion, Bobby was "always cheerful and extremely amusing, very sensible and competent ... among his personal luggage is always a large pillow, a marble ash-tray, a strainer, a waste-paper basket and a new box of chocolate biscuits. ... We have decided to settle in Cyprus. Bobby is going to have a small but expensive castle."

Cyprus, Rhodes, Delos, then Athens where he refused to rave over the Parthenon and where instead "the debauch of my nights ruined my days." Munich, Budapest, Vienna. Once he was back in Europe, his sense of superiority modified though it did not disappear. For the immense sum of a thousand pounds Bobby had bought a new model Mercedes and Alan liked to go alone in it as much as possible. He shared Bobby's fantasy about the Germans. "I certainly have the greatest admiration for the German way of life. . . . I suppose they are far more go-ahead than anyone else in Europe, and I am sure that it is largely because they have learnt not to be self-conscious when they haven't got any clothes on . . . everyone is interested in any new subject from internal combustion to Braque. Nothing could be more stimulating than to talk to such ready and individual creatures."

Vienna, he thought, seemed a little lifeless. The inability to speak German was humiliating. Then on 31 May Bobby took him to dine with Mitzi "whom everyone is expecting to marry Frank Wooster. I had long wanted to meet her, having heard so much of her enormous wealth, her eight palaces in France, Austria, Hungary, and Czechoslovakia, her energy at directing all the businesses that the old Baron Springer left, and her adoration of Frank. But as dinner came nearer I felt shy." It was Derby Day, and Mitzi's horse was the favourite. Meidling was the sort of house he didn't know existed outside Ireland. The little old lady arranging gramophone records and getting on the wrong side of Mitzi was Tante Bébé, otherwise Fraülein d'Italia, a member of the family and who lived in the house permanently. "Also were Poppy and Lily, two schoolroom daughters who never spoke except in family jokes, and the Baroness herself, very small, very Jewish, very chic in black and so forceful that she compelled me to think her attractive (I sat next to her) and brilliant. She has an active, malicious tongue and *great* charm, I thought at last. Conversation was difficult, being conducted simultaneously in three languages, and worst of all for me who knew no-one. However, I think everything went off quite well." On 3 June, his last day in Vienna, Alan was invited back to Meidling for lunch. This time Mitzi was very gracious, he thought, and whenever a new guest arrived the two daughters muttered "God help us," and giggled in the back of the room. (Poppy was just seventeen, Lily just fifteen.)

Alan departed to Vence in the south of France, and was soon describing to his parents how he had seen a *concours d'élégance* of men's bathing dresses and deportment: "Daddy would not have approved!" "I shall miss him awfully," Bobby told Vere and Harry, "I don't think a cross word has passed from one to the other of us all the time we have been together. He has, I really think, enjoyed everything. . . . And now I have something to tell you and do hope that Harry and you will agree. I have asked Alan to come with me to South America this next winter." In *The Bonus of Laughter* Alan held at bay anyone who might be wondering about his relationship with Bobby: "So successful was the human element in our little adventures that we spent the two following winters together, in South America and Central Africa. No doubt this looked strange to some. I was twenty-two, Bobby in his forties."

On the liner out to Brazil, Alan finished *Spring Journey*, and posted the manuscript to Kenneth Rae. Published by Cobden-Sanderson in 1931, the book had good reviews, one of which called him "perhaps the most brilliant and versatile of the youngest English writers ... he has already attracted wide notice as poet, critic, essayist and musician." Copying this praise into his diary, Alan supposed that Squire was responsible for it. (Visiting Australia, I found in a second-hand bookshop in Perth a copy on whose flyleaf

Jan Masaryk, the Czech Foreign Minister defenestrated by the Communists, had written his name – evidence of the book's reach.)

Journey to the South, retitled *Hot Places* for the American edition, is a hybrid of fact and fiction. The stories of invented characters supposedly convey the South American experience. Experimental at the time, the device does not wear well. Bobby and he reached Rio de Janeiro just before Christmas 1930. They were to move on to the Argentine, Chile, Cuba, Bolivia, Peru, and Ecuador. A sense of superiority again rose close to the surface. Santos was "a poisonous town," Valparaíso "really horrible," Quito "bijou." More inquisitive than before, however, Alan did meet a number of people, including the Argentine Foreign Minister, and Bobby Pryce-Jones, a cousin descended from one of Harry's brothers who had exchanged Dolerw for Buenos Aires. In Montevideo on 5 February 1931 he wrote to Patrick Kinross (who could never have enough of this kind of thing), "Here in the Plaza Zabala, there are pretty goings-on, very squalid, and for an elderly clientele of sailors and crossing-sweepers." In Lima, he was frightened momentarily by the revolution to depose the President. Still, an attachment to South America lasted for the rest of his life; he was to lecture there for the British Council; and Jorge Luis Borges had noticed his writing and more than once expressed approval of it in print. In the family Guy Dawnay told Vere that the book was extraordinarily clever: "More power to Alan's literary genius."

Extravagant by nature, he was not earning a living. Before leaving for South America, he had complained to Patrick Kinross, "Papa's income is exactly halved and his taxes precisely doubled, so I haven't the heart to take any more money off him which means getting a job at once. I suppose that means the B.B.C. if I can persuade them to have me. Isn't everything hell?" The two travel books were to earn in the order of a hundred pounds each. *Hot Places* was having an American *succès d'estime*, he again told Patrick Kinross, and a cheque would follow for £3.12.0 on account of six months' royalties. Journeying one last time with Bobby – to Kenya, Uganda and Sudan – produced no book, but at its conclusion he put a heartfelt cry into his diary: "Money! Money! Money! Will no-one give me £1,000 a year? Surely not much to ask." When Harry had to go back on his promise to furnish a flat for him, Alan hoped instead to retreat to some office that also served as a bolt-hole. For the purpose, "I mean to cheat Papa out of £100 if I can't get it any other way."

The exhibitionist in Alan was strong enough at that point to overcome the would-be artist pressed by dull financial reasons to finish his masterpiece. "I find I write more easily if I paint my lips scarlet," he told himself – an admission that writing for him means posing. Taking a flat in Paris for the summer of 1931, he spent the time indulging himself. It seems like an omen that he wrote to his father on 29 June to say that he had seen a good deal of Frank Wooster and Madame Fould-Springer as he calls her – two people Harry had surely never heard of previously. Friends arranged a meeting with Jean Cocteau. Writing it up in extremely vivid prose with the date 1 July, he comes out abruptly with the sentences, "I've taken cocaine. A clean medicinal smell, but no apparent sensation whatever." And then, "At about 2.30 we took to heroin and the effect improved; I talked copiously and felt great affection towards my friends ... at 5.00 I went home to my new flat, unpacked, arranged books and felt in superb humour, looking brown and quite untired." Returning to England by Dieppe and Newhaven towards the end of the month, he writes that he burnt the cocaine he had with him and all day long was in a stupor. "O, the nausea, the exhaustion, the hot pains, the collapse."

"I saw Pryce-Jones in Paris," Maurice Bowra wrote to Patrick Kinross, well aware of the glee the information in his letter would cause – Bowra was himself pursuing Adrian Bishop, another aesthete. "I telegraphed at great expense offering him his fare and keep in Italy, but he did not answer. His book is very bad and gets very amusing reviews in the Sunday press where he has not seduced the reviewers. . . . He was very odd in Paris, having a good deal of fun with Ironside [Robin, the artist], taking drugs, his eyes shooting in opposite directions on strings, and his face knee deep in slap."

(Bowra was writing salacious and supposedly satirical poems that he read to the select few. Published after his death, this excruciating drivel must owe something to Alan:

> Baronin Fould-Springer of a first-rate family
> Said to be the fattest woman in Europe
> Went to bed with a dud Czech
> Who talked French with a real French accent.
> He froze all her assets,
> And the psychologist takes over her guilt-edged
> securities.)

Back in Paris in January 1932, Alan might well have paid the cost of settling into this lifestyle. To wear make-up and take drugs was to be free from the arduous discipline of writing. Other men, richer and more in the social swim than Bobby, might be found to keep him, and one of them was Arturo Lopez. A Chilean, he had a huge fortune from minerals and mining. Everyone who was anyone gossiped about the extravagance of his house in Paris, and the debauchery that took place there. As he describes it, Alan's sense of superiority was again in play. Taking his distance, out to shock, he was far above anything respectable and boring. "I caught myself delighting when people stared – knowing my face was brilliantly made up and my eyes wide with cocaine. A glow of vice.... Nothing could uproot me and furious stares were the proof of it. The joy of Arturo's black enamel and looking-glass bathroom – with shelves of silver instruments, boxes, bottles, pencils. I spent half an hour experimenting – quite childishly, luxuriating."

"A first experiment with morphine in Maddox Street," is an entry in Alan's diary dated that April. Those injecting him were evidently addicts; protectively Alan identifies them by initials only; he omits the surname of Irene, one of these friends who had died from the drug. "Of all, heroin seems to work best on me," he decided. "By mixing it with opium, pernod, cocaine, and pâté de foie gras, however, I made myself ill."

Among contemporaries with much the same background and similar literary aspirations as Alan were several specialists in failure. One whose fate Alan might have shared was his friend Brian Howard, self-described as a poet, in circuit around the pleasure-spots of Europe, dissipating his gifts in drugs and the young men he picked up. Alan's two travel books had not matched the expectations they had raised. To judge by the works of André Breton and Marcel Duchamp that he kept to the end of his life, the Surrealism of the period was another possible route into a dead-end. For Surrealists, life and art spread the nihilistic premise that no one human being has anything in common with another. According to Alan's diary, he had admired and wanted to meet the Surrealist René Crevel, "struck by his great beauty," but before this could happen Crevel committed suicide. Into the 1950s Cocteau was still sending Alan copies of his books, with his usual doodles and inscriptions on the flyleaf.

Throughout 1932 and 1933 Alan pursued Joan Eyres-Monsell, the first woman who had meant anything to him. Both seem to have found the business of love rather erratic and unusual. When I was up at Oxford, Maurice Bowra, by then Warden of Wadham seemingly in perpetuity, invited me to dinner to meet Joan. Dark-haired, she was very attractive in a *grand bohème* way, and greeted me saying in a quite deep and seductive voice, "I could have been your mother." By then in her fifties, she was living in Greece with Paddy Leigh Fermor, who wrote the kind of stylised and idiosyncratic travel books that Alan had been expected to write. When she eventually married Paddy, as Artemis Cooper makes plain in her biography of him, Joan was finally resigning herself to the male selfishness that she had come up against. By then, she was too old to have a child.

The Eyres-Monsells lived at Dumbleton, a large Gloucestershire house with an estate. Joan's parents were forbidding; Sir Bolton Eyres-Monsell was First Lord of the Admiralty. "Lady Eyres-Monsell is immensely rich," according to the *Daily Express* of 2 April (possibly on a tip-off from Patrick Kinross). "The fortune she inherited cannot be less than £50,000 a year." Joan's brother Graham was cultivated, knowledgeable about music, and, as a friend from Alan's brief Oxford interlude and himself a homosexual, in a position to tell tales. On 2 January 1932 Alan was one of a large house party at Dumbleton, and by that August he was asking himself if he was in love with Joan. "She could not be more lovely; yet, could we be happy if she was as foolish as I fear she is?" A couple of days after that reflection, he proposed and was accepted. "Since then I've alternated between rapture and despair.... Is she stupid? Am I perverted? Are we poor?" One evening at this point Cyril Connolly talked to her about Alan, "whom she says won't marry her without a grand wedding. We all got tight at the Florida." Joan seems to have accepted that she had to indulge Alan. No sooner engaged than he sped off to Spain by himself, ostensibly to settle somewhere long enough to finish a play he was writing (there is no trace of it). At first Granada was a city where he would have liked to stay permanently. Quite soon the room he had found in the Villa Carmona, part of the Alhambra, the great Moorish palace in Granada, proved too cold and uncomfortable, "as bad as Eton." Once more a tourist, he took in Córdoba, Seville ("The bliss of bathrooms and cocktails"), and Cádiz from where he sent home a postcard, "Lady E-M has told Graham that she finds me an exceptionally nice young man. How could she not?" Then Algeciras, Tetuán, and Xauen in Spanish Morocco. "Only Joan is a comfort," he could still tell himself. "I think she is decided to marry me from the depth of herself." The Eyres-Monsells happened to be in Spain and a meeting back in Granada had been arranged. Joan's mother had no objection to him, Alan gathered, but her father would like someone who could be of use to him, "a politician or a duke, I suppose." At least, "the *atmosphere* is improved."

During the summer of 1933 Alan and Joan had a foretaste of the social life they might have had as a married couple. Meeting up with Evelyn Waugh at a late-night party, Alan found him "more like a carved potato than usual." Other guests at a weekend with Cyril and Jean Connolly were Eddie Gathorne-Hardy, Nigel Richards, Piers Synnott, Peter and Marcelle Quennell, Brian Howard, and John Strachey: a roll-call of the smart set. Alan was by himself at the Salzburg festival, however, and there was someone called Bobby Marshall, a friend of Joan's brother Graham. "I knew I was sunburnt and looking my best; but he is a 'hearty', who has always led a perfectly normal life, and I am engaged. . . . I don't want to go to bed with him (or do I?) nor he with me and yet we can't bear to be apart." An excursion across the border into Germany offered a preliminary glimpse of what was to come. "I saw Hitler, aquiline-eyed, bareheaded, and Goering later in a heavily-guarded car."

Needless to say, the Eyres-Monsell parents in reality were

having none of it and sent Joan away to India, pleased that Alan at the same time was going his separate way to Vienna. From Admiralty House on 21 November 1933 Joan wrote a farewell letter to Vere, the fond mother-in-law who was not to be. "I very nearly came to see Alan off on Friday but didn't in the end – Of all the depressing and unsatisfactory things, seeing people off is the worst. I'm sure I shall really enjoy India. . . . Anyway I would rather be there than in London if Alan is in Vienna."

Eight

Mr Pryce and Mrs Jones

DUCKWORTH WAS A small but successful publishing house, with Evelyn Waugh and Virginia Woolf among others on its list. One of its good ideas was Brief Lives, a series of short biographies of great men written for the general reader. Beethoven was Alan's subject, and throughout 1932 he was researching and writing what was more an extended essay or monograph than a book. *Harper's Bazaar* paid the flowery compliment that Alan "has deserted music for the primrose path of literature." The August diary entry in which he wondered if he was in love with Joan starts, "Days in the British Museum, reading up Beethoven. Musical lives are the dullest literature in the world. About Beethoven they are interminable and tedious to a degree beyond what I have ever conceived." Writing in a high and indeed superior tone, as though one genius taking the measure of another, Alan emphasizes Beethoven's bad temper and conceit at the expense of the universality of his music. He could apply the word "dull" to Beethoven's eighth symphony. The book was to come out in March 1933 and a friend, the writer Anne Fremantle, told him that Duckworth was "dotty with excitement" about it – news which he passed on to his parents. (Evidence of this book's reach: Benjamin Tammuz, author of *Minotaur*, a novel with touches of genius, used to tell me that reading the Hebrew language edition of *Beethoven* had been part of his education.)

As Joan set sail to India, Alan installed himself in a flat in the Schoenburgstrasse, in the Fourth District of Vienna. He paid his rent to a lady of "superb lineage" whose money had vanished in the postwar inflation. For under £50 a year, he said, he had the choice of dozens of modern flats. The intention now seems to have been to write a book of short stories (no trace of them) and to learn German (a skill that would have come in handy with *Beethoven*).

Vienna then was the capital city of an empire that had just been dismembered. Nothing remained of the Habsburg past except some splendid buildings now purposeless. Alan had strayed into a crisis of collapse and confusion whose outcome could not be predicted. The struggle for mastery between Nazis on the one hand and Communists on the other was already out on the streets, and many expected that the clash of ideologies was sure to spread from Austria right across Europe. Vienna was an early testing ground for those of Alan's generation who were committed politically to the Soviet Union and Marxist revolution. Engelbert Dollfuss, chancellor since 1932, was prepared to treat extremists as they treated him; traduced as an Austro-fascist, that is to say a Hitlerite, he had survived attempted assassination. Alan ignored the tide of violence or registered it as an inconvenience. English friends there included the writers Ethel Mannin, Jimmy Stern and John Lehmann. As for Austrians, "We know *nobody* who isn't a prince." Work went by the board almost at once. "My Christmas week has been almost too merry – though involving, I hasten to add, no disgrace," he wrote to his mother. The two of them began to correspond so frequently and in such detail that they numbered their letters. His skates had cost 78 schillings or £2.13.6. "There are literally about fifty people in all Vienna whom one wants to see and I see them, chiefly on the Rink [the Eislaufverein] before luncheon (very sure art!) and at the opera. Tea-parties merging into cocktails and an occasional ball are the recognized entertainments here and I go to a number of them."

"One night last week I was the victim of an outrage; when Nazis threw tear-gas bombs into a cinema where I was," Alan recounts in his Letter 13, dated January 1934, but omitting the actual day. "Luckily they only had time to throw two before they were arrested, so, as it was a large cinema, my eyes only watered a great deal." He then reverts to the familiar: "More parties. Melanie Hoyos, Mary Apponyi, and other of the names which quite fill my life, gave them ... and on Thursday there is the great party of the season: the Fould-Springers which is to last from six to six."

Letter 14 is headed with its full date, 8 February 1934. "Thérèse Fould is by now really almost my greatest friend. She's almost a Madame de Sévigné; brilliantly witty and quite delicious too. The awful thing is that I would quite as soon spend the rest of my life with her (no that's not really true) as with Joan; and what makes it worse is that she is even richer prospectively. I seem only to take to the daughters of millionaires. They left today for Kitzbühel and I'm inconsolable – so much that after being up very late, I went out to Meidling this morning to have breakfast with them. But I suppose one ought not to marry a Jewess anyhow; especially if one is marrying someone else." That letter's envelope contains photographs of a group of eight, arms linked, Alan and Poppy among them, and both wearing *Tracht*, Austrian costume – for her, this was habitual, for him, fancy dress.

Semmering is on the outskirts of Vienna, with an architectural monstrosity, the Grand Hotel Panhans, at its centre. Alan had stayed there previously and since he returned to the hotel, revolution broke out in Vienna. The letter of 14 February told Vere that his flat was shut up with his passport inside and the servants away in the country. He could therefore not pass through checkpoints. Trapped in the hotel, he was watching from the window of his room troops and machine-guns moving down the road. Three days later he was back in Vienna in the Hotel Sacher. "Every few yards one is stopped for one's passport, and there are bayonets on every street corner. I even saw a body in one of the main streets yesterday." Alan had had a brush with the shelling of the Karl-Marx-Hof, a housing estate built to socialist designs and a landmark for tourists still today. This episode was immediately enshrined in the martyrology of the Left. In July the political situation deteriorated further when Nazis disguised in police uniforms stormed Dollfuss's office and shot dead the Chancellor who might have held off Hitler and the Anschluss.

Marked "Private-ish," a lengthy post-script to that same letter discussed what mattered to Alan far more than public events. One reason for staying on in Vienna, he confided, was to shirk the whole issue of Joan Eyres-Monsell. Also "A new complication. I find Thérèse Fould so enchanting." Asking plaintively, "What am I to do?" he went on to remind his mother that she had heard Bobby talk about Baron Springer, "one of the great international bankers like the Rothschilds and the Schroeders" and also all about Mitzi and Frank Wooster. There were four Fould children – "as to being Jews I only meant that they are of Jewish extraction – but certainly have been Christian for three generations – nor was Fould a Jew at all!" (This deliberate lying has to be for fear of anti-Semitism at home.) "La baronne Thérèse and her sister are now with a governess at Kitzbühel – la baronne being about nineteen, and, as you guess, more than nice, as well as being extraordinarily intelligent in the most unassuming way, and very witty and natural. I can't resist following them to Kitzbühel."

Cameras were then novelties for the public at large, and a huge number of albums and wallets stuffed with snapshots evoke the life la baronne Thérèse, alias Poppy, was leading at that time. In the summer, she and her friends are photographed in bathing costumes at the edge of a lake or at the open-air tables of some Gasthaus. In the winter, she and the friends wear the thickest of jerseys as they sit again at open-air tables, only now in some ski resort. Healthy and happy, everyone seems to be laughing, on the best of terms with each other. Poppy is in the thick of it, and also in the photos is her sister Lily, younger by two years but as it were shadowing her. Hardly out of their teens, these all look like young and innocent beginners in flirtation.

Letter 17 on 19 February tells Vere that a telegram from Bobby invites Alan to meet him in Innsbruck, spend a few days in Monte Carlo and then go through Spain: "to be supported for four weeks free isn't to be sneezed at." Next day, Letter 18 is from the Hotel Tyrol in Innsbruck. Arturo Lopez, the supplier of heroin, was staying there.

> I had the greatest trouble in concealing from the respectable that I also knew the unrespectable, and vice versa. However, the Foulds were charming, and nearly made me break my neck on skis. . . . This is a squalid and ill-à-propos moment to introduce the fact that you need have no worry about their income. Mitzi has been having a lawsuit with the Czech government for eighteen million; and has finally compromised, as she says, very badly. But as the Czech properties are only part of the whole and leave the Fould-Springer bank quite out of the question, she must have enough to go on with.

Mitzi and Frank went out of their way to be matchmakers. When Alan reached Paris, they and the girls were already there, and he could be impressed by the family's possessions in France. "Yesterday we all went to Royaumont in the largest Rolls you ever saw," he wrote home, "I feeling a little, well, a little – owing to having been induced the night before to join some people after dinner (not by Frank). And you know what that leads to." The house was "miraculously beautiful," built like an Italian palace. He admired the avenues of trees, the park with formal sheets of water set with islands. The afternoon was extraordinarily hot, and he spent it in a boat with Poppy and Lily. The others were "so unnecessarily nice that I'm sure, no I'm not, though, that they actually *want* me to marry Thérèse. But I must be wrong. Or has *she* said something? The awful thing is that I want to marry *her*. Then Joan – oh, it's absolute hell."

From Monte Carlo on what was to be their final journey together, Alan took Bobby out to Cap Ferrat to meet Somerset Maugham. By mid-March they were in Tangier, "horrible place. Unfortunately Bobby likes it." Another candid postscript to a letter read, "I do wonder about these Foulds. Quite apart from anything else could one take on all that background of Rothschild cousins and Goldschmidt-Rothschilds and Kahns and Albus? Bobby, quite un-à-propos, said, 'How pleased Mitzi would be if you could bring yourself to marry one of her daughters,' and as she is almost his best friend I suppose he knows what he is talking about. I do know that she is particularly anxious for them all to marry Englishmen. . . . Also I know she likes me very much indeed – but; well, life is difficult, I've always heard."

Somerset Maugham pursued them to Spain. Written in the Hotel Alhambra Palace in Granada, Letter 25 on 2 April relates that Maugham has a huge car and he and Alan have spent most of their days driving in it to obscure and beautiful places. He wanted to hurry back to Vienna to finish a book that promised to be twice as long as *Anthony Adverse* and would take him the rest of the summer (no trace survives). "Dare I hope that Bobby will pay my fare home?" he wondered.

In fact, he spent the rest of the summer courting Poppy. All his life he was to consult fortune-tellers, and one in Vienna wondered if he would find out how miserable he had made someone in England. Frank continued to encourage him. On a drive from Salzburg into Germany Frank without warning told Alan that he knew Thérèse was very fond of him, and Mitzi would be delighted to have him as a son-in-law. "It is rather exciting," Alan concluded. In the photographs of that summer, he looks pleased with himself, a slim and attractive figure, the lederhosen showing off his legs and the white knee-socks that go with *Tracht*; and she in a dirndl, irresistibly pretty, doll-like as she turns her face up at his. Both were play-acting at being Austrian; otherwise they had nothing in common, not education, not religion or nationality, not experience, not even a mother tongue. Poppy and everyone in her world, even or sometimes especially the servants, were conditioned to believe that wealth and privilege must make everything come out for the best. She had no way of knowing how to judge Alan's intentions or to find out why his friends were almost exclusively homosexual. No means either of knowing whether to take him on his own terms as someone with a genuine literary vocation. The one person in possession of all the facts about Alan was Frank, and he was not about to reveal secrets that compromised him. Poppy and her siblings talked among themselves rather bitterly about the relationship between Frank and Eugène; otherwise here was another classic example of the sexual innocence deemed at that time to be proper for well-brought-up girls. Jessie used to say that one evening at Meidling she had found Poppy in tears. She must be pregnant, Poppy said, because Alan had kissed her on the lips. Many years later, Lily was putting her stamp on Royaumont, and made me open a trunk stored there with Poppy's initials on it. We found it to contain those pre-war Austrian clothes. In the pocket of Alan's lederhosen was a testimony of sorts, a contraceptive that had survived longer than the lovers who could perhaps have made use of it.

109

Another undated letter to Vere has to have been written as the moment of decision approached. Almost all of it is twisted or outright untrue, especially about Poppy's appearance and her religion. "I thought I told you all the facts about Thérèse. She is a Roman Catholic, I imagine, and has neither American nor Hungarian blood in her veins. Her father was created Baron Fould. Thérèse is therefore half French, half Austrian. The Springers are, I'm sorry to say, Jews, and cousins of the Rothschilds, Goldsmids, Goldsmid-Rothschilds [properly Goldschmidt], etc, but really very very *very* nice." Poppy was coming to Salzburg, "and there I can straighten things out finally." Mitzi was "absolutely simple and unsnobbish," and so wouldn't want the husbands of her daughters to have any money. "I've heard her say, 'I'm so stupidly rich.'" Even if Poppy had £100 a year, he'd still want to marry her. "She's got a comic little face, not in the least good-looking, but most awfully nice. Not much what you call 'painted.'"

Early in September, Mitzi and Frank were visiting different villages in the Salzkammergut. Among guests at meals were Alan and Oswald Fordham, Mrs. Rodd (Nancy Mitford, had Mitz only known it), Baron Stiebel from Florence, and Erwein Gecman. On the morning of the 10th Alan told her that he was longing to ask Poppy to marry him; he was sure she would say no but might later change her mind. Mitzi had been expecting this for months, she acknowledged in her diary. After a serious talk with Alan, "we were both ever so pleased with each other!" That day, the girls and Jessie went to the Hotel Post at Ischl. Nearby, at Traunkirch on the

Traunsee there is a tiny, very old chapel, and there on the 13th Alan proposed. By then, Mitzi and Frank were already away in Venice, where they went with clockwork punctuality at that time every year. In their hotel "there was a message, Mr Pryce and Mrs Jones have telephoned together." Poppy rang again next day. "What a sweet, young, clever, common-sense, agreeable little couple they will make. They ought to have a lovely and interesting life," commented a Mitzi delighted with the way things had worked out, and not failing to note two practical factors in favour of this marriage: Poppy would be acquiring a British passport and the sweet little couple's wish to live in Meidling spared her the complication of getting money out of Austria.

Nanny Stainer was at Royaumont while her rival Jessie was being Poppy's chaperone. The day after she became engaged, Poppy wrote to reassure her. "I knew always since the day I saw him in January in Vienna that I was in love with him but I never wanted to admit it to myself for I never dreamt he could be for me." Just five days after he became engaged, Alan got down to brass tacks: "I want Thérèse to have about £1,500 a year, and for us both to have permission to live at Meidling. I could not bear to be quite dependent on my in-laws, and I know that the need to make some money without the danger of starvation if one does not (and consequent worry) is the best incentive to work. I am, after all, before everything a writer. I *must* write. And if we were really rich it would make it terribly hard to work properly. The urge for £100 just supplies the spur."

A month later, on October 15, Alan was able to rejoice. "We are to have Meidling plus the two cars and about five servants. We shall only want a cook and a chauffeur-valet. Poppy is being given a maid, and we have one wing – with about four rooms, two bathrooms, and the big central hall of the house for a dining-room (Our living is practically free).

We shall have about £2,000 a year, clear, and allowances for children if any." The house was hideous but Poppy adored it, he told his mother, and the money would be enough "for us *just* to live on."

A letter from the jilted Joan that November is brief: "I'm so sorry you find it impossible even to see me. I thought that we should remain friends which is all I want."

Nine

The Only Duty

THE FIRST NIGHT of Alan and Poppy's married life was spent in the Hôtel de Crillon in Paris. Next morning, Erwein Gecman came to breakfast with them – one of the young men in lederhosen and white stockings who featured in the holiday photographs, he made the most of his youthful good looks and title of Baron. The Hotel Quirinale in Rome, the Grand Bretagne in Athens, the Pera Park Hotel in Istanbul, Sofia – the honeymoon continued in the most luxurious style. "It is unlucky that we look so very very rich," Alan pointed out with more pride than regret. "We arrive, with a mountain of luggage, in huge fur coats of obviously the best fur."

At Meidling on 28 January 1935 he gave some glimpses of his new lifestyle to Patrick Kinross, his correspondent from former travels and his recent best man. After a grand ball in Athens, he wrote, they had taken a Turkish liner to Smyrna. Soldiers in the custom-house there had "arrested" (Alan's word) a teddy bear of his, "a peaceable, non-political bear," as well as a small glass elephant and an ever smaller fibre horse found in his dressing-case. "They made a hole in the bear's arse, too, to see if he was carrying any heroin up it." Exorbitant bribery was needed "to bail them all out." In Istanbul, though, he had found much to admire. (In the market they bought an eighteenth-century timepiece with Arabic numerals that was an ornament in every house they were to live in; round and in a case, it was just too big for a hand or a pocket.)

"I wish you could have seen our arrival here," he continued, pulling out the stops. "We were met at the station by the Director of the Fould-Springersche Verwaltung [Management], with a humbler director and a quite little director. They had roses tied up in gold ribbon and electrified the whole platform. At the lodge gates there was a great deal of hand-kissing, and bowing, and a few tears from the more emotional gardeners. In the hall, there was a line of elderly, very elderly servants, with more roses; and, on the gallery a great expanse of purple velvet, framed, to which were pinned crowns of gilded laurel, and an entire rose garden, crazily hung with gold cords and horseshoes. Here, the Director, bowing, left us; and the humbler directors scuttled about...."

He insists that Patrick Kinross should come and stay. He could make the Connollys drive him out, or even Mitzi. "It was almost as much to be her son-in-law as to be Poppy's husband, that I married the girl. That, by the way, could not possibly be going better. Not only are the mechanics of marriage most satisfactory, but we don't bore each other; indeed, we find each other more and more interesting and self-sufficient, which is very gratifying."

He was almost as exuberant to his parents. "You don't know how nice it is to be well taken care of: to have one's pyjamas ironed every evening, to have an office which automatically sends architects, electricians, gardeners, decorators, at one moment's notice, cashes cheques and sends messengers out to one, pays bills without one knowing they exist, and says as Brüll [Dr Siegfried Brüll, in charge of the Verwaltung] did yesterday, '*Votre seul devoir ici c'est de vivre bien.*'" (Your only duty here is to live well.) Gusti was the head housemaid and Poppy had Mali, short for Amalia, to look after her. For the Opera Ball at the height of the season in Vienna, Franz the butler mounted a footman on the box "as we couldn't go simply with a chauffeur."

Twenty-Seven Poems, the dust-jacket as insipid as the title, was published by Heinemann in April 1935, three short months after the couple had settled into Meidling. Some of the poems had appeared previously in *The London Mercury* or the *New Statesman*. His itinerant life could be reconstructed from dates and place-names attached to many poems – Moustier-Sainte-Marie 1929, for instance, Belgrade 1930, St. Florent 1931. Allusive, composed of images rather than narrative, linguistic skill standing in for emotions, no scansion but rhymes and half-rhymes, the poems are very much the work of someone determined to prove that his literary taste has moved on from the Georgians of the previous generation and is properly à la page. "Perhaps Mr Pryce-Jones is worth watching after all," ran the review in *The London Mercury*. Coming from a friendly source, Alan took this back-handed compliment as "the most wounding sentence I have ever read about myself."

"I have already made my wife a present of my life; So, as I have nothing better to offer, she must expect things like this," is the inscription he wrote for Poppy in her copy of the poems. For her twenty-first birthday on May 2, he gave her an unexpected diamond bracelet costing £300 – "which I have not got" – and they drank one of the last remaining bottles of 50-year-old Imperial Tokay which must once have been laid down by Baron Gustav. They had already forged pet names and terms of endearment for one another. Poppy called him Min; Alan called her Boule. Borrowing from Beatrix Potter, she signed her letters Pigling. Both sometimes started or ended letters with the drawing of a mouse. Their sheets were pink, with white mice embroidered on them as a monogram. As tokens of love, they were in the habit of personalizing gifts to one another by having these pet names engraved or stamped in their own handwriting on anything suitable such as photograph frames or leather wallets.

Soon after that birthday, still in May, they visited London, and out walking one afternoon there Poppy said she thought she was pregnant. She had been taken by surprise, she felt ill and foretold disaster, Alan writes, because "a child should be planned for, dreamed of, aspired to." Seemingly no member of the family had told him that in childhood Poppy might sit on her bed and cry all night unaccountably and inconsolably. What they had become used to he was now to discover for himself. At Meidling again, and at night when she was tired, she would suddenly begin crying. "I have never known anybody with such wet tears: everything is soaked in a moment, and my pyjama jacket is glued to my chest – and then to be remorseful. 'I'm horrible. I'm not worth your love.'" This was all for no reason, he speculated, unless she was feeling alone or frightened.

Poppy's mental and physical condition had to accommodate plans. Salzburg was the place to be in August. Alan had arranged to meet there Evan Tredegar, his first love and now another of the visitors going native in Austrian costume. (In the summer of 1937, he took her to stay at Tredegar near Cardiff. Another guest was H. G. Wells who invited Poppy to row him on the lake while he corrected the proofs of his new book. In the boat he made a pass at her. Grabbing the proofs, she threatened to throw them into the water unless he stopped. He persisted; she threw.) They drove on into Germany, to a Kurhaus at Bad Reichenhall where another love, Bobby Pratt-Barlow, was staying. Poppy was suffering inexplicable pains. She might miscarry, Alan wrote to his mother, but there was a great specialist in the town who would advise whether to continue or return to Vienna. Changing the subject, he mentioned that Kenneth Rae, his previous publisher, had read the book of poems and his enthusiasm could be paraphrased: "Great as my admiration is for your earlier work, I never thought you capable.... [*sic*] Balm! Has anybody else reviewed my poems? I wouldn't mind a few laurels there, because they are a much better lot than any of my prose."

Towards the end of August, the first visit to Meidling of his parents and Adrian prompted some of the well-imagined observations that are the strongpoint of his style (the dots are his): "Papa's cough . . . Not disagreeably thick, but uniquely caparisoned: a tasselled cough . . . Mama's footstep, not exactly tired, but reticent, like a hall-clock ticking . . . Adrian's slightly troubled air: the drawers don't pull smoothly and the door handles, in his life, are too high." Smothered by his parents and overshadowed by his elder brother, no wonder Adrian had a troubled air. But he was becoming an ice-skater at Olympic Games level, winning silver cups and gold medals. Photographs show him skating gracefully at St Moritz by himself or with Sonja Henie, the foremost skater of her time.

To Alan's surprise, "Papa turns out to be such a very much nicer man than I had ever supposed, and Mama was divine." One evening alone with his mother, "we really opened our feelings to one another." On the same page of his diary he took stock of himself. "Too talented: too good at everything immediately. I could have been a notable dancer, painter, musician, artist of any kind. But, having no application, the thing would have stopped short at notability. I enjoy myself too much. After all, the consciousness of great powers is what one enjoys. That I have. The ability to exert them is another matter. . . . Contented, I love my wife. I like my books, food, wine, scenery. I enjoy being rich. I like being in a big car when others are on foot." A letter of 25 October 1935 to Vere shows Alan in his element. "Our horse won the second biggest race of the year," he rejoices. "We were quite beside ourselves, and led it in, and were congratulated by everyone, and quite lost our heads. I never thought I should live to see the day when a horse in which I had even the smallest interest would win a big race; and now of course, I think of nothing but racing." He rounds the letter off with a caution: "There is no doubt the rich have little fun. The only thing to do is to try not to lose the riches."

"My dearest Parents," Poppy begins her letters to Harry and Vere. On September 29 she filled them in with some typical chat. The day after Harry and Vere had left, Max and Lily arrived. Off the four of them went to Piešťany in Slovakia, where they were joined by Bubbles and Eduardo. Max had arranged a shoot on his property, Bucşani; Alan and Lily were proud of their shooting. "We bought lovely national costumes but had to have them made," and also "We have all been sitting out in the park wearing our Tyrolean clothes for the last time this year." Cyril and Jean Connolly had been to lunch; she had found them "rather extraordinary." Reynaldo Hahn, the Argentine composer, was in Vienna (he and Alan seem to have collaborated but no trace remains of whatever this may have been). "Alan has begun to work again seriously, I am so pleased about that."

Poppy must have taken a New Year's resolution on January 1, 1936 to keep a so-called Year-by-Year Diary in which the record of each day has to be crammed into just four lines. She was receiving and answering lots of letters. She went into the city centre; she was at the Burg Theater (Molnar), the opera (*The Flying Dutchman* and *The Tales of Hoffmann*), and a concert with Furtwängler conducting. She went for walks in the snowy parks of Meidling and Schönbrunn. Alan was having lessons in Czech. Beverley Nichols, Peter and Joan Hesketh, and Billa Creswell, later married to the economist Sir Roy Harrod, came for meals. (With a finger Billa had once inscribed, "Alan is a pansy," on his dusty car – "a tease and not a comment," he said, presumably in the expectation that at least some readers would believe him.) Erwein Gecman, Desy Fürstenberg, Wolly Seybel a well-known wit, were rare Austrian guests. Many years later Kari

Schwarzenberg, destined to be Václav Havel's Foreign Minister, took me to dine with his parents in their family palais. I asked if they had been to Meidling before the war. Since they appeared not to have heard of the place, I mentioned Alan's name. Shocked, Prince Schwarzenberg said, "*Jones? Aber in England das ist sehr vulgaire*" – which needs no translation. On February 14, the day before my birth, Poppy's cheerful little entries stop, and the rest of that diary is blank.

"*Il n'y a que les riches qui se font mal soigner,*" the Fould-Springers liked to say about doctors – only the rich get themselves bad medical treatment. In the practice of that day a woman having a child was treated as an invalid. Primarius Fleischmann, the family doctor, ordered Poppy to stay in bed. Phlebitis developed. For the rest of her life her ankles remained distended. She who had climbed for reassurance into her father's bed, or sat crying all night on her own bed, now on top of her physical condition had to endure her special form of post-natal depression. Sheets of paper survive on which she has scribbled with a pencil in letters sometimes at least an inch high, repetitively but incoherently protesting her love for Alan, begging to be forgiven for unspecified faults and pleading to be loved in return. Here was something kept secret from me. The first I heard of it was in 1987 when Alan published *The Bonus of Laughter*. He had not shown me the proofs, so the revelation on the page of the finished copy was all the more stark. Poppy, he says there, had been "gripped by some force outside her will." As the years went by, "this would recur every few weeks." This, he posited, was the same anguish that Virginia Woolf had suffered from. Reflecting about his wife's case, Leonard Woolf had ascribed her death to "loss of control over her mind." The inference is that Poppy too might one day have committed suicide. Now and again I did find her crying, but for real reasons that had nothing to do with supposed mental confusion.

At Meidling she wrote at some length to Vere on 18 April, complimenting her as "my one and only true Mummy." Apparently under the impression that she might die, she goes on, "With all my courage and God's help I am struggling to win a very hard battle against my end. I am living in perpetual anguish, every day worse, not so for myself but for my adored Alan and my precious David, but if ever God did call me back to him, I know you would be the only one to really help him and understand him and love him as I do." And then, "I suffer much more mental than physical pain."

For the remainder of the year, Poppy was in a specialized clinic at Malmaison, outside Paris. I spent my first few months at Royaumont. Miss Cutmore, otherwise Cutty, took care of me. She is remembered for saying as tea was being served on the terrace, "Who would have thought a year ago when I was looking after little Prince Dietrichstein that today I would have a little commoner." Writing from the clinic, Poppy continued to convey unhappiness without explanation or insight into the cause of it. An undated letter from that time again appeals to her mother-in-law rather than her mother. "I have been wanting to write to you since days but I have been feeling so much worse again that I couldn't. I really begin to absolutely despair of ever getting any better! Alan is more and more wonderful, patient and adorable and it absolutely breaks my heart to make him so miserable. I think his book is brilliant, and so exactly like him and all the descriptions and summaries make me know and understand him even better and remind me of some of the many happy days in the past. I sometimes hardly recognize myself. I have become horrible not only in looks but specially in mind! Please, darling Mama, help me. I need so much help to give me more courage. I feel I can't live here among much madness, doctors and nurses any longer and yet I know I can't either live with those I love! It is all so terrible and so dreadfully long. If only I could sleep a little and sometimes forget. I have lost continually confidence in everything and which is worst of all I don't believe any doctor because I see that there is not the slightest progress in my condition since two months. Please write to me, Mama darling, and give me courage." She signed, "Your very sad Poppy."

In another letter to Vere on 3 September she is still rehearsing her self-reproaches. "My son came to see me, he is lovely and so very sun-burnt which makes his blue eyes seem bluer than ever. I went for a little drive with Alan, it was a real treat to leave this horrid place for a hour. I haven't slept more than five minutes since a few days, but I am very pleased because Mummy saw my Viennese doctor . . . and he will be passing through Paris in September. I am already counting the days because he is really the only doctor in whom I have confidence. . . . I am trying very hard to be better but alas I don't think I will be." Four days later, she is still heaping obsessive reproach on to herself, while excusing Alan. Throughout this emotional breakdown, he is blameless in her eyes, "more and more and more perfect each second and no husband has ever been like him."

"Now that all is over," she was able to tell Vere on 7 November,

> I feel really grateful to have gone through all that, because it only makes one appreciate one's existence so much more. I suppose no couple in the world are quite as happy as Alan and me and really each day now I feel I am getting better. I wrote you before leaving Malmaison. . . . My sweet son came to see me today, he is too adorable now and tries so hard to talk! I hope it is quite decided that you are all coming to Vienna in January! How marvellous. Alan has begun to take Czech lessons again. All my friends are so nice, it is really such a joy to see them

all after so many months. I went to Lulu's wedding yesterday [this childhood friend had married Geoffroy de Waldner].

"I want to be in a large house in England," she confided to Alan a wish-fulfillment fostered by childhood in Meidling and Royaumont, "with lots of wonderful old servants and a French cook and four children in the nursery and lots of delightful neighbours and you working in the library on your masterpiece and me on my carpet and nothing but peace of every kind surrounding us." Petit-point tapestry was her pastime.

The book that Poppy thought brilliant was *Private Opinion*, published by Kenneth Rae of Cobden-Sanderson that June; its dedication to her must have been some consolation in her clinic. Subtitled *A Commonplace Book*, it is a collection of observations on everything and anything that Alan has been reading, enlivened with recollections of important influences and events in his upbringing. Already in the book's second paragraph he lets drop that a cousin has married a duke. A high point is the description of the shoot at Bucşani to which Max had recently invited him. Some judgements are amusing: "There is too much in Gide of mittens," or in the case of Aldous Huxley, manifestations of the intellect have been turned out "half asleep, like his applauding readers." The style is opinionated, thickened by resort to unusual words: ataxic, paregoric and such-like. Many of his targets are minor writers and Alan's familiarity with their work risks either seeming precious or making the reader feel small. In a review in the *Sunday Times*, Edward Shanks objected to Alan's projected superiority. "There seems to be no one whom he cannot patronize when he is in the mood."

Ten

Storm Clouds

"I GO MAD in this country," Alan told himself after walking in the mountains from Berchtesgaden to the Hintersee, "wanting to crush and distil each valley into its essence and carry it round with me." The pleasure of "bead-blue lakes, the mossy parks among rocks and pines" was so intense that he could express it as a positive torture. Poppy was pleased but slightly bewildered that his response to her Austria should be so aesthetic. When someone climbed into the park at Meidling and carved swastikas on trees, Alan found nothing stronger to say than this was an "obscure threat."

The moment Hitler came to power in January 1933, Mitzi had to confront a threat that was not obscure. The disposition of her fortune became a preoccupation. Always abreast of events, she read newspapers thoroughly in at least three languages, and she also read journalistic books of the day by the likes of G. E. R. Gedye, László Hatvany, Berta Szeps and Ferdinand Czernin, annotating them with her own observations. Friends and acquaintances, some of them actively political – Philippe Berthelot of the Quai d'Orsay, Robert Vansittart the strongly anti-Hitler permanent under-secretary at the Foreign Office – kept her informed. Wherever she was, she was regularly in touch with the staff she employed to manage her interests. In addition to Brüll in Vienna, Hans Mailath-Pokorny moved between Budapest and Prague overseeing her affairs. In Paris, George Hickman ran an office for her, conveniently situated on the floors below her apartment in the Rue de Surène. Known as Hickie, or Mr Hickie, he was a model of tact and good humour, an efficient bureaucrat willing and able to stand up to Mitzi and to give way gracefully. A light growl in his voice suggested something was wrong with his vocal cords. Where he was all restraint, Gladys, his wife, was all exuberance. In the war, he was a Group Captain engaged in staff work at Biggin Hill, the R.A.F. base. At Mr Hickie's insistence, Mitzi moved a small amount of money to Canada. To deal with expenses that Frank might incur in sterling, she also opened an account at Hambros Bank in London. By way of investment, she purchased founder shares in Singer and Friedlander, a merchant bank just launched in London by two men, both refugees, whom she had known in Vienna. Her father's daughter, she could not bring herself to take advice to sell inherited properties. Awareness of the approaching storm did not overcome a lifetime's cast of mind.

On 14 February 1933 she and Frank were in London dining in the Savoy Grill. Also there was Leopold Hoesch, the skeptical but pliant German ambassador who was soon replaced by Joachim von Ribbentrop, a dyed-in-the-wool Nazi. He came over to sit with them. "He told us that the country had such a strong longing for Hitler that he *had* to come." On another occasion at that time, Prince Philip of Hesse described to her how he had told Hitler that he himself had Jewish friends and could never do anything against them. Hitler had answered that this was right, that he had nothing against Jews already settled in Germany but wanted to stop immigrants from Poland. "Hesse of course believes Hitler," Mitzi concluded, adding with obvious disbelief, "*qui vivra verra.*" (He who lives will see.)

Visiting Nazi Germany in the summer of 1933, Mitzi was shocked by the swastikas everywhere. She and Frank stopped at Baden-Baden. "I never thought Germany wanted war, now I believe everything is possible. I admire some things in Hitler, I believe him to be sincere, but all the nation seems as if gone mad.... I fear we may all face the same situation in Austria even if their temperament makes them say, '*Ja, wir wollen zu Hitler halten, aber unsere Juden muss er uns lassen.*'"

124 (Yes, we'd like to go along with Hitler but he must leave us our Jews. Elsewhere she reproduces an alternative version, "*unsere Juden muss er nie fressen,*" he must never gobble up our Jews.) "Who can understand Hitler?" is a rhetorical question in her diary. "These Germans behave again like badly brought up children. The anti-Jewish movement is very cruel though I can understand the reasons that have taken hold of Hitler and his men." Then they spent a night at Heidelberg, catching up with Max Springer, a cousin who had just been deprived of his post as a professor at the university of Mannheim. "All the professors there and all his students asked him to come back; he did so but of course could not get paid. His wife and children are born Christians, but the boys after 15 will not be able to go to school like Christian boys whose four grandparents are or were Christians."

As they did every autumn, they drove on to Venice, a city that she sentimentalized because it had been a backdrop while she was convincing herself that her triangle of love with Eugène and Frank was sincere and innocent. The Dollfuss crisis was erupting and Mitzi wrote that Austria could be lost to Germany any day: "The Nazis will finally win but the country will not be anti-Semitic like Germany. It will be Nazism à l'autrichienne." Now Frank met a young German boy who was a friend of Paul Goldschmidt, and he told them that Hitler was a real god and not a bit anti-Jewish. Another encounter was with Lord Lloyd, whom Frank had known since Gallipoli where Lloyd had been on the staff of General Sir Ian Hamilton. A Conservative member of Parliament, he had been High Commissioner in Egypt, and was just publishing a political book about it. Like Frank, he moved in the company of handsome young men. Following a telephone call from Hitler, Lloyd left Venice for Berlin, "one of those who think Hitler a saviour," as Mitzi put it. (She may have been assuming mistakenly that because he was a notorious anti-Semite he had to be a Nazi too. In 1940 Churchill appointed him Secretary of State for the colonies and then Leader of the House of Lords.) The First World War had shaken Sir Ian Hamilton into pacifism and appeasement of Germany. At a lunch, he was to recount to Mitzi and Frank that on his recent visit to Germany "all seemed contented there." At the Adlon Hotel in Berlin he had observed 30 or 40 Jews happily dining together. According to Mitzi, he said, "Nations ought to leave Germany alone these days. I should not like to be the nation to attack her now. She is capable of everything." Robert Vansittart at the Foreign Office had taken the trouble to ask Sir Ian not to see Hitler.

"The Jewish question," as Mitzi then perceived it, "is something I understand in many a way and not at all in others. There are always masses suffering for the wrong-doing of others, and what horrors we shall still see God alone knows. All countries will take up anti-Semitism again, I fear. Where are these miserable Jews going to settle down – Francis de Croisset [born Franz Wiener in Vienna, a family friend, Jewish, a successful playwright] says one ought to find them an island in the Pacific as Palestine is not safe for them either." This passage goes on to relate the story of another friend, the aristocratic Count Yorck, known as Sonny and married to Ruth Landsberg, a member of the Jewish family that owned Mazer, the Palladian villa in the Veneto as perfect architecturally as Royaumont. On a flight from Venice to Berlin, there had been "a little Jew to whom Yorck poured out his worries. This man next morning denounced him. Hitler's officials want to force the Jews back into the mentality one says they have, and bad treatment is the way to get them there quickly. Sonny Yorck lost his situation in a bank for having a Jewish wife. The Jewish father of Ruth has got a new job in a Nazi undertaking. *Comprendre qui pourra* [let him understand it who can]. My Jewish question is concentrated on Max Springer and his family. What will happen to them?"

As Austrians identified more and more openly with Nazi Germany, the family's centre of gravity shifted away from Meidling. For most of the time Mitzi and Frank were at Montreuil, treating it as headquarters. Her children felt they could not reject summons to go there, although the heart might sink. On their own at Royaumont, Max and Lily had the time of their lives in a house so close to Paris and so ideal for entertaining. The two English nannies substituted for the missing domesticity. In innumerable photographs I am to be seen, with aunts and uncles, or sometimes Harry and Vere and the teenage Adrian on a summer visit, bending over a gigantic pram or holding me in their arms.

Bubbles, the eldest daughter, in old age liked to present an idealized portrait of herself as artist, painter, socialite, cosmopolitan, the friend of royal persons, author whose memoir has a title that is the equivalent of a handwave, *I Loved My Stay*. Eduardo Propper de Callejon had not been Mitzi's choice for a son-in-law. The one and only time I ever heard her say anything in Yiddish was years later when she had an expression for the Proppers as "Jews from Galicia with lice in their side-locks." A monarchist by conviction, Eduardo had joined the Spanish diplomatic service and been posted to Vienna after the First War. He left the service in 1931 when King Alfonso XIII resigned. In exile in France, Eduardo and Bubbles lived either at Royaumont, in Mitzi's flat in the rue de Surène, or in the Hotel Meurice with other Spanish exiles whom he referred to as "a Spanish nationalist colony." During the civil war he spent several days in Berlin on a mission to buy arms for Franco. For much of the Thirties Mitzi was paying them an allowance.

After the birth in October 1930 of Philip, their son and my first cousin, Bubbles had a post-natal depression or psychological collapse exactly as Poppy was to have, though longer lasting. The birth in May 1934 of their daughter Elena, or Elly, prolonged it. With Bubbles weeping in a hotel room and Poppy weeping in the Malmaison clinic, Eduardo and Alan discussed how to come to terms with married life and fatherhood. "At first David meant nothing to me," Alan wrote. "Sometimes I have hated him for making Poppy suffer so. Only when I saw the faculty of *searching* grow in him could I recognize him. He looked for something. His contented feet, and his sash, however, made me recognize him as a possibly lovable human being."

One idea was to put in order Poppy's property at Kostolany in Slovakia. In preparation, Alan continued his Czech language lessons, and bought himself a Tatra, a car of Czech design whose advanced engineering gave it a scarcity value but a headache to mechanics. Off the road a good deal, the Tatra nevertheless was Alan's pride and joy. Another idea was to rent Herstmonceux, a huge and well-know country house in Sussex. The owner, Sir Paul Latham, was a friend of Max, and used to visit Royaumont. Caught in a park with a soldier, he was sent to prison. "I am feeling very John Bullish just now," Alan confided in a letter to his parents on 21 October 1936 with a cheeriness contrary to the tone of the letters Poppy was writing to them, "and long to be in London: or Herstmonceux Place. Poppy is very excited about that." On 26 October he was explaining to them that she had "a peri-flébite – which sounds more alarming than it is. There is nothing to be done except to stay in bed." Next day she would move into her mother's Paris flat in the rue de Surène, while he attended a party given by the duc de Gramont at Vallière, the duke's country house. "The Herstmonceux plan has gone down very well – and with a little careful nursing we shall bring it off. Poppy wants it, Max thinks the idea splendid – and Mitzi is going to look the whole thing over, at my request." Four days later, he wrote again to tell them that Poppy was "absolutely herself," looking at Molyneux dresses and coming out for a drive in the Bois de Boulogne. One week more, and they had decided to take Herstmonceux, "though I don't quite see how we can afford to live in it. One must not, however, be sordid in plan-making, must one."

Instead Mitzi looked after them financially as she did Bubbles and Eduardo, buying the lease of a house in London, in Marylebone. Coming to stay there, Mitzi found it "adorable . . . they are ever so sweet. . . . I do hope I can manage to let them keep it, but *how*." 4 York Gate was in the middle of an imposing terrace which is part of John Nash's masterful town-planning for that area. The uniformity is eye-catching. One end of the street is closed by St Mary's church and the other is the edge of Regent's Park. In childhood, Poppy had spent two or three summer holidays with the Esmonds at North Berwick, but otherwise knew nothing about the country she now found herself in. Aged twenty-three, she had a housekeeper, Mrs Kay, and a butler, Saunders, noting their wages in a special diary bound in pig-skin. Ruth Harris, a long-standing friend, used to maintain that Poppy spoke with a French accent, but by the time I could judge this for myself, she spoke English like a native. In the process of anglification, she was presented at court, a ceremony that required a formal dress as for a wedding, ostrich feathers and elbow-length white kid gloves. In a white tie and tails Alan escorted her to Buckingham Palace, and with them were Vere and a Harry very solemn as a Gentleman at Arms complete with helmet and sword. (They sent a photograph of themselves in a group to Brüll, because after my birth he had written to them in English, "From Meidling I can only report the best. The little David, his mother and grandmother are all right and very happy.... This child may bring you good luck." I was grown-up when his son Hans returned this photograph to me just before he emigrated to Israel.)

That York Gate house was made for entertaining. Voices of guests arriving in the hall reached up the staircase. Alan picked up literary life as though he had never been away in Vienna, and his absence had only served to establish him as a man of letters on his own terms. He propelled Poppy into the world of Harold Nicolson, Eddie Marsh, Charles Morgan and Squire. Among his contemporaries, he didn't like Evelyn Waugh, he thought Raymond Mortimer "the most brown person I know," therefore destined not to be remembered. After some dinner party or social encounter he could turn a phrase that exactly summed up a character. Stephen Spender had, "The head of a beautiful turnip." Again, "We ran into Stephen Spender on Chiswick Mall. He thinks I am frivolous, I think he is half-prefect, half sarg [sergeant]. He was sunburnt, handsome – and I like him. But the sincerity and strength of his politics, even though I agree with them, hopelessly divide us. There was a sort of tension – the combat between an open shirt and a blue overcoat. 'I live near here,' he said." Christopher Isherwood "seduced more boys than any other individual in Berlin, one is told with aghast admiration." Cecil Day-Lewis was "a memorial. A cape gooseberry. There is no trace of poetry left, no fire; an accent so genteelly *ow-ow* that it seems to have been acquired along with party membership." The adjectives for Cyril Connolly tell the whole story: "Easily wounded, unforgiving, dislikeable, delightful."

Every day, columns of horses from the cavalry barracks in Albany Street would clatter and jingle down York Gate on the way to exercising in Regent's Park. Hearing that evocative sound, I would stand on furniture and crane out of the window. Someone called Margaret was filling in for the proper nannies at Royaumont, and she forbade me from taking up my watch on the grounds that I might fall out of the window. Catching me red-handed one day, she undressed me and stood me in the corner, forbidding me to move while she went to the kitchen for tea. As luck would have it, she was still out of the room when I heard the heavy tread of grandfather Harry coming upstairs. He may have been calling my name. Ashamed to be naked, I shot under the bed, and there he found me, poking his head upside down below the valance, and then dragging me out. When Margaret re-entered the room, he gave her an hour to pack her bags and leave.

Eleven

Adolfo Chamberlini

ALL GRANNY WOOSTER needed to be happy was a pen and paper. Every day she wrote up her diary in the belief that she had in hand a document of historic importance. When she fled in 1940 she entrusted the volumes to Madame Provins, her housekeeper and mother of her maid Paulette – they had a house of their own in Montreuil. Buried by Madame Provins in the garden without adequate protection, a good many volumes were spoiled beyond recovery. Mitzi never forgot, let alone forgave, what she considered criminal negligence.

A grandson and a published writer, I was handed the remaining volumes. Mitzi had the highest expectations. Editing a coherent book out of these hundreds of thousands of words was supposed to be my task but it was something she alone could do. She wrote in a manner that assumed the reader to have been as familiar with this material as she was. Statement has to stand for explanation. Suddenly switching from one topic to another, she lets drop names, places, references, amid random reflections of fear or hope about the politics of the day, without any attempt to be discursive. She comments for instance, "The law against Jews in Hungary is pretty bad. My children cannot visit our properties," without spelling out what that law specified, and almost immediately contradicting herself: "We are all making plans to go to Hungary in September." (This was 1939, so war overtook plans.) Then early in 1940 she expressed her disappointment and anger more explicitly: "As for Hungary they want the certificates of baptism of Frank's parents and grandparents, mine and the one of Bubbles." Which led her to exclaim,

"When I think of the years of hard work that all these places gave me! And for what!"

Another sketchy incident concerns a tax demand in Czechoslovakia for eighteen million crowns. How the demand arose is not clear. Pokorny appears to have negotiated it down to a few millions. Bitterness remained: "I will always hate the Czechs and never forgive the way they treated me and made special laws to steal from me all they could." Again, what laws were these? The Munich toing and froing, she hazarded, could have had a different outcome. "These famous Czech patriots will not once try to kill Hitler. Old President Hácha ought to have done it during the death of his country." Her Czech properties grew beet, and through Pokorny she appears to have bought or gone into partnership with Teplà, a factory producing sugar from beet. Alan was put on the board of Teplà (which may also explain why he took Czech lessons and passed the test for a driving licence in Bratislava, where he may have had an eye on his Tatra car.) When someone Jewish, whom she refers to as "*le malheureux Wolf*" (the wretched Wolf) somehow made trouble for the Teplà board, Pokorny drove him by car from Slovakia to the Protectorate of Bohemia. On the face of it, this means handing him to the Nazis. Mitzi concludes an incomplete summary of this episode with what might be an admission of guilt: "the Jews who are refugees from Vienna in Prague, what about them? *Tout cela déborde la charité privée* [private charity can't cope with this] and although I feel nothing but pity for these unfortunate people my conscience is clear. Confronting a mess like this, an individual can do nothing." Pokorny informs her that he has advised their accountant, a man called Hinteregger, to acquire protective covering by becoming a Nazi – this didn't take much persuasion, Mitzi notes with sarcasm that was probably deserved but still needs to be backed with evidence. References to one Lauf are murkier still. His first name is not given. Turning up in Vienna and accepting bribes to stand between the Nazis and the Springer interests, he was really running a protection racket.

Two opinions exist about a German lawyer, Geutebruch, someone else whose first name is not recorded. Mitzi seems to believe he was acting in her interest. Not only did he oversee the sequestration of Meidling but in the war turned up in Paris at the office in the rue de Surène and at the Maisons-Alfort factory. Protected by his French passport, Max went once to Meidling after the Anschluss. Describing Geutebruch as a Gauleiter, he loved to relate an exchange they had had in Vienna, saying with an exaggerated German accent, "*Herr Gauleiter, was behalten Sie für Italien?*" To which the answer was, "*Italien bedeutet kein Problem.*" (Herr Gauleiter, what's your opinion about Italy? Italy presents no problem.) At the end of the war, according to Max, Geutebruch had had himself sent to the front and been killed.

Mitzi was at Montreuil on 12 March 1938 when the Wehrmacht overran Austria, and Hitler annexed the country next day. In the course of a triumphal visit to Vienna, he appeared on a balcony of the Hotel Imperial, according to Mitzi the balcony of the room that her father had reserved for himself. Overstating an important friendship, Mitzi put in her diary, "Vansittart says England would stand behind me if one touches our houses in Vienna." She was practical enough to add, "We are ruined by events in Austria."

Alan had shunned the anti-fascist posturing of so many intellectuals at the time, and now he was to come up against political reality. "Brüll's voice at the telephone," he records, "I must come at once to Vienna. He can give no explanations, I surmise, because of the Gestapo. Advice, letters to be got from Vansittart, instructions from Mitzi." British and not Jewish, Alan did not have to feel afraid. Brüll was among the

Jews whom the Gestapo humiliated by forcing them down on their hands and knees to scrub pavements. A fortnight after the Anschluss Alan flew to Vienna. The Consulate was thronged with Jews trying to obtain visas and Alan had a spasm of guilt when he was shown into the Consul's office ahead of these desperate people. At lunch in the Grand Hotel, where the presence of German officers imposed silence on everyone else, the British Consul put Alan in the picture. Then at Meidling he learnt that Brüll had taken responsibility for a large loan to the shady Lauf in the hope of saving the situation.

A letter to his parents dated Wednesday, 6 April 1938 shows Alan rising to the crisis. "I left Berlin by the night train on Monday," he writes, "arriving in Vienna at 8.0 yesterday morning. Then out to Meidling: then a three hours conference with a Berlin lawyer [Geutebruch?], a Vienna one, and the people of the bureau. Then out to Meidling again, to arrange the packing of books, clothes and pictures. Then another conference from 3.30 till 7.0 broken by a visit to the Consul. Then a talk to one of the Legation secretaries; very interesting but only to be described verbally. Dinner at 9.0 in Meidling; more packing; and the 11.15 night train to Prague with the Centraldirektor that involved discussions with him until 1 A.M. in my wagon-lit." He was due to fly to Paris, he tells them, take a train to Montreuil, probably cross to London for a few hours and then back to Vienna. "I think I have accomplished quite a lot by my going; and anyhow I have collected some fascinating snapshots of Central European life at the moment. Also, I may tell you, that apart from Unity Mitford, few people stand higher in the esteem of the Dritter Reich than your loving son. Sieg Heil! I don't think!"

The same spirit infuses a letter written from Royaumont on 11 April. He and Mr Hickman plan to fly out of Le Bourget airport at 6.45 the following morning. He has to spend a few

ABOVE: Baron Gustav Springer (1842–1920), whose interests extended from Austria and Hungary to Maisons-Alfort, his yeast factory in Paris.

RIGHT: Gustav with his only child, Mitzi, standing behind him. His wife, Hélène Koenigswarter had died giving birth to Mitzi.

ABOVE: "What a pity the little Springer girl looks so Jewish," Mitzi heard one army officer say to another. At eighteen, she married.

OPPOSITE, FROM TOP:
Meidling, the house Gustav built in a park of some fifty acres adjoining the imperial palace of Schönbrunn.

Pokvár, the house with an estate and a partridge shoot near Györ in western Hungary where the family spent the summer.

The great Cistertian abbey of Royaumont was destroyed in the French Revolution, but the Palladian palace built in the 1780s for the Abbott survived in secular hands. Mitzi and Eugène bought it in 1923.

Marrying Mitzi, Eugène Fould (1876–1929) insisted on retaining French nationality but placated Gustav by hyphenating the family surnames.

Frank Wooster was the illegitimate son of the industrialist Sir Frank Leyland, and the friend Eugène came to regret.

Born and brought up in Meidling, Poppy stood out for her unusual background, singular prettiness and unaccountable moods.

Alan and Poppy became engaged in September 1934 at Traunkirchen, a village on a lake in the Tyrol, and married that December.

Colonel Harry Pryce-Jones ended his military career as Harbinger of the Gentlemen at Arms. He and Granny Vere lived in one of the Grace-and-Favour houses at Windsor Castle.

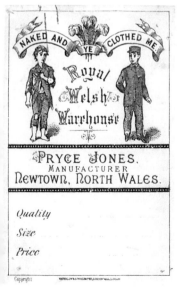

Sir Pryce Pryce-Jones's Royal Welsh Warehouse in Newtown, Montgomery, had 6,000 employees and sold goods by mail order all over the world.

LEFT: Alan was at some pains to show the world the face of a dedicated man of letters.

BELOW: At Royaumont in the summer of 1960.
FAR LEFT: Philip Propper; FAR RIGHT: Elly, married to Raymond Bonham-Carter (standing behind her); next to him Elie de Rothschild and then Lily.

days relieving Brüll of his functions, and hand everything over to some suitable person whom he has still to find. Then he will go on to Prague because the last interview at the Legation there had been very rushed. He reassures his par- ents by telling them that he is enjoying himself in his new role and has just received a charming letter from Vansittart who can hardly have a minute to spare for the affairs of Eng- land. "And then – isn't it sad – I must arrange for Meidling to be dismantled: for the pictures to be sent to London, and the house closed, I suppose for ever. But under present con- ditions with a huge garage for armoured cars and camou- flaged police wagons at the lodge gates, and a twenty foot swastika flag flying from the windows of your room (I had it taken away and replaced by the Union Jack!), it isn't much fun. All the servants, too, have turned into Nazis, and to hear Heil Hitler spoken by those silly old things is, to say the least, unexpected. Though they're so silly that they assume, as a matter of course, that we are delighted too. You are being angelic to take such care of David and York Gate, and I can't ever tell you how grateful we are."

Permission was not forthcoming to dismantle the house or pack up possessions to be sent abroad. The Nazis had wasted no time passing the decrees that enabled them even- tually to steal everything owned by Jews. Alan managed to slip into his luggage a very small picture by Rudolf von Alt of the Belvedere, the magnificent palace built by Johann Lukas von Hildebrandt for Prince Eugène of Savoy. More danger- ous still, at Brüll's request he agreed to fly home via Berlin in order to smuggle currency. As he describes it in *The Bonus of Laughter*, he was to meet a German contact at Tempelhof airport and hand over to him all the cash available in the Springer office. Ostensibly the money was to buy Mercedes- Benz patents. What with his anxiety, the size of the package and the flimsiness of its brown paper wrapping, Alan was fortunate to pass undetected. Nothing was ever heard of the German stranger, the money or the patents, and it seems probable that this was extortion on the part of the shadowy Lauf.

These experiences were not going to prevent Alan from doing as he pleased so long as peace lasted. Austria was now excluded, but other countries had comfortable houses, expensive hotels and sights for him and Poppy to enjoy. Fresh from being an observer at military exercises at Tidworth, Harry had a soldier's perspective that war with Hitler was ultimately inevitable but he wrote some lines of doggerel that celebrate arrangements to spend the summer in France in the place of the absent Alan and Poppy:

> In August nineteen thirty eight
> From the Duke of York's through the big main gate
> Went Harry and Vere and Adrian
> Off to the sea at Le Touquet.

From Montreuil, about half an hour away, I had already arrived at Le Touquet with the nannies and my cousins. We were staying in Paris-Plage, part of the resort with all sorts of facilities right on the beach. One family album has a series of photographs of Granny Vere in an ankle-length dress and waving a parasol above her head as she cavorts on the sand like a commedia dell'arte dancer. Writing from Royaumont, Alan informed them of his "rather bleak visit" to Montreuil. "Mitzi not at all well, and in a bad state of nerves, Frank with a sprained foot: panic about money, etc. None of it, luckily, was directed at *us*; but I had to hold both their hands a lot, and they were getting on one another's nerves into the bargain."

Royaumont was the setting for domestic drama. The Proppers had decided to part. There had been a scene.

Everybody said exactly what they thought in no measured terms: that Bubbles was this and this and this; and
Eduardo that and that and that! The upshot of it all is
that he is leaving for Spain apparently in a week – but
only to go to the Ministry at Burgos. I don't suppose
he'll go in the end. Bubbles has announced suddenly
that she will go to Burgos too; but my impression is that
he has made up his mind not to cope any more. And she
has no mind to make up, as you know! Neither of them
speak of all this; and though I lunched with *both* on the
only occasion since that scene on which they have met,
neither has told me anything about anything, and I had
to be manful indeed to break the silence. It may have
crossed Eduardo's mind that the fact of his wife's religion
can only wreck his career after the war is over; and that
there is less and less to hope for from anyone's efforts
except his own. I am very sorry for the poor old thing.

Visiting Pokvár six months after his wedding, he had told
his parents that he was contemplating "early retirement into
an eccentric Hungarian country life." On the last day of July
1938 Alan and Poppy drove off to Hungary in a Daimler
that Mitzi put at their disposal. For Poppy, Hungary meant
time out of life, with villagers who kissed your hand, gypsy
music, shoots with lunch served in a tent specially put up for
an hour or two in a convenient field. Accompanying the guns,
Poppy one day had said, "*Ich habe zu viel geschiessen*" – that
is shit instead of shot – and was surprised to be offered
boiled rice at dinner. A postcard home makes a good story of
losing the way to Pokvár in the dark without having the language to ask for directions. Standing on the running board,
three gypsies eventually escorted them home on a back road
across fields and ditches.

Pokvár is hidden away in a landscape of deep forests,

a place of fantasy, the house that a Central European under the influence of Walter Scott might have built. The entrance hall and wooden staircase leading up to a gallery has a baronial feel. The setting and the immemorial way of life captured Alan's imagination. The prose with which he evokes Pokvár in his diary is so observant and lush that it is possible to miss the sense of regret that all this is too good to last much longer. The park there, he begins, is very shady and green.

> One has to walk warily, because someone is always on the verge of dropping his (or more likely her) hoe and coming to kiss one's hand; if not, a house servant is creeping along the shrubberies waiting for a chance to carry something. And suddenly the paths debouch into an acacia forest, or a vast open golden prairie, or a great muddy enclosure full of geese, with white glittering cottages, like pieces of sugar and huge white barns all round out of which the peasants stare, with the sightless stare of magnificent respectfulness, or an occasional hand-kissing. The air smells like a spicy exhilarating cupboard. The corn is stacked into broad cathedrals, the colour of no natural thing except golden hair; the whole country drips biblically with fatness. And in a few yards the house is always invisible. But once in sight again, how welcoming! The absurd central block ends in a dazzling stepped pediment, built over a big canopied entrance. The windows have round tops and carved corbels, with stucco eyebrows on the first floor. At one end, there is a round battlemented tower like a sand-mould. All blindingly white.

Lovingly he picks out the "ugly and delightful things" furnishing the interior of the house. Large double doors led from his room into Poppy's. The furniture was in an old-fashioned rustic style. On account of the heat, the windows were shuttered all day. "I can see nothing, but the sounds are violent and odd. Carriages drive past . . . there is a great deal of shouting, punishing, crackling of whips, rattling of heavy axles, clopping of horses, and childish singing, going on all evening."

Callers include "the *Verwalter* [manager] of one place or another who arrives with tuberoses wrapped up in ribbon; the postman who bows and walks out backwards; the forester, the secretary, the *Gestutmeister* [director of the stud] who expects monetary orders – it contrasts so oddly with my letters, which tell me that if I sent out even £20 of cheques in England they will probably be returned by the bank!" In this idyllic setting for his own writing, he was reading *Les Grands Cimetières sous la lune*, Georges Bernanos's recently published polemic that did much to turn public opinion against Franco's Falange; and on top of it all trying to learn Italian.

At the Lesvár stud were nine brood mares, three yearlings and a number of foals. Mitzi, they learnt, was putting more horses into training. In front of stable hands shoo'ing the horses through their paces, "We looked as wise as we could." Driving through Kapuvár on a Sunday, they admired people who had put on national costume for the church service and were now filling the main square, women to one side, men to the other. Out sightseeing, they found the great palace of Esterháza closed except for the stables. "I have never seen any harness rooms of such size and splendour," Alan enthused. In another part of the building, even more praiseworthy, were "some forty carriages, carrioles, victorias, coupés, landaus, goat-carriages . . . the 1866 coach lined with yellow watered silk . . . the cream landau which the Regent uses when he comes." Esztergom is the seat of the Catholic Church in Hungary, and the 900th anniversary of St Stephen, the country's founder-king, was being celebrated there. Alan and Poppy stayed to witness the arrival of Admiral Miklós Horthy, the Regent of Hungary with a part to play on the European stage. A huge crowd had assembled, with a guard of honour and a cordon of girls marshaled by nuns. "Officers in magnificent hussar uniforms with moustaches like a child's harrow, and expressions of the most bellicose order, drove up in taxis. The Cardinal came out by a side door, surrounded by bishops in full fig. At last the Regent, of course in Admiral's uniform, very spry and contented, drove up to the National Hymn and walked along the lines."

This Grand Tour took in Brno and Prague, then Zagreb where they bought "some wonderful clothes from peasants in the market," and on down the Dalmatian coast to enter Italy at Fiume. Their objective was the Villa San Carlo at Lerici, the isolated spot in the Gulf of Spezia where Shelley had set sail in a storm and drowned. On arrival, they had no less than twelve suitcases to unpack. Kenneth Rae came to stay and Conradine Hobhouse, "with whom we spend our whole days lying on the flat rocks and tumbling about in a warm sea." Distinguished people to be visited included the artist Aubrey Waterfield in the Fortezza at Aulla. At Lerici were Percy Lubbock and his wife Lady Sybil – he was the author of *The Craft of Fiction*, a book influenced by his friend Henry James, and she was the mother of Iris Origo by a previous husband. "I liked Lady Sybil very much," Alan described to Vere an afternoon with the Lubbocks, "and he sent messages to Daddy, on the strength of knowing him at Eton. 'Very neat-looking, I remember,' he said."

Alan and Poppy had spent a week in the Villa San Carlo when on 15 September Neville Chamberlain undertook his first flight to meet Hitler, and the Munich crisis began. War looked probable and sometimes certain. "Freddy dangerously ill," ran the telegram Kenneth Rae had received from a friend in London, code that they were to return home at once. They went to ask advice from the British Consul in Spezia, "A mild, flowerless, un-watered bit of a man," he knew less than they did. Telephoned, Vere told them that war was indeed imminent. The Speech further spelt the end of peace – as if to exorcise Hitler, Alan capitalized key euphemisms for him: "It was pretty frightening to hear the Voice last night in this remote little town, booming over the wireless from the bay, which is full of cafés. Nobody understood a word of course; and nobody seemed to care much."

Returning to Royaumont, they found themselves trying on gas-masks in the drawing room. Hitler would surely put the democracies before a fait accompli, "and everyone will say that any humiliation is better than war." Alan told himself that he would probably not be killed in war, he had already enlisted in the Intelligence Service and "they will probably think I speak better Czech than I do." There was no war, then, no honour, no peace, "yet we are all passionately relieved." We would not be selling York Gate and moving to New Mexico for ever, as he had fantasized. "Bubbles is back, in a great state of nerves," was the latest news there. "Eduardo has left the house for good, and set up at the hotel in Paris – so altogether disharmony reigns unchallenged."

"France and England have been worse than useless since 1938," is one of several combative entries in Mitzi's diaries. She followed the build-up to war closely, yet changed little or nothing in her way of life. In mid-July 1938 she and Frank stayed with friends, Guido and Pat Accame near Castiglione della Pescaia. Italy, she found, was "hysterical and miserable." In spite of the talk of war, they decided they would drive through Germany for their usual summer month in Czech resorts. Harlé the chauffeur and Robert the valet were to accompany them. At the frontier on August 12, she says, she flirted with "a very good-looking S.S. officer," who against orders let her keep her jewels and stamped the box with a swastika. At the pension in Freudenstadt were "three non-Aryans," and in the evening one of them did not return; the police arrived instead. In Heidelberg a cousin Max Springer, his wife and twin boys had been trying to leave for South America and she had arranged the necessary funding. Their contact in the bank said to Frank, "never believe anything said against our Führer." Frank's retort was, "What about these famous camps?" "Not a word of truth." The bank manager then explained that the money could be handed over only in Switzerland. Caught in any such transaction in Germany, the cousin was certain to disappear.

The German-Czech frontier was a formality. From Marienbad, they went on to Karlsbad where Pokorny was waiting for them. On the 22nd Konrad Henlein, the Sudeten German leader and agitator, arrived "amid great shouting of Sieg Heil and arms stretched out in welcome. All the local people are, pockets, hearts and souls, pro-German." The time for Hungary seems to be coming, she noted. After a stopover in Prague, Mitzi and Frank went on to Brno. There in the course of dinner with Melczinsky, the agent from Bucşani, they listened to Hitler's speech. "One could not call it speaking, it was yelling, so much so that the windows rattled ... no one seemed interested in the least." Max was shooting at Pokvár; she booked tickets for his immediate return to Paris, but he paid no attention. In spite of apprehensions, they were already in Hungary when news came through on September 14 that Chamberlain was to fly to see Hitler. "It is glorious to be English!" Hungarians, she wrote quite unselfconsciously, "all are radiant when they see an Englishwoman in a Rolls, talking Hungarian."

Every September brought them to Venice, and a world crisis was not about to interfere with Mitzi's schedule. "Felt a lump in my throat saying goodbye to Pokorny," was a rare concession of hers to reality. "What I want to know so badly is: are we going to be Hungarian or Slovaks." Pokorny was left to deal with this question upon which a large portion of her fortune depended. "Accord at Munich! Peace! It all seems too wonderful after having been too awful. Even if Hitler has had it all his own way what does it matter, compared to the end of our world." Through ill will, as her prejudice would have it, Edvard Beneš and the Czechs had brought this disaster on themselves.

Most of the French, she wrote regretfully, felt ashamed at abandoning Czechoslovakia. Back in Paris, she lunched at Maxim's with Paul Goldschmidt and agreed with his view that it was mostly Jews who deplored Munich. Every passing week brought news that raised her Jewish anxiety. After Christmas at Royaumont, she and Frank retreated to Montreuil for the New Year 1939. There, on 31 January, she listened on the radio to Hitler's speech that evening in the Reichstag. This was his most overt challenge to the world, and in particular to Jews, foreshadowing the Holocaust. "What hate of the Jews," Mitzi wrote, "but very true much of what he says. He wants Germany for the Germans, and if the Jews are as wonderful as the other nations say they are, how very queer the other nations are not delighted to take them in, but on the contrary do not let them in. He says that war is wanted by Jews alone and predicts it would be their end. That last part is also true. I think anti-Semitism can be seen growing in every country."

She had heard how wretched life in Vienna was from Clarice, wife of Alphonse Rothschild whose brother Louis had been in the hands of the Vienna Gestapo since the Anschluss. The Gestapo now made a move against Mitzi. "The Waisenhaus in Vienna has been taken. We get nothing for the house or for all that is in it, nothing for the ground it stands on! And so the robbing goes on. As the house etc belonged to a Jewish charity and was not in our name we can do nothing." (Early in 1939 the Gestapo closed the Waisenhaus, and most of the boys were murdered in Auschwitz. One survivor has been traced to an old peoples' home in Haifa. That April, the Stillhaltekommissar set up by the Nazis to control all institutions took over the orphanage and transferred it to the IKG, the German acronym for the Jewish Community Organisation which had to do as it was ordered. The building was immediately valued at 300,000 Reichsmarks. On 14 April the orphanage became a hospital for the elderly. The IKG was obliged to submit to the Gestapo lists of all the Jews in Vienna. In 1942, the list for the former orphanage shows 138 women and two men. They were all deported to Auschwitz, 44 of them on Transport 29. The director Dr Ludwig Margulies was deported to Theresienstadt where he died. Compelled to accept about half the recent Gestapo valuation, the IKG in September sold the empty building to the city of Vienna for 155,700 Reichsmarks. Expert profiteers from mass-murder, the Viennese authorities after the war haggled over restitution to the IKG, making sure to keep possession of the orphanage, knocking it down and building profitable condominiums in the grounds where it had stood. Asked to pay Frau Margulies a pension out of the money received from the developed Waisenhaus property, the authorities decided that they had no contractual obligation and refused.)

On the face of it, Alan's prewar travels might well have been on behalf of the Intelligence Service. Questioned, he was always vague. If he was going on Mitzi's business, she said that she had begged him not to go to Vienna for fear of what the Austrians might do to him. On 7 March 1939 he was in Berlin, giving dinner to Pokorny and Dr Pietsch, a lawyer who may or may not have had something to do with Geutebruch. Next day Prague, with a Teplà board meeting:

"a ridiculous scene, the English poet among Central European businessmen, declining enormous cigars, and lolling in a deep leather chair." "*Juden raus*" was chalked on walls everywhere, and there was a dreadful air of expectancy. Alan is no fool, Mitzi wrote, yet Prague gave him the impression that the Czechs were more anti-German than ever. "Under Hitler all goes so shockingly that what is true one minute is an old story the next." In fact when he went to dine at Meidling the main change was that the house was now unheated. Giving him tea, Tante Bébé, the last family member still in Vienna, was in floods of tears. An atmosphere of complaint was everywhere: "It was like watching the thunder roll round an empty desolate plain."

Two days later, the Wehrmacht marched into Prague and Czechoslovakia ceased to exist. Mitzi felt this newest blow: "The Germans are entering Bucşani this afternoon at the same time as Hitler is entering Pressburg," as Bratislava under German occupation had to be renamed. "The factory is our last possession, our only hope," she wrote. Daily the factory was producing 27,000 kilos of yeast. For once giving a figure, she recorded that it had brought her 496,000 francs in April, with the comment, "not bad." She and the family would be all right, she thought, if the annual figure came to four million francs. A competent businessman and industrialist, the managing director, Dr Albert Metzl, was likely to deliver, but for reasons that are not clear – maybe to do with Springer properties or perhaps his own Czech background – he was in Prague when the Germans took over what remained of Czechoslovakia and for a number of days they prevented him from returning to France.

That same April, Mitzi heard from Alan that he wanted to go into politics. Like everyone who knew him, she thought this was out of character. "There also I cannot help," she signed off with a sniff. Alan's disposition was always to see both sides of any question and to make light of commitment. However, he had witnessed Nazism enough to take a stand against it. In a letter to the *Spectator*, he declared himself a Liberal because it was the only party with a policy of full and immediate rearmament.

A by-election was due in the constituency of Louth in Lincolnshire. At a meeting of the party association on 12 May, Alan was adopted as Liberal candidate. The president was Mrs Margaret Wintringham, and next day a local paper *The Advertiser* reported what she said. She had evidently been briefed about how to present Alan without being constrained by the facts. Here, she told Liberal party members, was a candidate prepared to devote practically the whole of his time to the requirements of so important an office. He was a young man "who had studied many aspects of the agricultural industry in other countries." No doubt she meant it sincerely when she went on, "A Liberal foreign policy, backed by a live League of Nations, is in my judgment the world's salvation." Alan, she said, was "an ardent temperance advocate and a non-smoker." Presumably with a face as straight as Mrs Wintringham's, Alan announced that if he won, he and his family intended to take up residence in the Louth Division. According to the paper, he was received with repeated applause.

For something like twelve weeks he campaigned. Poppy accompanied him. Trading on connections, he persuaded the Liberal James de Rothschild to pay a flying visit, though regretfully aware that this might not be a vote-catcher. Briefly at some point he hired a truck and put a piano on it, playing to attract attention. Writing from a hotel in Lincoln on 28 May, he told his mother that at a meeting there cannot have been more than a hundred people but they had seemed to like it. He was just off to Worksop, Chesterfield, Chatsworth, Warrington, and Liverpool. Here he is on 10

June in the hotel in Lincoln: "I have made three long open-air speeches – and three impromptu ones – and now I know that speaking in public is the only thing I like. The short ones were rather terrifying. I drove into a village – any village – and summoned the people through a microphone; spoke for a few minutes, and then climbed out of the car and went among them shaking hands. The nicest people you ever saw each time! So far I have not been asked a single question; and have had, for fine summer evenings quite good audiences: 100 or so in a market place, and a lot more listening from behind their curtains. I am terrified by my own fluency: the Hitler of Lincolnshire, oh God." And he signed, "Adolfo Chamberlini." In Woodhall Spa on 3 August, he was writing, "I hope I converted some young Socialists. . . . Poppy's temper was made very uncertain by the sea air at Sutton, where we slept yesterday." The Conservative candidate was elected, but by a slimmer margin than had been expected.

At a time with so many demands on him in such different contexts, it speaks well for his energy that he had managed to cram in writing a novel. *Pink Danube* was published by Martin Secker in the summer of 1939. In the copy Alan presented to Poppy he took his turn at writing doggerel:

> There is no need, my love, to pine
> Rather for *Arthur's* love than mine;
> But damn the crisis, and galumph, re-
> -joicing, through the life of *Pumphrey*.

The *nom de plume* suggests that Alan was hiding his identity in the expectation of a *succès de scandale.* Precautions were not necessary. The novel fell flat. The reason for this failure was laid out very well in the review in the *New Statesman* of 29 July 1939 by Brian Howard – it must have been galling to be pulled to pieces by someone already a certified failure as a writer as well as a human disaster. Among considerable basic faults, he found, "The construction is wildly haphazard; there is very little feeling of inevitability, and, most disturbing of all, one senses that the author has not made up his mind about his own relationship towards his characters. His sympathies rise and fall, and revolve, and all one can do is bump along behind, swearing that detachment is the prime literary virtue."

Occasional sentences in the novel are flashes in keeping with Alan's outlook, for example "Money is simply a short cut," or "I was, I had to admit, too gifted." In the period covered by *Pink Danube*, Nazis were putting Vienna fatefully to the test, and if he had found a narrative that took account of that he might have fulfilled the Tolstoyan ambition of his younger self. The novel has a first person narrator whose encounters with other people serve not to illuminate time or place, but only to illustrate his inner feelings and in particular his sexual ambiguity. He is made to say, "Half the queers in the world are only queer out of snobbery." And Naomi, the leading female character, mirrors Mitzi as she was taking up with Frank, "If I ever marry again, I shall marry a queer man.... After all, many of the nicest men are. And they're very easy to live with, everybody says."

Living in Hitler's Berlin at that same period, Christopher Isherwood was writing comparable novels of self-discovery, but with just enough reference to the surrounding Nazism to give him the reputation of being a chronicler of the Thirties. Familiar as Alan was with Nazism in Vienna, he treats it here as incidental, as if it were operetta, so losing the chance even to be a pseudo-Isherwood. Deprived of any general issues, *Pink Danube* is harmfully one-dimensional. More telling still, here is a comedy of manners concealing a reality that was not comic at all. Alan knew himself but could not be open about it. Someone called Simon Wardell had stayed with him. "Eighteen, with very clear features and very bright blue eyes. Since I have tried to change, I found myself taking a new pleasure: 'No, I shall never discover.' I would not go to his part of the room, nor look at him when I talked to him. He talked almost exactly as I used to at eighteen; and when we went for a walk together I tried to be honest with myself. The attraction, I decided, was at least half non-physical. By a certain amount of self-deception, I would say that it was not physical at all . . . there was no active will to do anything about it, so I suppose the process of sublimation must have gone on. I think that perhaps if I could talk to Poppy about such things the sublimation would become complete. I should be released from my unwilling prison."

Poppy was twenty-five when this novel and the diary entry about Simon Wardell were written. No longer a girl kept in ignorance, she was familiar with Alan's friends, incessant gossips virtually all of them. Perhaps she had moods and bouts of feeling unwell because she could observe for herself this complicated and incomplete process of sublimation, and found it not so easy to live with. At any rate, giving up as impulsively as he had set out in the first place, Alan never again engaged in active politics, and made no further sustained effort to write fiction.

Twelve

Exodus

THE HOUSE THAT Mitzi and Frank built at Montreuil is now a hotel. At the end of the park a footbridge leads to the eighteenth-century "dream house" that had caught the eye of Eugène and Frank. Mitzi waited until the 1960s before repairing the war damage and the looting. I didn't like to tell her that in an antique shop we had found glass and linen initialed M W. The whole place would one day belong to us, she would say, encouraging us to spend as much time there as we could.

To return is to discover that everything has changed yet everything is also the same as ever. That part of the town is so quiet that it seems deserted. There's a green with, on one side, the great defensive ramparts designed by Vauban and on the other a high wall with a suitably fortress-like door opening on to the garden surrounding the house. Frank took a lot of trouble over his flowerbeds. The bricks on the garden paths are laid out in a striking pattern of diagonals. The pool is as shallow as a bath so I could splash about in it unsupervised. Secure and spacious, here is some corner of a foreign field that is forever the Home Counties. As would-be squire, Frank was slightly over-dressed with his plus-fours and silk scarf knotted round his neck. Sometimes he carried me around on his shoulders. George, his huge dog, shaggy and white, is so good-natured that I am allowed to ride on its back. In search of distraction, Frank used to go to the golf course at Le Touquet, though not so often as he sidled off to the casino.

"David was with us for a week," my grandmother records in the last summer before the war. "We took him to Royaumont. He returns here with Elena in a few days." I have Jessie; Elena has Nanny Stainer. Madame Provins is at the service of all of us. She is small, neat, unhurried and smiling. Her daughter Paulette has the bright looks and manners of a typecast French lady's maid, and her husband Robert puts on a formal jacket and white gloves to wait at table. There is a chauffeur but on expeditions to Le Touquet Robert, faithful and watchful, often accompanies Frank.

Fresh from the campaigning in Lincolnshire, Poppy took a cure at Bagnoles. She and Alan met up later in Nice, where they were joined on yet one more holiday by their old friend Kenneth Rae, this time bringing his young niece Jean Fort, (fifty years later she would be the formidable headmistress of Roedean). At the end of June 1939, Mitzi was in London. Harry and Vere had lunch with her, and during the course of it he forecast that if Hitler took Danzig there would be war. Back in Paris, she went on 20 July to the Gare de l'Est to greet Max Springer, a relation escaping at last from Germany with his wife Elizabeth and their twin sons. Georg and Heinrich were thirteen, lively and clever, "*les enfants du miracle*," in her phrase, the miracle being that they were free. The Maisons-Alfort factory owned a house in Provence, and she arranged for them to live in it.

"I am writing on the morning of 29 August. It could not look worse for England and France. Now one sees how the people were right who said one ought to have made war last year." Several times Mitzi repeats that the crisis is playing havoc with her nerves. They were listening to the news on the wireless four or five times a day and kept themselves occupied blacking out the windows as a precaution against the coming air-raids.

Reinforcing his warning, Grandpa Harry cabled that Alan and Poppy should come home urgently. Max had lent them a Peugeot, and they set off in it from Nice at six o'clock in the evening of Friday, 1 September, the day of the German invasion of Poland. To make room for Kenneth Rae and his niece they had to abandon almost all their luggage. Thanking Max for the car in a hurriedly written letter, Poppy described how the roads had been jammed by thousands of people who didn't know how to drive – she'd never known anything so frightful. It was half past eleven before they reached Aix, where they had to spend the night on deck-chairs in the salon of a hotel along with four Swedes, a Dutch couple and a dozen English people. Invited into one of the hotel corridors, they had had an hour's sleep before taking to the road again at five in the morning. She'd put in a call to Max but the hotel owner didn't come to find her when it came through. Half dead with exhaustion by the time they'd reached Royaumont, they met up with Bubbles and Eduardo. Lily was about to go to the factory. Telephone communications had been cut off. Next stop Montreuil, then England. "Like you," she signed off to Max, "I haven't stopped hoping."

Alan had a shot at teasing. "In the intervals of struggling into my own khaki, I must write to you, dearest Max, to offer my sincerest sympathy in your misfortune in being born a European. Think of those happy blacks in Guiana and on the banks of the Limpopo river. They think of it as a perfectly natural thing to boil one another in large pots – a war would, to them, be simply a waste of cutlets – nothing more. We are hurrying back to London on the evening boat, so I have no time to write a proper letter."

"And so the Crusade has started. God help us." Mitzi followed up this invocation with the thought that the two nannies had been with her since 1906, therefore throughout the First War and now the Second War. "Poor old Chamberlain. His speech is wonderful." Having heard it, she put her thoughts down on two closely written pages to Max. "Till last night I feared we would still give way to the lunatic and his gang. We have to finish the whole lot off, as life in Europe these last two years is no life at all. Poland is only one of the hundreds of reasons for which we are going to war and we iboks [family code for Jews] have more reason than anyone to give them all the hell we can. I know you will do your bit just as you can trust us all to do ours." For the moment, she had all the cash she needed. The key to the safe in the rue de Surène was kept at the factory. She listed valuable possessions that Max was to hide in the farm: pictures by Vigée-Lebrun and de Dreux, the portrait of Jules Ephrussi, works by Falconet and Clodion, wall brackets from downstairs, the hall table. A thousand things had to be done. She was staying where she was. The children are fine, the duchesses [her term for the nannies had its element of getting her own back] holding up well. All meals at Montreuil would be taken together, lunch at 12.30 and dinner at 7.30, with paper napkins instead of linen. Alan has a job in London, she thought at the Foreign Office. Poppy could come over from York Gate any moment she wanted.

"Nothing can be worse," was Mitzi's reaction on 17 September when the Soviet Union took over eastern Poland as agreed by the pact of Hitler and Stalin in the final days of peace. She was already aware of the developing persecution: "One can never change a German and I hate them all. . . . All the Jews are sent without their families to Lublin, worst of places in Poland where a terrible famine rules." Dealing with her properties, she was pleased to see, Pokorny "dislikes the brute force and manners of the Germans." More and more anxious, he was expecting the sequestration of the properties in Slovakia, and she instructed him to try to let them to the Teplà factory. He was free to make deals but he was never to sell anything anywhere to whoever it might be. In the event that any property was stolen, he was to note every detail with a view to recovering it after the war. She dreaded the day that Hungary might have to go over to Germany or Germany would walk in there – that would be "terrible." When Pokorny appealed to the British Consul in Budapest for help, he was snubbed. The consul, he reported, had said that just because Mitzi had married an Englishman did not make her any less Jewish. Besides, how was the consul to know if she had made this marriage solely in order to safeguard her possessions. So angered was Pokorny by this interview that he had sent a letter of complaint to Vansittart.

Painfully removed from reality, the authorities antici-pated taking large numbers of German prisoners of war and had made arrangements to hold them in Dieppe. In mid-October Alan was posted there on military duty. British offi-cers were not allowed to have their wives with them, but Poppy had her family in France and therefore obtained per-mission to cross the Channel. She and Lily drove via Montreuil to visit him in Dieppe, and for his birthday on 18 November he had leave to spend the day with Poppy.

A particular Thirties touch that has survived the transi-tion from private house to hotel is the painted or plaster-work decoration of the bedrooms, one with the theme of monkeys, another with the theme of parrots. Jessie and I shared a room. For much of that November I was kept in bed with earache. The pain was excruciating. The doctor diag-nosed otitis and sent nuns to look after me. They wore hab-its. When they bent over me to pour some sort of oil into my ears their starched white wimples were ghost-like, monstrous. I resisted the one who strapped a hot water bottle to the side of my head. "It is too pathetic to see him with his poor head all bandaged up, so upset and feverish," Poppy reported to Alan. Pushed away by these nuns, Jessie must have been dis-pleased. She taught me to kneel at the foot of the bed to say my prayers and ask God to make me a good boy, amen. Her compact with the Almighty was a private matter between them. Churchgoing was merely another of her household duties. "Old crows" was her term for lumping together everyone in religious orders.

That Christmas was "merry, happy, lovely," adjectives that
didn't come so easily to Mitzi. Bubbles and Eduardo, Poppy and Lily were staying there. On the day itself, Alan arrived from Dieppe for lunch and later drove back with Poppy who remained with him for 24 hours. Under the mistletoe Jessie kissed Frank and called him "Darling." Bella Braun was also present. Ernst Braun, her husband and a Springer employee from Vienna, was away trying to obtain the papers to escape from Europe. (A letter of his, written in Chicago in 1948, reminds Mitzi that at Montreuil on 3 September 1939 he had heard her say that the eventual victor in this world war "will have to carry out the victory with Russia.") "Poor Mandeliks," is all she says of a Czech-Jewish refugee who was also there, with everything about him, including his first name, unrecorded. Accepted by the Intelligence Service, in the first days of 1940 Alan was posted to an introductory course in Cambridge. The Tatra could not be serviced, and on his departure from Montreuil he had himself photographed standing close to this trophy he was about to abandon in the garage.

A few days after his departure, Poppy sent him an early account of the relationship developing with me. After lunch in the well-known restaurant in Inxent, a village close to Montreuil, we had walked some of the way home. But, "He was dreadfully naughty with me this morning, pied-de-nez, pulled his tongue out etc. I had to get out of bed and threaten. I admire him as he isn't frightened in the least but holds his own. *Il a beaucoup de qualités mais il a besoin d'être dompté* [He has many qualities but needs to be brought under control]. I nearly had giggles in the middle of the drama. I am sure you would have laughed if you could have seen us."

Meidling, the "dear old place" as Mitzi thought of it, must have seemed at a great distance from Montreuil at that moment, and altogether a plaything of fate. On 1 December 1939 an official in Vienna with the title of Head of State Collections had written to the Gestapo to draw attention to what he calls the "rich inventory" and "outstanding things" to be found at Meidling. In his opening paragraph he makes the all-important point that the owner is a "Jewess with English citizenship." The sheet of paper bears the stamp of the Nazi eagle. Below the typewritten greeting "Heil Hitler!" is an illegible signature.

Six weeks later, on 14 January 1940, almost a year after the Waisenhaus had been taken, the Gestapo duly drove up to Meidling and expropriated everything in it, all the furniture, linen, silver, amassed by Gustav Springer. The full list of stolen pictures comes to 57, carefully inventoried by the Gestapo. A further selection of 22 was made on behalf of the State Collections. One of the paintings listed is a Van Dyck of Saint John, a favourite subject of that artist. The Head of State Collections had his eye on this, and he was particularly disappointed that this picture had gone missing. Within 24 hours of moving into Meidling, he was already recommending an investigation into its whereabouts. To this day, it is still unaccounted for, and the only plausible explanation is that one of these Nazis had been quick enough to lay hands on it for himself. The Head of State Collections was equally eager to acquire several pictures by Rudolf von Alt, and one of these was also not to be found. One Gestapo agent is on record accusing Eduardo of removing this picture. Another Gestapo agent, however, corrects this. He has interrogated the old servants and they inform him that the Pryce-Jones son-in-law had the Alt with him when he last left the house. In the Gestapo dossier is a sheet of paper with Mitzi's name and an exclamation mark drawn on it in a huge ungainly hand, giving a total estimate for the looted pictures of 33,000 Reichsmarks. Another expert later confirmed this valuation. The house in which I had been born then became a school to train senior Nazi party officials and future Gauleiters. Meidling had meant everything to Mitzi and she can hardly have expected that it would ever be restored but she did not give way to sentimentality or self-pity, merely commenting, "We go on doing our best to be practical and to keep our spirits up."

(In 1999 the law changed and Austrian authorities were obliged to restore stolen art to rightful owners. One of the paintings missing from Meidling was a small study by the nineteenth-century artist Johann Gualbert Raffalt of a Hungarian shepherd boy. The Belvedere museum now had to confess that since 1945 this painting had been in their possession and on exhibition. Providing the documents to establish our rights to the painting involved a bureaucratic procedure that lasted eleven years. On the day that the picture was finally returned I received a letter from the Belvedere to say that the Raffalt was an important part of the national heritage and they would like to have it back for an exhibition. Making themselves out to be deprived of what was really theirs, the authorities were evidently hoping to cast former owners in the role of grasping and vindictive Jews going to extreme lengths in pursuit of their property and so bent on damaging the nation. All the other paintings are still unaccounted for.)

In the months of the Phoney War members of the family came and went much as they had done in peacetime. At the end of the Spanish civil war Eduardo resumed his diplomatic career as a secretary in the embassy in Paris. To quote from a Harvard thesis written about him by a young historian, James K. McAuley, he proved "a loyal servant of Franco's Spain and a committed Nationalist ... deeply conservative, almost reactionary." Their marital discord now behind them, Eduardo and Bubbles divided their time between Mitzi's flat in the Rue de Surène and Royaumont. On 12 January 1940 the Spanish embassy informed the Quai d'Orsay that Royaumont was Eduardo's "*résidence habituelle.*"

Whenever Mitzi was in Paris at this time, she stayed in the Hotel Lancaster. Once she took Max, Poppy and Cécile de Rothschild to a Sacha Guitry play. In early February Poppy went home to York Gate, never imagining that she would not be able to return to Montreuil. In the Ritz on another occasion, Mitzi was displeased to see "the Windsor woman," as she dismissively called the Duchess of Windsor who was lunching with the Polignacs. On the walls of the house of her old and Jewish friend Marie-Thérèse de Croisset, she could not fail to notice the daubed slogans "*Mort aux Juifs*" and "*Méfiez-vous des Juifs.*"

In the Lancaster Hotel on 8 May Lily had tears in her eyes when she told her mother that she was engaged to Elie de Rothschild – she was about to be twenty-three, he was a year younger. They had known one another since childhood. "I hugged her and told her that as it had not been that awful Guy de Rothschild I was delighted." Elie's father Robert de Rothschild had been Eugène's great friend, only to have a row with him that was never made up and now Robert's youngest son was marrying Eugène's youngest daughter – "How queer life is!" she concluded with a favourite exclamation of hers. Robert de Rothschild came round to the hotel to celebrate with her. "They are impossible, these Rothschilds!" but she then does not explain what had given rise to this no doubt heartfelt outburst. After a course at Saumur, Elie himself had just been commissioned in the Onzième Cuirassiers, an elite cavalry regiment. When he reported for duty, however, the colonel commanding said that he was not prepared to accept Jews in the regiment. After the war,

Elie would often speak about this rejection. The colonel of the colonial Moroccan regiment that he finally joined on the contrary called his officers together and told them he would not tolerate anything anti-Jewish. Elie was unable to accompany Liliane or his father that day of the engagement because he was in the field in the north of France.

At Montreuil we were issued with gas-masks. The air-raid sirens had turned out to be false alarms. The so-called "dream house" that had attracted Eugène and Frank in the first place had served no purpose since the building of the new house. French officers back from Poland were now billeted in it. Mitzi did not like it that General du Ranguet was sleeping in what had been her bed there. Poppy had explained that she and Alan had left York Gate for the time being and were staying at Rockley Manor, on the edge of the Marlborough Downs. This house belonged to Mary Loder, a relation of Alan's because her mother, Lady Wakehurst, otherwise Cousin Cuckoo, was born Grey. Enlisted in the French air force, Max was stationed at Soissons within range of the Maginot Line. Wing Commander Hesketh DFC, commanding 150 Squadron, gave him a testimonial that also served as a pass: "His excellent command of the French and English languages has proved invaluable to me, and I wish, if possible, to retain his services permanently as an interpreter."

As luck would have it, Mitzi was in Paris on May 9 in order to take to the Hungarian Legation the documents proving that Frank was Aryan. The blitzkrieg had opened when Bubbles telephoned at ten o'clock the next morning, a Friday, to say that Max had arrived at Royaumont in the middle of the night. In his view, Montreuil was not safe and we should all flee from the war zone as soon as we could. Charras is a small town near Angoulême, and Dr Metzl had a house there. He would take us in. The children were to leave at once. Already for Mitzi, "The news of the greatest battle of all time was not good." The tempo of the German army was "terrific." And also, "Every moment, you have to be saying goodbye to everyone around." Since Frank could not drive, Mitzi arranged for René Dupas, the deputy managing director of the factory, to take them that Sunday one last time to Montreuil. To be travelling towards the fighting was frightening. She imagined the Germans bombing everywhere as they had bombed Rotterdam. "It is a wonder we were not killed. It is queer to be alive and wonderful not to have gone mad."

In the crisis, Frank was drinking. The husband whom she habitually referred to as "My angel," said things that "made me not care what happened." She praised herself for keeping "calm and peaceful" about Frank, but there was more. "At dinner Frank was awful, screaming that Jews are terrible people, they run about town with pessimistic news, all of it false. Just as bad are the Spaniards, they are the last people who should be told anything. Eduardo was always anti-English."

Through the Spanish Embassy Eduardo was in touch with the latest news of the disaster now in the making. He agreed with Max that we should go south. He took charge. We were to assemble at Royaumont. Max lent them his old Peugeot, and through friends Frank and Mitzi heard of a chauffeur called Whitworth, a sixty-three-year-old English-man who seemed to have no objection to driving away from the Channel; we went in convoy with Dupas. Perhaps the château was shut or there were no servants; at any rate Jessie and I slept in the laiterie. From then on, I am in the hands of Jessie. Poppy had no means of knowing our whereabouts or circumstances except what Jessie was able to communicate.

From Royaumont, Jessie wrote: "Things look very black just now but no doubt we shall tide over it all. You see, the Germans are so deceitful, dishonest, crafty, fake, dishonour-able, that it is like fighting a white lie. Anyway we must not look on the black side, but believe that right must prevail over might.... I know you must be very anxious wondering where Alan might be sent.... Now my dear, courage and stay there until Alan makes a move."

Without warning, I was woken up one night and had to dress. This was unprecedented. It was exciting to hear that we were about to go on a long journey running away from the Germans. We would be driving to a place called Charras. A miniature pigskin suitcase, about twelve inches by eight, contained my treasures – toy soldiers, the stamps I had begun to collect – and made me feel grown-up. From Charras, Jessie described our flight to Poppy. "Your brother came home at 3.30 A.M. Thursday morning, saying it was wiser to send the children here, he himself went off again at 4.30, so, as children always complicate everything we made a move, and were off at ten o'clock that same day, arriving at about 7.30, time for bed. They were very good but towards the end they were rather tired and slept all night; now Propper and Co will feel more free to do, and go, as they like." She finishes, "Make no mistake, we are going to win this war, or if we don't and it's the Germans that gain, then it is the end of everything, religion and everything it stands for, falls to the ground, and if England falls, then every other nation falls also, so you see, think, and know, also pray, that the Allies come through victorious, right must win, and will. I've implicit faith in my country. Now! Your son is quite well and having a fine time here where it is not so nerve-wracking for them as at Royaumont or Paris although myself I would rather be there to see what's going on, but, children first is the order of the day."

On that drive to Charras, I had sat in the back of the car next to Elly. Millions of panicking people for days on end fled from the Germans in this exodus which set the seal on the defeat of France. I retain an image of the Spanish flag fluttering on the front mudguard; also at some point when the throng on the road obliged the car to slow down a woman dressed in black stared in at the window. At Charras, Dr Metzl's extremely pretty eighteenth-century house gave on to a street. Jessie didn't see fit to tell Poppy about my mishap there. Somewhere round the side of the house there was a patch of gravel and groundsel sprouting up through it. Persuading Elly that we should clear out these unsightly weeds, I found a piece of sharp slate to serve as a tool. Hacking too hard at the groundsel, I cut myself inside my left arm, just at the joint of the elbow. I hadn't known I had so much blood. I was convinced that now the Germans wouldn't need to catch me, I'd done myself in.

Jessie reassured Poppy that she still had 3,000 francs left, and later received another 3,000 francs via Granny and Maisons-Alfort. She kept repeating that Poppy shouldn't leave Alan until they knew where he was going to be sent. "I think you will find it difficult to get over, as all regulations are changed, but we'll hope for the best. The struggle will be long and many valuable lives lost, but the Allies will win through at terrible cost; keep well and don't worry needlessly." Every other day she wrote a letter on the grounds that some at least would be delivered. "Never mind about the things I asked you for," runs the letter of 24 May. "All that matters is to win this war. I hear Mosley has been arrested, good job too.... I don't suppose we shall ever see Montreuil again, and Royaumont? Your little man is quite well and happy, thank God, it was quite touching the way he received your two sisters when they came, I thought he would never let them go.... I would like to know you are out of London, because they will surely pepper a bit over there and my Poppy, be sure to believe we shall win, and I hope God willing one day we'll all meet again, even if in poorer circumstances." On 31 May, a Sunday, Jessie and I went walking in the fields, picked a poppy and enclosed it in a letter. I was putting on a piece of strap from an old pram and calling it my Sam Browne belt. She thought I would turn out "very self-willed and determined which is a good thing. You can laugh but he will make a fine man and you will be proud of him. . . . Your place is by your hubby, and your boy is alright here."

"We are all unhappy to know you are still in London, and you must really make a move for somewhere," she repeats herself in a letter on Tuesday 2 June. "The beast's movements are always very sudden and one never knows where the brute will hit next . . . however he may want to dominate the world, we *must must* win and for him 'Great will be the Fall thereby.'" A week later, she credits me with saying, "Where is God? Why does he not kill the Germans?" And then, "I hear the vermin are not far from Paris, God help poor France, but where is he? If we have to make a move from here I'll wire at once, so don't worry, for this state of affairs can't go on for long. What worries us much more is to know that you are still in London. Calm is the order of the day and we shall win. Getting to Paris does not win the war. England's might has still got to show what she can and will do, to defend the right; and her shores, so as in Nelson's time, 'England expects' etc. Come they from the three corners of the earth and we shall shoot them etc." In a final letter from Charras she says that I will want for nothing in the way of clothes until the winter. About 300 children are arriving in the village from Angoulême. Passport in hand, she is off to fetch what she calls "sugar cards" for herself and me. "Goodbye my duck, useless to tell you, you are never out of my thoughts . . . look on the bright side . . . we'll give Adolf on land what we have already given him in the air and on sea. So chins up and we'll pull through. It's marvelous how they got all those men over to England from Dunkirk. She still rules the waves."

"Every day one wakes up wondering in what a state of misery one will be on going to bed." Mitzi was furious and despairing when King Leopold of the Belgians capitulated. The mood changed daily. "Can we resist on the Somme and the Aisne? I believe so, I think the German losses are terrific, worse even than ours." The French government fled from Paris to Bordeaux. Arriving at Charras at this moment of national collapse, Eduardo insisted that his duties took him to Bordeaux and we all had to move there.

Next morning, "We left at 8.30 in four cars – packed *and how!* Oh what tears." The cars reached Bordeaux at half past twelve. "Indescribable!" is Mitzi's word for what she found. This was *sauve qui peut*, especially for Jews. The Hotel Splendide had no more room for anyone. Spotted by Frank, the Splendide bar was the one quiet spot in Bordeaux. After lunching there badly and quickly, Mitzi sat talking for a long time to Nelly de Rothschild, wife of Robert, and their daughter Cécile. There was no news of Elie. "Nelly is the portrait of misery. She tells us that Mrs Kramer, mother of Alix de Rothschild's first husband, has just killed herself. Suicide. Perhaps the first Jewish suicide in France."

Everybody was asking questions, but they did not await or expect answers. "Most of those asking questions are Jews of course. It's understandable but not pretty to see. Poor things, they never have peace." In a Rolls-Royce were Eric Goldschmidt-Rothschild, his wife and son, and mother-in-law. At three in the morning, they were to leave by ship for San Domingo, hoping later to go to America. Lily was to spend the night at Lafite, the famous Rothschild vineyard. Bubbles took the nannies and children to a château taken over as the Spanish embassy. Remembering her former wine merchant, Mitzi telephoned him and he was willing to let her sleep in his daughter's bed. The house was "big, cold, dusty, dark, Dickens-like," and yet "I couldn't help laughing as I sat on her bidet that tragic evening."

Refugees leaving France with papers that allowed them to escape via Spain or Portugal to foreign destinations still were required to obtain Spanish transit visas. In a bureaucratic bind evidently designed to keep such refugees out of the country, these were issued in very moderate numbers. Frightened either to grant or to withhold these visas, the Spanish consul in Bordeaux had shut the consulate and made himself scarce. Mostly Jewish, refugees frantic at this extra last-minute impediment to survival and freedom were milling outside the building. Without authority to be doing so, Eduardo opened the consulate and set about issuing visas. At the request of the French government, his ambassador, José Félix de Lequerica, was engaged in negotiating the terms of the armistice with the Germans. A former mayor of Bilbao, Lequerica was known for his political influence and his anti-Semitism. A note from him to Eduardo survives and it ought to have covered him. "Eduardo, do whatever you think you should, and let me know before you start." Years later at a dinner party in London, I happened to meet Maurice Ohana, who ran an art gallery. A Moroccan Jew, he told me with emotion that Eduardo had saved his life by issuing him the indispensible transit visa.

"Eduardo has all the visas for all of us!" Mitzi understood what an extraordinary stroke of fortune it was that he was willing and able to steer us to safety, evidently at the risk of his career. "If he'd wanted us to take a trip from Bordeaux to England we were ready to do it at once." Some were trapped, for instance friends of hers who were unable to set off from Bayonne on a coaling ship because they did not have what she calls a military visa.

The armistice on June 22 divided France. The unoccupied

southern zone took its name of Vichy France from the spa where Marshal Pétain now set up his government. Those with reasons to be afraid of the Germans immediately fled there. To return to Royaumont would have meant living under German occupation and Max was receiving news of it that didn't scotch the idea completely. I cannot identify the man whose signature looks like Jacquet, but he must have been an employee. One letter of his to Max on 13 July says that the complete evacuation of Royaumont had lasted six days. It wasn't Germans but retreating French soldiers who had moved into the château, "leaving the disorder you can imagine." German soldiers were having a good time fishing in the lake or swimming, but that was all. Ten days later he was reassuring Max that he'd been to the Kommandatur for advice, the property had suffered no damage to speak of, "the Germans, it must be recognized, are very correct." Max's other informant from Royaumont, Carlos Moore, a man of Spanish origins writing in French, had been the estate manager before Marcel Vernois. Having fled as far as Versailles in what he calls a caravan of sixty people, he too consulted the Kommandatur where he was told to go home. At Royaumont, he'd found the cows out on the road, all the doors of the house left wide open, but only the gramophone and some linen was missing. Franto, the Slovak odd-job man, was patrolling the estate with Attila, Max's fierce dog.

In a letter dated 25 June 1940 Jessie in Bordeaux brought Poppy in London up to date about what the others had decided. "Your mother left here with Frank this morning early, and in a short time she hopes to be with you. There was a lot of hesitation as to whether the boy ought to come but in the end she decided not, the risk was too great. Then Lily said she wanted to go to be with you, and that also was ruled out so here we are with none of our usual newspapers and the wireless and as we sit beside this instrument of torture we know you are listening to the same and this is the only tiny link we have at present." Her closing exhortation was perhaps not as robust as usual. "We are not down-hearted. I wonder if you will get this and how soon?"

"That terrible day of 25 June," is Mitzi's account. "We got up at 6.30. Packed. The girls sat with me. We gave each other addresses all over the world to meet at. Bubbles keeps having panics and the wish to leave Europe. Lily does not see how she could stand life away from Europe but also has panics sometimes. I did not go and see the babies who were still sleeping. I did not feel I could face it. The girls and nannies came to the car. Frank and I kissed each of them, we were all in tears. Will we ever see them again? I looked and looked at them as the car rolled away, my eyes and heart seemed to leave my body."

Whitworth drove them out across the frontier into Spain. In Madrid they found themselves among people whom they had known before the war – old Mrs David-Weill and her daughter Mrs Seligmann, Kitty Rothschild, Tricia Landau and her husband, Lucie Goldschmidt and her daughter Simone. Mr Esmond was with his daughter Lulu, Poppy's old friend, and Lulu's little daughter Emmeline. Mitzi portrays him, "This Indian Jew has always lived in real luxury and comfort," and now is "a broken old man who has lost all his racehorses."

The talk was only of "visas, Clippers [flights to the United States], ships, dollars." She quickly concluded that she couldn't look after Bubbles and Lily, and didn't expect them to look after her. Poppy and Alan had all they needed. Regulations prevented Hambros Bank from sending to Spain more than £150. With the permission of the National Bank of Slovakia, Pokorny had wired 300,000 Slovak crowns to New York. Soon Pokorny was communicating bad news. Geutebruch, supervisor of the sequestration of all she owned in Austria, was now in Paris living in the Hôtel de Castiglione. Going round to her flat in the rue de Surène, he had found it occupied by a Frenchman, a Monsieur Brunard. German soldiers were living in Montreuil and had gone through all her papers.

As Jews, Max and Lily were forbidden to be on the board of the factory, and Geutebruch was trying to get in touch with them. The Gestapo had been asking for details about the Brauns and the Brülls. (Already in London, Brüll and his wife Erna expected to be interned any moment. On 12 July 1940 Brüll appealed to Granny Vere. They would not be in a concentration camp, he realized, but separated from their young son who was in Bournemouth. "I personally never had the idea to apply to Mr. Alan," Brüll apologized, "but think Mr. Alan did not forget us and would do something in our favour if he could." He hoped all was well with the Wooster family: "How happy I should be if I could be at their service in these difficult days.")

Jewish property in Slovakia was being expropriated, and Pokorny asks what he should do. "If we feel sure of our victory, he says, just wait and see. He believes England will be invaded and taken over but he does not know if this will stop the war. From where he is he cannot judge what the world thinks." Mitzi answered that she was not of his opinion and would only sell the Slovak properties without the Teplà shares on condition of a single payment of 500,000 dollars in US currency to a New York bank. "Should England go down she will do so nobly, not like France" – in her view, the wish to do down the Jews was enough to make France pro-German. Her adopted identity led her to an unlikely flourish, "Our people are grand, led by our King and Queen." When Frank called at the British Embassy, the ambassador Sir Samuel Hoare had said, "Are you worried about England? Don't be. We are perfectly prepared now."

Lourenço Marques was a possible destination for some. Kurt Reininghaus and his wife Biba (née Springer, from Sitzenberg near Vienna) were on their way to Brazil. Mitzi suggested Canada or even the Azores, Frank preferred South Africa. In a telegram, Alan was anxious that Jessie and I were not safe, and he'd help financially for us to fly by Clipper to America with Mitzi and Frank and Lily in tow. Mitzi objected: first of all there were no seats on the Clippers till the end of September, some twelve weeks away. There was no money to pay for this trip for five people, and nothing for them to live on over there. Alan did not specify what financial help he could provide. Finally, it was virtually impossible to obtain visas.

Mitzi and Frank moved from Madrid to Lisbon around the middle of July 1940 – at this point, her diaries carry even fewer dates than usual. Whitworth drove them one last time, and he then caught a ship to England. On 25 July 1940 at any rate, Mitzi and Frank settled into the house they rented, the Villa Preciosa at Estoril. She had never lived anywhere so nondescript, but was soon expressing a hope to spend the rest of the war there. Mitzi volunteered to do charity work packing up parcels, and greatly enjoyed it perhaps because this too was unlike anything she had ever done. Otherwise they settled into a routine of lunches and dinners in this or that restaurant and hotel, mostly yet again in the company of Jews with the means to pay to escape the Germans. However much she may have disliked Jews, she tells herself, at the present moment when they are blamed for everything, "I cannot help standing up for them. Oh, how bruised my heart is. The world is so ugly, such horrors everywhere." The company she keeps in Lisbon is a roll-call of what had been smart Jewish society: Jacques Stern, Lucienne Kann, Rudi and Marianne Gutmann, the Pierre de Gunzbourgs, Michel and Dolores Porgès, Pamela Frankau the daughter of Gilbert Frankau, and so on. One day Raoul Helbronner turns up at the Avenida Bar to say he's on his way to New York in order to propose marriage to Cécile de Rothschild (he was turned down) and another day she meets Poppy's childhood friend Aline de Gunzbourg with her little boy Michel Strauss, they too off to New York.

A flicker of cosmopolitanism survives when she entertains Somerset Maugham distressed by the fall of France (about which he was writing a book), Noël Coward on his way back from Australia, two local correspondents, Moore of *The Daily Telegraph* and Lucas of *The Times* (no first names given), the anti-Nazi German Baron von Friesen and his wife Walpurga, Prince Radziwiłł and his wife formerly Princess Eugénie of Greece. The Duke and Duchess of Windsor had stayed in Lisbon with Ricardo Espírito Santo, and Mitzi was "horrified" to hear from their relations, José Espírito Santo and his wife, that the Windsor woman hadn't even sent flowers by way of thanks.

In need of a power of attorney for Pokorny to deal with her affairs, she was obliged to apply in person to the German Embassy. In an atmosphere of embarrassment and hostility, she obtained the requisite document. Her visit to the Hungarian Legation took place on 1 August. She and the minister, André de Vodianer, talked politics as much as they dared. The future of the Balkans, they agreed, was changing from one day to another. Mitzi then asked about Trissolin (one of the horses that Alan and Poppy had seen in training at Lesvár). Mitzi had what was surely a unique experience for a refugee of learning that Trissolin had just won the Alagar Preis, the Hungarian Derby. Trissolin was unbeaten that season, and an article in a Hungarian newspaper congratulated "the little Baroness Mitzi" on winning all the big races even though the new anti-Jewish laws made life in Hungary impossible for her. Minister Vodianer came to dinner in

November, and she quotes him saying that if Hitler took Palestine he would make it a Jewish national state. He also told her what other diplomats would have been glad to know, that Germany was already massing troops against the Soviet Union in order to save Europe from Bolshevism.

What to do about me puzzled them all. Letters and telegrams with proposals and objections passed between Mitzi in Lisbon, Poppy in London, and Eduardo and Bubbles. Mitzi did not want to have to take me with her to Canada, but she was not happy that I stayed in France. "People coming from Nice say they are starting to starve there and that the Jews will be put into camps." She wondered, "How will I ever get David and Jessie out?" Jessie refused to fly alone with me to Canada. If Mitzi was to take care of me she would have had to postpone departing from Lisbon, and she imagined Frank would blame her for paying attention to the children "if anything happened," that is, if they were deported from Portugal or somehow forced back under Nazi rule. Visas and tickets, she said, were unobtainable but they obtained them all the same.

Round about 10 June 1941, she and Frank sailed to New York on the *Serpa Pinto*, a Portuguese liner that had seen better days. No tears were shed when she threw off what she calls "poor mad Europe," not even on quitting the Villa Preciosa that had so suited her. The other passengers on the voyage were a cross-section: 29 survivors of an Egyptian ship that had been torpedoed; a young rabbi, "dark, sad and upsetting;" Germans huddled in the third class "like animals," playing the refugee card. Some woman misinformed her on 22 June that the Soviet Union had entered the war as Hitler's ally – the ship's captain put her straight. Next day, the ship docked at Pier B on Staten Island. She and Frank checked into the Best Western hotel on Fiftieth and the corner of Madison, where the charge was $225 a month. The year in

Portugal had cost her $9,500. In New York she had $11,000 in the bank. The presence of Robert and Nelly de Rothschild, and their daughter Cécile, allowed her to pick up social life more or less where she had left it. But determined to live in the British Empire, they chose to spend the war in Montreal. The judgment she passed on herself after the change of continent is characteristic: "Mitzel Springer from Vienna, what different things you do and how you love it."

THIRTEEN

Villa to Villa

THE VILLA LES OEILLETS is on the Boulevard Alexandre III, a short walk down to the Croisette, the Cannes seaside so much more glamorous than Le Touquet's Paris-Plage where Jessie had previously taken me. Built in stone in spacious and leafy surroundings, here is a summer-house that might have belonged to one of those Frenchmen advised by President Adolphe Thiers in the previous century to enrich themselves. Shallow steps lead up to the entrance. At the rear is a patio, slightly sunken. Out there one day, I somehow contrived to collapse the deckchair I was lolling on, pinching a finger and unable to lift my weight off it. A balcony on the first floor overlooks the patio. From time to time, a priest would call round, stand on that balcony and throw sweets to Elly and me below.

Max rented this villa, and in mid-July 1940, a few days after we had arrived there, Jessie was writing to Poppy, "I hope in the near future I'll be able to hand you over your saucy son, he's grown and getting quite brown from the sea air here." Letters, the one and only lifeline, had to be mailed via a neutral country. In Spain and then Portugal, Mitzi had the vital function of forwarding communications between Cannes and London. Inevitably, some letters went undelivered and some questions had to be left unanswered.

Jessie's letter of 19 July must have given Poppy as much reassurance as information. The opening paragraph declares, "I have never lost confidence in what England can, and will, do, but it will be a hard struggle." Royaumont, she then says, so far is intact, with the Spanish flag flying over it, thanks to Eduardo. "Your mother is still in Portugal, very unhappy and I think it takes her all her time to keep the baby [Frank, that is] good-tempered, and I think perhaps she is beginning to understand that." There follows one of the many quotes that she had memorised:

> Every man will be thy friend
> Whils't thou hath wherewith to spend.
> But if the store of crowns be short
> No man will supply their want.

A family discussion was to be held next day in order to see what was the best thing to do for the children. "For the time being, they are having a good fling here by the sea. I don't know what you would say to see David going down to dinner after his bath at eight o'clock. He has breakfast in bed at nine o'clock, lunch at one o'clock. We are out until after seven o'clock sometimes, and he is not in bed much before 9.30 and he sleeps like a top. He has grown but not very fat, no!" Lily has just heard that Elie had been taken prisoner in the fighting at the time of the Dunkirk evacuation. "I was so thankful I could have cried."

We were to spend the summer of 1940 from the end of July to early October at Zarouz, a resort on the Spanish coast, half an hour from San Sebastián. For Eduardo and his immediate family no particular formalities were involved. Jessie and Nanny Stainer could still travel legally on British passports and both may have been too old to be interned. Hitherto I had traveled on Poppy's passport. This had been issued at the British Consulate in Paris and dated on the day of her wedding in December 1934. After crossing from Austria into Germany on 12 July 1935, she had acquired a page with swastika stamps. I am entered as her child as from 30 April 1936. Once the war had begun, she received special permits stating that she was returning to her mother at Montreuil but with the qualification, "This passport is not valid for any military zone overseas." She was taking liberties. An Immigration official stamped her entry to Southampton on 4 February 1940. After that date, we were separated and I had no identification papers of any kind.

In the course of innumerable conversations with Eduardo towards the end of his life, I never thought to ask how he had arranged for me to be waved across the frontier between France and Spain. For many, this was to be a matter of life and death. Some chose to find an illegal route over the mountains into Spain – Jacqueline Propper, a cousin, borrowed Lily's ski boots for her long hike. The eminent literary critic Walter Benjamin was one among many denied entry – he committed suicide rather than face the consequences. I have to assume that Eduardo passed me off as Spanish, a relation, even his son.

The Grand Hotel at Zarouz had a French owner, Madame Bringeon. Philip, then aged ten, remembers the deprivation and poverty left by the civil war. Children were barefoot. The hotel served only one good meal in the week. Out to re-assure, Jessie on the contrary depicts "a lovely place, here, wonderful beach and the children are looking fine, good appetites and plenty to eat so far." She had only one criticism. "Any amount of sausages [i.e. Germans] walking about here, so we have to shut our eyes, ears and mouths." German soldiers were allowed to wear their uniform in Franco's Spain but not to carry side-arms. Jessie was sitting on a bench one day when one of them suddenly appeared and sat down next to her. Behind the bench was a concrete ramp which I used to run up from bottom to top. Playing at this, I saw Jessie turn to this soldier, and I heard her say in English, "Do you think I am going to sit next to you? Get off this bench at once." Probably the sight of an angry old woman made him think he was doing something wrong. He stood up, saluted, and walked away.

Elly and I climbed up that ramp, we paddled carefree in the sea and we built sandcastles and jumped on and off a rock shaped like a mouse. "He is having a glory time," Jessie wanted Poppy to know. There I was speaking French to be able to play with boys who had no English. *Merde* was a word I was forbidden to use, but Jessie was pleased to pass on my retort, "I can think what you won't let me say." We were invited to a tea party in a local villa and I came back with the potato I'd won in the potato race. "He says he is going to marry Elly, she wants a real live baby and he will buy her one. I hope not." Once when I was supposed to be having a siesta, I was watching Jessie sitting in a chair in our bedroom and soaking her feet in an enamel bowl full of water. Suddenly she unrolled her stockings. I piped up to ask what she was doing, and she answered that she was drowning the fleas that had gathered on her legs.

A two-way link between my parents and me, Jessie accepted without any hesitation the responsibility put on her so capriciously. If ever you get lost, she would say to me, I'll be able to find you because you'll be the boy with two moles on his back. Far from usurping motherhood as another might have done, in letter after letter she is at pains to stress that I miss my parents, I cherish their photographs and often speak of them: "his last thought is of you two when he goes to bed." She had lived through Poppy's post-natal depression, and I imagine that she was afraid of some sort of relapse. Poppy had to be re-assured that she still had the son she always had. Explicitly she exhorts, "I pray you are keeping yourself well in hand, my Poppy, and not letting your nerves run away with you."

Jessie was also providing bulletins of family news. Lily

had received her first letter from Elie, in which he says that as a prisoner he is being well treated. Lily had been afflicted with boils, and Bubbles went back into France, to Biarritz, to fetch medication for her. Throughout the summer, Eduardo was at Vichy but he had contrived to go to Royaumont and Paris; "everything very sad looking." The Spanish flag protected Royaumont, but the cellars and the provisions there had been looted. The cows were let out of the farm. The gardener was the ringleader, she believes, his expression when the family left showed that he was thinking he could take whatever he liked. Max expected everyone to live with him in the Villa in Cannes. "There is always that question of food but I think it will be the same for all countries this end of the world. Roast beef [i.e. England] will be alright as she keeps the key of the larder, so far we have had plenty of everything, may it continue."

"Are we down-hearted? No!" Right is bound to prevail, she repeats. It must have encouraged – perhaps amazed – Poppy to see how the inflexible Jessie was refusing any thought of surrender:

> Hitler is neither master of the seas nor the skies but until he is, invasion is bound to failure. The awe-inspiring courage of the British people, wrote W. Lippmann in the *New York Herald Tribune* in September could not be sustained if along with their brave hearts they did not also have clear heads, they fight on and are determined to fight back, not in the manner of men resisting blindly, but as men who know their position and odds and real alternatives. Only a great people could do this. The British are a great people and now they are led by a man who knows their history, and having the quality of greatness and being greatly led, their reason does not undermine but on the contrary strengthens the courage of their hearts.

Early in the blitz, on 8 September, a bomb hit York Gate. That night Alan and Poppy had been sleeping in the dining-room on the ground floor. At three in the morning, bombs seemed to be dropping so close that they went down to the kitchen in the basement. Minutes later, the bomb fell, breaking windows, cracking a wall and filling their beds with glass and brick. "I know that you are the bravest of the three girls," Jessie commiserated to Poppy, "but this was too much and how grateful we are all of us that you and Alan were spared. Happily David was not there."

The choice was between joining Mitzi at the Villa Preciosa or Max in the Villa Les Oeillets. Portugal was an unknown quantity. Jessie was frank with Poppy, "I don't care to go on such a journey on my own, but if you insist, I must. One is safe *nowhere*." Then, "Bubbles says she can't take David without your consent so I suppose you will be getting a wire to that effect. Granny wants him to go to her but I say of two evils choose the least, and I think we had better go to Max but will abide by your decision whatever that may be. . . . I would like you to write to Bubbles and tell her to do for David as she would for her own two, in every way. . . . Bubbles has just been in to say a wire from Eduardo says it will be alright for myself and Nannie, and with papers to fill up and finger prints to take, I don't care so long as they don't take David away from me. For me, it is a sacred charge, and I *must* deliver him over to his Mummy."

With hindsight, to leave neutral Spain and re-enter Vichy France was tempting providence. Heedlessly, we were going towards the dangers that so many others around us, including friends and relations, were trying to get away from. Exceptionally, Philippe de Gunzbourg, Aline's brother, was already set on a heroic course as head of a resistance movement in the south-west. Like the sort of conceptual artwork that contains its own comment, a photograph exists of Bubbles and Philippe smiling as they pose on the Croisette beside a photograph of him on a wall-poster that offers a reward for his capture.

"In a way I'm pleased to be here," Jessie reports from the Villa Les Oeillets at the end of October 1940, "it will lengthen their summer a little, and for Max who is always lost without his sisters, and we miss you, my Poppy." Her own attitude remained Churchillian. "We still have faith, hope and confidence that right will be victorious over might; and you have the honour to be living in a very plucky, right little, tight little island. I hope you are not worrying, for we must take things as we find them." Another letter ends, "A great poet said what I've told you before, 'Come they from the three corners of the earth and we shall shock them, and nothing rue, if England to herself do be but true.' Oh what a nice little island."

Those who could afford it were finding somewhere to live and if possible arranging to escape abroad while it was still legal to do so. *Au Pilori*, the French publication as viciously anti-Jewish as *Der Stürmer* in Germany, was soon jeering that Jews were turning Cannes into Kann-sur-mer. There was a social life of sorts, involving visits from friends or relations whom Poppy had known – women at present without husbands – and Jessie names: Rose d'Ormesson, Sylvia de Castellane, Claude Getting, Nadine Blondel. Another English nanny, identified simply as Bradbury, had been in Paris and Jessie tells Poppy her story, "they rounded up all the roast beefs and took them away to a camp. . . . I am sorry for Bradbury as she is old but it will give her time to think about all the good dinners she used to give her dog." Antoinette, wife of Philippe de Gunzbourg, had bought a house nearby [the Germans would have been glad to know that]. Dr Metzl has come to Cannes to see his dentist. Max has taken the house on for another three months; he is very thin, "not unhappy, but where will it all end?" Eduardo is also looking for a farm or place in the country for his family – no respecter of persons, Jessie nicknames him Flopsy Bunny. Bubbles went to winter sports for a week and broke her leg: "She has taken up a good bit of my time." Strangely she refers to Lily in many of her letters without once mentioning that Lily had married Elie by "procuration." Conducted by a mayor, this civil procedure in France allows one party to marry in the absence of the other. Photographs caught the rather grim little bureaucratic ceremony attended only by her brother and sister. All her life Lily was to quip about having married an empty chair.

Attic-like, my room was on the top floor of the Villa. I was allowed to read in bed. The books had elaborate pictorial covers and told thrilling tales of adventure about dashing spahis and zouaves, cruel Barbarossa and even crueller Bluebeard, with illustrations in primary colours. For Christmas 1940 Jessie bought two books, addressed and stamped them herself and had the postman tell me that this parcel came from my parents in England. "David has had a very happy time as far as we could make it, the usual tree but very small, about thirty candles on it and a small quantity of silver trimming and a few mandarines."

Our life in Vichy France, she tries to get across to Poppy, was almost normal. She could write, "Until now they get plenty to eat, thank goodness." Knock on wood, David is marvellous, "no bad colds, no earache, no tummy aches, in fact it seems to suit him here, rosy cheeks, grown, one meter ten and weighs just nineteen kilos. I can't seem to get him over that weight but so long as he does not lose I don't mind." I played marbles with Philip, and cards with Elly. "Elly is Spanish, isn't she?" I apparently asked one day, and hearing the answer yes, I said exactly what would have pleased Jessie, "Well I'm an Englishman, thank God." Elly and I fight, she says, but can't do without each other. David "talks to himself as if he were writing a book, knows all the capitals of Europe which for the time being have changed a bit." I had a toy pistol whose caps went off with a loud crack and some satisfactory smoke. Twice a week I had a bath. Philip developed severe whooping cough, Elly had it less badly, and I was hardly aware that I was even ill with it.

Jessie had a bicycle and bought me one too, again pretending that it was a birthday present from my parents. The two of us would go round the local streets foraging for food. My weight didn't increase because we were in fact not getting plenty to eat. To keep Poppy's spirits up, she would mask reality. "I assure you the children have enough to eat, parcels from Granny also from Eduardo make up what we can't get here, condensed milk etc." Among the questions I never thought to ask Bubbles or Eduardo was whether we qualified for ration cards – probably not. Jessie had spotted a garden with a hole in its wire netting and would wait for the moment to send me in to pull up vegetables while she stood guard. In a local shop the sole thing for sale that gave some impression of filling and sustaining were little round red tins of Réglisses, a brand of licorice bits either a centimeter long or cone-shaped, for obvious reasons known to Jessie as Mouse's Number One and Mouse's Number Two. When hungry, you are at the mercy of the pit of your stomach. Meals in the Villa were brief and joyless. At one point we shared a single cauliflower between us all, and on another occasion we were reduced to sucking fish-bones. Mouse's Number One or Two did nothing to help. The aunts used to bicycle to country farms to buy what they could – Jessie praised Lily for going about 25 kilometers in search of some eggs. One day they didn't pay attention to a piece of meat left on one of their bicycles, and a passing dog snatched it. Once on the Croisette, the aunts gave me an oyster, but it was so slithery and slimy in the mouth that I vomited. Furious at the waste, the aunts went for me, and I have never eaten an oyster since. Years later I found out that Jessie and Nannie Stainer had been competing, each getting up early and creeping downstairs in the hope of being undetected as they made sure that their charges had the best of anything there was to eat. Jessie couldn't resist making cracks to Poppy about her lifelong counterpart and rival. "Nannie has not been very well, old age I think, and Philip is one too many for her." Or when it came to travel, "Can't you see Nannie up in the plane, Oh! Oh! Oh!"

To me, Eduardo was "Mon Oncle," and as a small boy I was Flannelfoot to him, the nickname borrowed from some film. During the years when he had retired we frequently discussed the events of 1940. Prewar contacts with personalities like Pierre Laval, Pétain's Prime Minister at Vichy and the prime mover of collaboration with Hitler, ought to have stood him in good stead in Madrid. Spanish foreign policy was in the hands of Ramón Serrano Suñer, at that time an unqualified supporter of his brother-in-law General Franco and an outright Nazi sympathizer who expected Hitler to win the war. In the civil war Hitler had greatly helped the Nationalists to victory, and now that he was redrawing boundaries in Europe even greater spoils might be had. Getting in first, Mussolini declared war on the Allies on 10 June in the belief that he was laying the foundations of a Mediterranean empire. Four days later, with the limelight on the Wehrmacht marching into Paris, Spanish troops occupied Tangier, hitherto an international zone. The difficult course now was to befriend Hitler enough to assure his continuing approval of Spanish aims but not enough to alienate the Allies and risk the punishment they could inflict. At the meeting with Hitler at Hendaye on 23 October, Franco got this balance right, skillfully arguing that Spain was in too desperate a state to help the common cause but was obliged to stay neutral until the damage of the civil war was repaired. In words often quoted, a disappointed Hitler remarked afterwards that he would rather have teeth drawn than negotiate again with Franco.

The initiative Eduardo had taken in Bordeaux to issue transit visas for Spain was bound to be seen in Madrid as a favour to the Allies which exposed Franco and his regime unnecessarily to German pressure. In a letter to Lequerica, in charge of the embassy in Vichy, Serrano Suñer gave vent to his prejudice, describing Eduardo as someone "who served the interests of French Jewry." Rumour has it that Eduardo took jewels and a valuable picture out of France in his wagon-lit on behalf of the Rothschilds. His repudiation, quoted by James K. McAuley, is certainly equivocal, "What need had the Rothschilds of my intervention?" At any rate on 2 February Serrano Suñer demoted Eduardo. A telegram had the brutal order, "You have 24 hours to leave your post and you go to Larache." – he had been more or less dispatched into exile as vice-consul in what was then a small fishing village on the Atlantic coast of Morocco. (Serrano Suñer eventually apologized, Eduardo became an ambassador, and after his death Yad Vashem, the Holocaust Museum in Jerusalem, honoured him as a Righteous Gentile for saving Jews in the hour of need.)

Jessie well understood that our fate depended on the international political configuration. Someone so patriotic can't have enjoyed suggesting, "as for Gibraltar we may perhaps have to lend it to them for a short time." She had been kept in the picture, for on 1 February she wrote that there had been some question of Eduardo leaving his post, "but I think it has been arranged and he is staying where he is for the time being." Whether or not she knew about Eduardo's punishing telegram that very next day, she gives her reason for staying out of England, "I quite understand that you want your little boy" but "I think I should be taking him into worse danger than here." She repeats herself, "David and I shall come as soon as it is reasonably possible to do so, but we must wait until the sausage has tried to swallow the roast beef, pray let it be soon." Six weeks later, on 14 March, she was putting it more strongly: "Yes! I'll bring him when the time is ripe, as promised, but friends and family are against it now, the risk is far too great for the time being. I know this is very hard on you both. 'I know, don't tell me,' as David would say." (At the same time, she asks Poppy to send a card to her sisters in Horspath and "tell them that half a gammon of bacon does not come our way.")

During the course of March, the family had to re-adjust to Eduardo's new post. We were to live in Tangier rather than Larache. At the end of the month, Mitzi in Estoril heard from Eduardo that he had left Vichy for good. "He says the reason given him that he helped too many Jews out of France is surely not the real one. He is very upset to have left his family and not to be able to look after them, Alfort etc. What will happen to Alfort etc now, God alone knows." Only if he and Bubbles were able to look after me could she leave for Canada with a clear conscience. Sure enough, she concluded, "They asked me if I thought David ought to go to Tangier. How difficult to know! But I do feel he ought to stay with Phil and Elena and so be under Eduardo's protection."

The second bomb to fall on York Gate was an incendiary that burnt out the house. That night (9 May as far as I can make out) Alan and Poppy happened not to be there. Mrs Kay and her two sons were unharmed. "I send her a hand-shake." Jessie was rather perfunctory considering how lucky everybody had been, and that now we had no home to come back to. Her final letters from Cannes show that she was in several minds. She is sorry that Poppy can't have me back.

"I made a false move when I brought him here instead of taking him to Granny, but we can't always see how things are
going to turn out." She explains, "Fate has decided that I
shall go with the Proppers which is much against my will.
I had so hoped I would be able to hand you over your little
boy. There have been plenty of chances which we have not
taken as we all agreed we were sending him into danger. Anyway you must think, and know, that we've done for the best
where he is concerned. The voyage from here to Lisbon is terrible, everyone is agreed on that point. If we go with Eduardo
it is not so terrible, in two hours we are at Lisbon by air, the
family will be separated again, it will only be for a short time."

The departure from Cannes of the Propper parents and
children, the two nannies and me – seven of us in all, because
Max and Lily chose to remain behind – was on 5 July 1941.
The heavy luggage went separately via Marseilles and Oran.
Between us, we carried 21 bits of hand luggage and parcels,
including the little pigskin suitcase that I clung to. Accompanying us was a Mrs FL – unidentified, presumably English – who claimed to know Alan and promised to deliver
photographs of me to him. "We are on the move again," Jessie writes, "but with all these ups and downs I can't seem to
put my mind to letter-writing." The crucial letter containing
some information is on paper of the Ritz Hotel in Madrid
but undated. In it, Jessie says the journey has been very tir-
ing for everyone. We were detained at the frontier for four
hours. Missing the train, she goes on, we went into the station buffet "where we all ate two bananas each and a bottle
of lemonade." Dinner was in a hotel nearby "and they did
put it away." Woken at three in the morning, an hour later
we caught the train to Barcelona. "They brought up fourteen
boiled eggs for our breakfast," Bubbles and Philip each ate
three. "I am not sorry in a way to change places, it was necessary for the children's food question." Her weight has gone

down 14 kilos. During this part of the journey I lost my purse with 80 francs in it, and Eduardo lost the box with his brand new official hat in it, but no name or address on it.

After a pause in Madrid, we went by train from Cádiz to Algeciras and then by boat to Tangier, landing finally in Morocco on 24 July. The Minzah Hotel was, and still is, a repository of the Oriental charm of which Edward Said so disapproved. On arrival, we ordered a meal. The waiter who brought it to the rooms wore a red tarboosh that set off his white jacket. His spherical figure showed that he was a serious eater. Watching us devour the food, he stayed wobbling with laughter and pleasure, becoming an instant living legend for us as The Fat Man of the Minzah. That night I slept for the first time in the mysterious half-light of a mosquito net.

The mail service to and from Tangier was normal. From the Minzah, Eduardo wrote to Alan that Jessie had lost a lot of kilos but "is still capable of slapping you or me if we have the bad luck of displeasing our ladies. She was magnificent on the journey when she did everything for the children and Nannie." David, he says, is "exactly my third child," and he wonders what Elly will make of it when we have to part. The costs at the Minzah are 1,100 Moroccan francs, and could Alan ask Lord Bute, the owner of the hotel, for a reduction. Then there's the rent. Eduardo has paid June and July at £16 each, and now Alan should pay August, September and part of October. Would he also please remit to the Bank of British West Africa, 37 Gracechurch Street, expenses of £32 for my journey.

Now rented by Eduardo, the Villa Ritchie took its name from Anne and Richmond Ritchie who built it. A Victorian literary lady, Anne was the daughter of the novelist William Makepeace Thackeray. Their one-time house is on the Marshan, a hill overlooking the town below and with Gibraltar a visible smudge on the far side of the Straits. Two squat pillars enclose the entrance, and a short drive curls up towards the house. Opposite the front door is a wall with a tiled bench built against it. "There's plenty of room to move about, six bedrooms and three servants' rooms," Jessie is quick to tell Poppy, "only one bath and just jugs and basins but that can't be helped."

In my mind, the Moroccan sky is a permanent Prussian blue. Under a copper-bright sun, we go down to the beach. In the garden Muhammad Driss enjoys showing me the lilies and orchids he is growing. The house is cool. Eating at last, we are "like full fed ponies" in Jessie's expression. Philip goes to the lycée, and a tutor by the name of Isaac Abekassis comes to the house. I play football with boys my age on an open space of the Marshan. These boys have djellabas that flap around their ankles when they run, and heads closely shaved except for a tuft in the middle of the scalp. This, I hear, is for Allah to lift them up to him if he must. After every game, Jessie suspects I will have caught nits, ticks, even lice, and inspects my head minutely. Wearing baboush that are pointed and flat-heeled, neither shoes nor slippers, in goatskin dyed a shiny yellow, I imagine myself properly Moroccan.

Next door, out of sight behind a high wall is a large forbidden mansion. The owner is a great Berber chieftain, the Glaoui, and if he's in residence weird music will shatter the silence. Sitting against one of our pillars is the *fiqh*, an elderly unkempt witch doctor, the soles of her feet dyed orange with henna. She has bangles up her arms. The little footballers stand around while she works her spells, burning feathers and mumbling to herself. Suddenly frightened by a curse, we all run away. One day we are driving through the Petit Socco when an Arab spits at the car, and saliva dribbles down my window. Everyone pretends not to notice. At dawn, Bubbles and Eduardo get me out of bed, and from a seat in the garden we watch British warships passing through the Straits.

Dark grey shapes are silhouetted against a light grey background. You'll never forget it, the grown-ups impress on me.

In a hectic exchange of telegrams, Bubbles argues that it is better, safer, for me to stay where I am. Poppy presses that we be reunited, though she back-pedals too: "Very worried nothing organized from here, we always insisted David should leave only if the remainder of the journey was fixed and we beg to have instructions about what to do." "Papers are getting filled up, photos stuck on," Jessie tells her, "I don't altogether relish the idea of a long air trip, but if you can you must, and if you must, you can." Sir Alvary Gascoigne, the Consul in Tangier, and John Mallet, in the Lisbon embassy, were informed. On 3 September Poppy was in a fret, "Have cabled money and tickets Schreiber. Please wire David's address in Lisbon." Two days later, "So relieved, no news from Schreiber but everything well organized now, thanks and forgive panic."

Years later, I met Mrs Schreiber and was able to thank her for putting up Jessie and me in Lisbon. She was the wife of the air attaché and mother of Mark, afterwards editor of *The Economist*. Somewhere in Lisbon a toyshop had laid out a battlefield with lead soldiers, guns and tanks and electric lights flashing like explosions. I spent my days spellbound by these war games until Mrs Schreiber saw us off on the plane to Bristol – in 1943 the Germans shot down the flight and the actor Leslie Howard was among those killed. In one hand I gripped my little suitcase and in the other a bunch of bananas, which Jessie warned would be the last I'd see. Not until 1968 did I return to Morocco, this time accompanied by Clarissa. Isaac Abekassis, the former tutor, was almost too frightened to meet us. For him, the stabbing in the street of the rabbi of Tangier was the start of a pogrom and he couldn't wait to take up a position he'd been offered in the University of Strasbourg. At the Villa Ritchie, I could show Clarissa the

pillar where the *fiqh* had squatted to work her magic. Tres-
passers, we walked up the drive. Approaching, the gardener
came to shoo us out. From some way off, Muhammad Driss
recognized me, came running and we were both weeping as
we embraced.

On 10 September 1941, I met my parents again. With
painful self-awareness heightened by literary skill, Alan wrote
up the moment.

I showed the constable my war office pass and he agreed
to let me on to the aerodrome. "But who," he asked, "is
this young lady? Is she your daughter?" Poppy was wearing her W.V.S. [Women's Voluntary Service] uniform
and looked, in fact, about twelve, which made it all the
stranger that we should *really* be going to pick up David,
after so many false starts. We waited for an hour in a cautious waiting-room; modern and antiseptic; built to face
the wrong way (for security); built for tea and the *Sketch*
as a balance to nerves. Chintz and sycamore. When I'm
waiting for something anxiously I can't talk. I want to be
part of the furniture, a bracket for a newspaper. "Talk to
me," Poppy kept saying, and I couldn't. People rushed in
and out, slamming the door. We stood on the grass verge
outside the open window, while an engine in the shops
made an unbearable noise. At last someone said, "Here
comes the little boy," and David ran round the corner, just
as when I last saw him asleep at Montreuil on New Year's
Eve 1939, only a little larger and speaking with a French
accent. He buried his head in our arms, not so much shy
as recollecting his courage; then took me off, as if nothing had happened, to look at an aeroplane. We came
back to London ... [*sic*] and when I think of Bristol, it is
I who am shy, who concentrates on the Clifton terraces
and the chapter-house – almost, it oddly seems, from

laziness. Do other people spend as much of their time avoiding emotions? I live in them so vigorously that they become an imposition, and a kind of wooden silence my refuge. Now, having David, my self-preservation instinct is to read the paper, in order to avoid the wonder of having him in the room, of enjoying him.

In a crowded carriage of the train to London I sat next to Jessie and wondered what this man and woman opposite had to do with me, and why we weren't speaking. They wouldn't know about my yellow baboush and the little pigskin suitcase that had come the whole way with me. Bananas were unobtainable in the war and I was conscious that everyone setting eyes on the bunch I was carrying threw me a special look.

―――――

The Pretender to the French throne, the Comte de Paris, was living with his family at Larache and saw a lot of Eduardo and Bubbles. In a murky incident in Algeria, a young Royalist, Bonnier de la Chapelle, murdered the collaborator Admiral Darlan, was caught and executed. Eduardo was in touch with influential Americans, for instance the diplomat Robert Murphy and Kenneth Pendar, the agent charged with keeping the Moroccan elite from going over to Hitler. Demarçay, the French Consul in Tangier, was a Gaullist, and when the battleship *Repulse* sailed from Gibraltar only to be sunk in the Far East, he had rolled in despair on the drawing-room floor of the Villa Ritchie. Our family doctors were Lucia and Federico Bedarida, Italian Jews who had fled Mussolini. (My daughter Candida married Owen Mostyn-Owen, whose maternal grandmother was the sister of Lucia. After the 1973 war, Lucia, a widow by then, had to flee again and so we met up after half a century in a chain of events a novelist would not dare invent.)

I had already left by the time Lily and Max arrived and settled in with their sister and brother-in-law. They had been exposed a great deal more than most people to the reality and consequences of Nazism. Yet in 1942 they chose to return to the Villa Les Oeillets. In reaction to the Allied invasion of North Africa on 8 November 1942, the Germans occupied Vichy France. Caught in a trap, more tens of thousands of Jews were then deported. In all probability, their Austrian background would have sealed the fate of Lily and Max. At the very last minute, Eduardo cabled false papers to be collected at the PLM hotel in Marseilles. A faithful family chauffeur, François Boyer, drove them from Cannes. Typical of Lily, she noted he was "very *bon genre*" (turned out like a gentleman), with his bowler hat and a magnificent pair of gloves, one finger filled with gold coins. German soldiers were already at the station. Max knew a passageway into the hotel. The concierge handed them the papers, they returned to the station and boarded the train. In a third-class compartment they found Iya, the Russian-born wife of Sir Robert Abdy, a rich English dilettante, also leaving for Spain. Hours passed before the train finally started; there was nothing to eat; they spent the night in a grim hotel at Cerbère, the frontier town. But they were out once more.

To the end of their lives, they were unable to put into words that they had been dicing with death. They believed people like them were essentially immune to persecution and murder. Bad things were what happened to the poor, to Jews unable to call on lawyers and bankers. They couldn't imagine that the Germans and a good many French made no such distinctions about Jews and were determined to kill off the lot. The belief that their primary identity was French had put their lives at risk for no purpose. After Max and Lily had returned safely to Tangier, Poppy's letter to them on 4 December 1942 began, "It's too wonderful and moving to know that at last you are all re-united, although waiting to have details is making us ill." In a separate letter with a Bletchley postmark and the censor's tape on the envelope as usual, Alan said that he had been following their emotions and anxieties closely, and "after all you have been through, words fail." Bubbles took a vow that if we all survived the war she would convert to Catholicism – and so she did.

FOURTEEN

War in Kent

NOW THAT YORK GATE had been destroyed, we had to find somewhere to live. Rockley Manor is a handsome eighteenth-century house at the foot of the Wiltshire Downs. Mary Loder and her mother, Lady Wakehurst, were living there. Strongly built and rather plain, Mary Loder shared her life with a graphic designer, Mildred Farrer, also rather plain but mousy. In my bedroom I read for the first time a book in English and ran downstairs to the library to test out whether this new trick would allow me to read that day's *Times*.

Alan was working in the War Office and found a flat within walking distance in Athenaeum Court, a modern block in Piccadilly. We moved. At night, the air raid siren was so loud that it seemed indoors. We put clothes on and gathered in one room. Poppy refused to go into the shelter, saying that it was better to be killed outright than trapped and buried alive. She would open all the windows as a precaution against blast, and we would sit waiting. At last the searchlights began to probe the night sky, and we could see each other silhouetted in grainy intermittent flashes as memorable as the ghostly half-light under a mosquito net in Tangier. As the raid got under way, the beams of the searchlights criss-crossed high overhead in the form of letters, a *v* or an *x* or a *w*. This much steadier illumination gave Jessie's white hair the look of a turban.

I cannot be sure exactly how long Harold Acton stayed in the flat. Much too well-mannered to do anything that might offend his host and hostess, he too would sit by the open window. Bald and sinuous in his movements, Harold had spent so long in Peking that he had come almost to impersonate a Confucian sage. To pass the time, he taught us Chinese, and we would have to repeat delicate sounds against the uproar outside. The searchlights sometimes pinpointed a bomber, though cloud or smoke might quickly obscure it again. Anti-aircraft guns or bombs falling close shook the building. Never perturbed, Harold kept up the exaggerated tones that were such a distinctive feature of his personality. Later in life, I would greet him with a Chinese phrase from our bombardment tutorials and he might do a reprise of one of the Chinese songs he had sung for us.

Poppy and Alan lost no time getting out of Athenaeum Court and into Castle Hill Farm. "This pretty new mousetrap of Pigling," Poppy described it in a letter to Alan. "I feel that wherever and whatever happens we can and *will* be happy and this house has already got a stimmung of gemütlichkeit [a cosy atmosphere]. I thank God for being so very kind to us: our Baba back and a new house is, I suppose, a unique cause of happiness in this horrible year."

The house and farm belonged to the Somerhill estate, one of the largest in Kent, consisting of the huge and historic Jacobean mansion and some thousands of acres midway between Tonbridge and Tunbridge Wells. Somerhill belonged to Sir Henry d'Avigdor-Goldsmid, otherwise Harry, baronet, member of Parliament, bullion broker, master of foxhounds, high sheriff, at that time a soldier commanding his regiment, and at all times one of the most eminent Jews in the country and one of the most generous of men. Harry had friends who were aesthetes like Alan, and Alan had friends who were influential like Harry. Large and slightly ungainly, he had an occasional impediment in his speech, especially when he was amused. Somerhill was a sort of architectural complement to his character, with varied rooms of all sizes, an immense entrance hall, a ground floor library that ran from the front of the house to the back, the cosy Justice Room, a dining room seating twenty-four, a courtyard and whole wings with stable and garages to explore. I was to see Harry brought home from Normandy, badly wounded and almost mummified with bandages. To me, he was one of the men who won the war. "Pas mal," Poppy wrote to Aline de Gunzbourg then in New York when Harry received the M.C. to add to his D.S.O.

On a Sunday, Jessie would take me to tea at Somerhill. The park had a private nine-hole golf course, a herd of Jerseys and a prisoner of war camp, the huts symmetrical behind barbed wire. We'd walk past one of the lodges, where the drive was closed off by an iron chain on which swung a board with the prohibition, "*È vietato ingresso*." The Italian prisoners in fact seemed to go where they liked, singing as they marched down the road and worked in the fields. One of them gave Poppy a ring he had made out of a sardine tin.

In Harry's absence, Somerhill was in the hands of Rosie, his wife. She had the stylised beautician's looks that society ladies copied from film stars of the period: white face, red pursed lips, hair with a permanent curl. There was no holding her back; she did as she pleased. During the battle of Britain, she had lain out of doors on a rug watching through field glasses the dog-fights overhead. The butler brought out martinis. Almost to the end of her life Rosie would tease me because she had first known me speaking with a French accent.

It was possible to be lost up the stairs and along the corridors on the way to the nursery. Sarah and Chloe were a few years younger than me, and their nanny was no match for Jessie. When she was not being observed, and as though we were still at the Villa Les Oeillets, Jessie took a bottle out of her bag and filled it with milk from the Jerseys in the park.

If Goldsmid can have it, she'd say, why can't my boy? Besides, they don't miss it.

Castle Hill was cheerful and unpretentious, white clapboard at the front, brick at the back. You came out of the porch on to an uneven path across scrawny grass within a picket fence. Ground elder had invaded the flowerbeds, and grubbing out its spaghetti-like roots pre-occupied Poppy. On the other side of the fence a duck-pond glistened with greenish scum. The oast house was full of mysterious sacks that were never shifted, and in the cowsheds Mr Carter, the nearest neighbour, milked the herd and churned butter of a yellow so deep it was almost orange. The name of his bull was William III, which I misread as William ill.

To the right of the porch was an extension. Alan's Bechstein stood in the room downstairs, and on the floor above Jessie and I shared a bedroom. More lawn reached towards the wall of a granary, and beyond in an open field was the cottage of Mr and Mrs Brown and their tomboy daughter. At the top of the hill beyond the Browns' cottage lived Mr Hickmott, a quiet and respectable man of a certain age who had some business to do with the nearby timber yard. His daughter Frieda, quiet and respectable and spinsterish, walked down the road every morning to help Jessie in the house.

On the sixth step of the narrow stairs (and never any other) Nikki the Maltese terrier lay like a ball of fluffy wool. Floors were uneven, latches didn't close properly, the bathroom had to be shared but there was an outdoor privy as well. A dusty semi-secret backstairs led from my parents' bedroom down to the kitchen. What looked like a cupboard door opened on to stairs up to a tiny bedroom in the attic, also dusty. Rescued from York Gate, grand French furniture originally from Royaumont looked incongruous in this setting. Surfaces were crammed with bric-a-brac, a Russian silver cigarette case, vases, odds and ends of porcelain, little boxes in gilt and semi-precious stones, ornaments and trinkets, bibelots, statuettes, framed photographs, keepsakes, the fruit of innumerable hours spent in junkshops. On Poppy's bedside table was a tiny pig in gold, an even smaller gold mouse, a scaled-down gold basket holding jewelled flowers. In his dressing room Alan had a collection of figurines including soldiers in silver about an inch high, and a tiny silver coach and horses. Within the turbulent real world outside was a miniaturised make-believe world of their own. The window there was too wide for black-out material, so Alan commissioned Martin Battersby to paint on a board of the right size a romanticised picture of Traunkirchen where he and Poppy had become engaged. One of my jobs was to fit the board in place at nightfall.

I was expected to bicycle with my mother to Tonbridge for the groceries. It was downhill all the way, but we'd push our bicycles and full saddle-bags uphill in a race to see who was first to pass the Somerhill lodge with the *Vietato Ingresso* sign. Sometimes we'd come home to find the postman had delivered a letter or a parcel from Mitzi in Montreal. For days at a time, these might remain on a table in the entrance. She missed her family, she'd say, but didn't want to know what a wonderful time her mother and Frank were having with no idea how we were living. In the parcels were clothes and shoes destined for me but too large even for Mr Carter, or tins of food and glass jars of cooking fat that stood untouched on shelves in the pantry.

Leaving me with Jessie, Poppy in her green tweed W V S uniform with mauve trimmings was away a good deal in London, settling refugees, interpreting, arranging transport and shelter. The nannies had seen to it that she spoke English without an accent. A refugee herself, she had around her a few people from her past. On 28 December 1941, Kenneth Rae was the first guest to sign the Castle Hill visitors' book. Four weeks later, his sister Gwynedd stayed. Both lived with their old mother at Knowles Bank, a short walk away through Harry's woods whose chestnut trees were cropped for hop-poles. We'd have tea and play spillikins with old Mrs Rae. Gwynedd wrote and illustrated books about Mary Plain, an adventurous bear from the Berne bear-pits and a prototype for Paddington Bear. Mary Plain's admirers included the Owl Man, evidently modelled on Kenneth Rae and drawn with unmistakable likeness. In one of these books, my six-year-old self plays a part under my own name. The drawing, also very lifelike, shows me holding the little pigskin suit-case that had come with me from Vichy France.

Elisabeth de Waal was the one and only relation Poppy had in England. A cousin through the Ephrussi connection, she and her brother Ignaz – Iggy – had spent the First War in Meidling and they both recalled Baron Gustav. In his book her grandson Edmund de Waal captures her independent spirit; he also arranged the publication of a fine novel she had written about the complex attitudes she encountered returning to Vienna after the war. She and her Dutch hus-band had finished up in Bletchington Road in suburban Tunbridge Wells. We'd bicycle there to hear tales about Mitzi and good old days. Her eldest son, Tascha, became Dean of Canterbury, a deserter in uniform Eugène would have called him. In a cottage in the nearby village of Pembury was Mary Apponyi, a close friend from Vienna. Born into the Hungar-ian aristocracy, she had married Anthony Irby, then an offi-cer in the Rifle Brigade. Their three sons were my friends. Mary had beautiful, proud looks, and a temperament to match. She and Poppy egged one another on. Once when Mary had come to tea, the two of them laughed so much they started chucking sandwiches and scones at one another. (Poppy lived long enough to know that Mary had died of cancer.)

The Castle Hill visitors' book all the same testifies to vestiges of the pre-war social round. Among guests were Raymond Mortimer, Cyril Connolly, Patrick Kinross, Janet and Reynolds Stone, and James Pope-Hennessy. Noel Annan's bald head gleamed as he stooped over the bed to kiss me goodnight. Commissioned by Alan, Kenneth Rowntree stayed for a month to do a water-colour of the house. Stanley Morison of the *Times Literary Supplement* came to sound out whether Alan might succeed him as its editor. Every so often Harry and Vere visited. In the hope that I would be as good a shot as him, Harry gave me a single-barrel 410. I had permission to shoot rabbits, and Mr Carter taught me to skin them. Adrian, now a lieutenant in the Welsh Guards, brought Betty Elliot, a cousin of Poppy's childhood friend Lulu Esmond. Independent and generous, Betty cared for him with a devotion that was surely unrequited love. Passionate about the theatre and opera, she introduced us after the war to famous friends of hers in the musical world, Tito Gobbi, Carlo Maria Giulini and the cellist Gregor Piatigorsky. Torpedoed during an Atlantic convoy, Guy de Rothschild had survived many days on a raft, and came to Castle Hill whenever he could. The close encounter with death by starvation or drowning had left him gaunt and white. To me, he was another of the men winning the war.

"David is very intelligent," Poppy boasted in correspondence to Aline de Gunzbourg. She kept my French going by reciting or reading French poetry with me. My French accent, she and Alan feared, would not be understood by boys my own age, and accordingly I might be bullied. Kent College for Girls was at the edge of Pembury, a little more than a mile away, and it had already admitted one other boy. Neil Willson and his parents, Sir Walter and Lady Willson, lived in a house a few hundred yards from the school. The headmistress was prepared to make another exception for me. Neil had a splendid train set that I envied. Out of pure mischief, one cold day when he and I were alone in the grounds, I pushed him fully dressed into the deep end of the swimming pool. He could not swim. There was nobody to help us. As he was gasping and going under the water again I could just reach his outstretched hand, and with difficulty pull him out. By the time I got home, Poppy was waiting in the porch, to greet me with, "What have you done?"

The girls were not bullies, it was true, but between lessons they were likely to take me into a convenient shed and remove my clothes. We were all far too young to go any further. Miss Earnshaw (as I shall call her) taught the class. Blond and with sparkling blue eyes, she was very attractive, very energetic and I felt something close to love for her. She wanted us to learn about things like wild flowers. In the course of one lesson, she happened to remark that Jews were wicked, the war was their fault, they had wanted it. I sat up. We came into this somehow. I had heard of Jews without knowing who or what they were, and here was Miss Earnshaw dropping a clue that sounded like an opening to the adult world. After school, I could hardly wait to tell Poppy. We went out of the door at the back of the house. In a corner of the field where I used to shoot rabbits was a ruined orchard. Poppy sat on the trunk of a fallen apple tree, and said, You've been with the family and you know them all, do you think they wanted the war? In order to lose everything and have to run for their lives away from home? I asked if they really were Jews and we went through them one by one: Granny yes, Uncle Max yes, Aunty Bubbles yes, Aunty Lily yes – and then Poppy herself, Yes. So why had this pretty teacher been making things up like this? We went back to the house and Poppy drove off to the school.

In Alan's papers is an unpublished poem, "Ash Vale 1940."

> Under the Surrey common, the horrible cheap hotel
> A wind roared round in the dark like a sea-shell
> Killed the Capstan smoke, the bitter-slops
>   on a tiled table,
> Guzzling up the dust, winnowing the foul bath
>   of beard-stubble,
> Bucking the bed, the stiff Tate Gallery bed where I was
> Loving in oils the accurate body splashed on the canvas.
> Our bed kicked. I worked a poor seam, used a scrap
>   of night
> Mining for sex in the usual discomfort and plain fright,
> When to the brilliantine pillow that wind came;
>   and there
> Suddenly a diamond shone in the roots of his hair
> And live love, the expensive and successful, burst
>   like a next-door
> Neighbour in the room, calling us names and
>   shocking for
> The reckless, the impossible, the huge catastrophe,
> Bullying us with the size of the moment. But we
> Lay fascinated, spilled and blown, shiftily.

Lightly deleted on the typescript, the concluding word originally had been "wonderingly," which would have transformed this account of a chance sexual encounter into open celebration. "Shiftily" implies guilt. "You and your pansy friends," Poppy sometimes said. For much of the war, Alan was away from Castle Hill, and she cannot have been privy to "the huge catastrophe" of his private secrets.

From the War Office Alan was posted to Bletchley. His particular responsibility was the battle order of the German army. This involved analysing everything from Enigma and other sources that might indicate the likely performance of units in the field: where in Germany the men had been recruited and trained, whether morale was high or low, what equipment they had. Attention was paid to the character of senior officers, their political convictions, the strengths and weaknesses that might be clues to their responses and decisions. One colleague was Eric Birley, whose area of scholarship was the battle order of the Roman army. For security reasons, everyone employed at Bletchley was forbidden to keep a diary. Alan regretted that he had not recorded this period of his life, and almost invariably claimed he couldn't remember anything about it. Bletchley, he once summed up, "was a place where the office boys quoted T. S. Eliot and whistled themes from Bartók."

In 1943 John Murray published on behalf of the Ministry of War a paperback of sixty pages with the title *The Enemy*, a collection of photographs edited by Alan (the hyphen omitted from his surname) from material at Bletchley. My imagination moved on from Mary Plain. The cover shows a helmeted German soldier holding by the handle the grenade he is about to throw. Here are other Wehrmacht soldiers, parachute troops and members of the S. S. Totenkopf division in action, manning mortars and machineguns, and the whole range of artillery. At the time I knew by heart the captions under photographs of the tanks and guns we were up against. With Jessie beside me, I spent hours at the table in our room drawing maps of the various fronts where these men and their weapons were engaged. We had crayons to mark positions with national flags, a little swastika and hammer and sickle out in Eastern Europe, the Union Jack in the Western desert, the tricolore at Bir Hakeim.

A day came early in June 1944 when military traffic started to build up on the road that ran in front of the house. After some hours the three-ton trucks had become an interminable slow-moving convoy. I sat on the five-bar gate at the entrance to Castle Hill as this tremendous force ground up the hill towards Mr Hickmott's house and so on to the Channel and D-Day. The men in the trucks were solemn and silent. In the afternoon, the bomber squadrons came over one after the other in continuous formations as though the skies were picked out with a pattern of black dots. Two Mustang fighters collided. One pilot bailed out somewhere over the horizon. The other plane crashed several fields beyond the ruined orchard where Poppy and I had talked. By the time I joined the little crowd that had gathered to gape, the wreckage had been on fire and the charred figure of the pilot was silhouetted in the cockpit.

In the dawn some days later I was woken up by a spluttering across the sky overhead. I hurried to the window, and there was a missile flying close and low in the direction of London. Castle Hill was directly in the flight path of the V1s. And then there was another. Within days, anti-aircraft batteries surrounded the house and barrage balloons rose like giant mushrooms. Talkative elderly men for the most part, the gunners spent much of their time drinking tea in the kitchen. However incessantly they fired, they never hit anything, and we had become accustomed to the racket.

Tomatoes were growing in the vegetable bed planted up against the wall of the granary close to the house. Poppy and I were out there to pick what we could when without warning a V1 came over. On its tail was a Spitfire firing bursts to shoot it down. Beginning to veer and lose height, the V1 looked as if it must hit the house. Bullets from the Spitfire's guns thudded across the garden and against the end wall of the house. Next to the tomato plants, Poppy pulled me down on the path and lay on top of me. It happened too quickly for me to feel the deep fear of death or to appreciate what Poppy had done.

Ironing in her room upstairs, Jessie thought that the crumps behind her back meant that a fuse had blown, and so her reaction was to switch off the electricity. At what seemed the last moment, the V1 glided over and landed a few hundred yards away in woods belonging to Harry on the far side of the main road. We were among the first to get there. Eventually a small crowd stood around the crater in which the V1 was stuck, its fin more or less at eye level. The Home Guard figure or ARP warden who arrived was absurdly wearing a tin helmet. He started copying down in a notebook the instructions in black lettering on the fuselage, and saying what a pity it was that none of us could translate them. Poppy stepped forward and he took down her dictation.

As I lay in bed that night I could see stars through the holes in the wall where Jessie had been standing.

FIFTEEN

Post-Mortem

FIRST TO RETURN to Royaumont was Uncle Adrian. A fortnight or so after D-Day the Guards Armoured Division had landed in Normandy. He and Rex Whistler had been in the same company, two aesthetes in the unlikely role of commanding tanks. In paintings done in the early years of the war, Whistler had portrayed Adrian in uniform, reading a book in the officers' mess. In action, Adrian had seen him climb out of his tank to help another that had been hit, only to be decapitated by a shell.

The German general quartered in Royaumont had taken care of it. Nothing had been stolen from the house except the leather, cut off chairs and even golf bags, destined presumably for Wehrmacht boots. On high ground nearby, the Germans had prepared defensive positions, and had they not pulled out in time the house almost certainly would have been destroyed. In the second week of September 1944 Adrian liberated it by walking up the terrace steps and slipping a note under the closed and locked main door.

Without the Spanish flag flying there thanks to Eduardo, Royaumont would have been expropriated as property abandoned by its Jewish owners. That was not his only service to Royaumont. Called up to the army, Marcel Vernois the estate manager had been taken prisoner in the collapse of 1940, and sent to some camp in Germany. Eduardo negotiated his release and Marcel protected the family's interests throughout the occupation. He could be relied on to do the right thing. Bombers and fighter escorts passed regularly over Royaumont. Marcel was watching a dogfight one day when an Allied fighter plane was shot down. The pilot managed a parachute jump that was bound to land him in the Royaumont woods. Marcel hurried to the spot. The pilot had injuries. Having done his best to bury the parachute, Marcel got the pilot as fast as he could to the farm and hid him there. The Germans had also seen the pilot coming down, and they soon discovered the parachute in the woods. Searching the farm but finding nothing, they suspected Marcel and threatened to put him up against the wall. If they shot him, he replied, they wouldn't be able to find out anything from him.

The hide-out was never discovered. Bicycling down from Viarmes in full view of any Germans who might be on duty, Dr Darène treated the injured pilot. His courage was also undoubted. At the back of his very bald head was a huge disfiguring hole where he had operated on himself, looking into a mirror to gouge out a tumour. When the pilot had recovered, Marcel and Dr Darène contacted the network specialising in returning shot-down airmen, and they sent him back to England. On a page of the Royaumont visitors' book is the entry, "Flight Lieutenant Tony Vidler, arrived the first time (unwillingly!) by parachute 20.4.1944. Stayed until 21. 5. 1944. Arrived second time (willingly) 12.12.1946."

Visas to travel to France were virtually unobtainable. Poppy pleaded that she had a French family and it says something about her will and ability to pull strings that six short weeks after the end of the war she was at Royaumont. Another entry in that visitors' book reads, "Thérèse Pryce-Jones (née Fould-Springer) left 2 February 1940, returned 23 June 1945." On the terrace that summer she was photographed with Adrian still in battle dress and so presumably on leave, come back to celebrate. Again on the terrace, Mitzi's four children lined up for a photograph of their homecoming. Max's letter to his mother about the occasion prompted an entry in her diary, "Max was impressed by Poppy who has turned into a grand little woman." For her part Poppy found that "Max has aged terribly and alas, his eyes are full of anxiety," which led Mitzi to reflect, "I wouldn't be astonished if that poor old boy went off his head. What a sad life he has had because of his odd mentality." After five years of separation she still could not query a bed-rock conviction that where her children were concerned she was always the innocent and wrongfully harmed party. So Max's odd mentality was the cause of his sad life, rather than her spontaneous suppression of him.

Poppy had travelled alone. Alan was away in Vienna, a liaison officer with the Russians, coincidentally but conveniently stationed next to Meidling at Schönbrunn. I was refused a visa for France and in any case my English accent had improved enough for me to move on to Beachborough, a preparatory school in Northamptonshire, selected sight unseen because my cousin Philip had spent a term there before the war. In honour of the German surrender, the boys were given a holiday. That same day, *The Times* published photographs of the dead and dying discovered in concentration camps in Germany. Mr Chapple, the headmaster, pinned this page up on the school notice board. We stood about in the corridor silent before the reality of mass-murder.

Preparing her return to Europe, Mitzi was selling her apartment in Montreal and packing up a quantity of possessions to be shipped. She had Canadian friends and for the longest time in her life had been her own cook. In a writing desk of hers, I once found a notebook in which she had recorded income on the left-hand page and expenditure on the right-hand page. Day after day, she had placed a single Canadian dollar on the kitchen table for Frank, pocket money for a drink, but only one. "My angel," as she makes plain in her diaries, had had quite enough of Canada. On 8 August they sailed on a Danish liner, the *Euria*, from New York.

"I am not frightened of hardship in Europe," she told herself, but, "I should so much rather live anywhere than in France." She makes some immediate but banal reflections on the atom bomb and typically derives sentimental satisfaction from the fact that, while she was at sea, peace with Japan was declared on 14 August, which would have been Eugène's sixty-ninth birthday.

Docking at Liverpool, by chance encountering their old friend Noël Coward in the station, they made their way to London, to the Dorchester Hotel. "I was alone when my little one arrived. We were just pure joy and delight. Just kissed and hugged and laughed. She found me quite unchanged and she is a magnificent little lady.... Then we called up David. Can't note all the wonderful stories Poppy told about him. He said, 'I must say I don't remember you, Granny, but I am so happy to see you soon.' etc. etc." When at last my mother brought me round to the Dorchester, "My angel took him to have his hair cut, they got on like a house on fire and a lovely sight they are together."

The weekend of 25 August was the first of several she spent at Castle Hill Farm, "an adorable cottage, too beautifully arranged. What taste we have in the family. Jessie much older but still the pillar! What devotion." Harry d'Avigdor-Goldsmid lunched that first Sunday and showed her round Somerhill in the afternoon. (A few years later Alan and Poppy left, and he sent them these mysterious lines:

The pheasants that shine in the Colebrook Fields
Call Alan Alan Alan from over the wall
And the chestnut cants on Castle Hill
Whisper Poppy Poppy Poppy as the brown leaves fall.)

In the manner of a medieval monarch on a royal procession, Mitzi congratulates deserving inferiors, whether family members, hotel servants, or old friends like the Vansittarts. Either out of a sense of superiority, or perhaps because her usage of the English language owed a lot to Frank and made her sound jaunty and condescending, she seems to be rejoicing that she is one who had got away in time, and it was her privilege to do so. Details that Poppy gave her about concentration camps, she writes, were "just not to be taken in." All the same, she did take in the sadism the camp personnel had inflicted on victims of typhus and women expecting babies. Julius Reinach from one of the most prominent Jewish families had told Poppy that he and his wife had been in Drancy, the Paris holding camp for Auschwitz. With them were Springer relations, Eric and Hélène Allatini, and the latter "had lived like a saint" before they were both deported to their death. Reinach and his wife somehow got out, but his brother Léon and his wife Béatrice, née Camondo, and their two children were killed. Her friends Jacques and Jeanne Helbronner, members of another prominent Jewish family, had also been murdered. "Lucie de Langlade will never come back nor will the Michel Proppers." Mitzi knew that Dr Metzl, the director of the factory, had lost two brothers and a sister, and the Brülls had lost every member on both sides of their family.

Writing from Budapest, Zoltánné Blum was only one of those appealing to Mitzi for financial help. She was the daughter of Dora Springer, a relation though not close. In a dignified tone, she gives the tragic details of her immediate past. In 1944 her mother had been deported to Auschwitz and never returned. Zoltánné's husband had spent several years in labour camps before he was dragged off (*verschleppt* is the word she uses) to Germany and murdered there. Her only brother, an engineer, was sent to Ukraine in 1942 as a slave labourer, and she has had no word from him since. Acquiring false papers, she had survived deportation but

everything in her home had been stolen, and she'd got back
the hairdressing salon she ran but not its most important
contents. Nothing indicates whether Mitzi responded by
sending money.

In the autumn she and Frank caught the Golden Arrow
to Paris. At the station Elie was waiting, along with Max
"green with emotion" and Adrian who once more happened
to be in France. The flat in the rue de Surène had been
recovered, and Bubbles and Lily joined them there. "We all
drank, ate, talked and kissed till 2.15 in the morning. It was
all very very lovely." Just released from a prisoner of war camp,
Robert was once again her butler and his wife Paulette the
lady's maid. Also originally from Montreuil, her chauffeur
Harlé had spent the war working at the factory and was at
her service. Being driven in the nearby rue François I a few
days later, she couldn't help remembering the van den
Brecks who had entertained her and Eugène in their house
in that street, "among their charming things and wonderful
food. She starved to death in a German camp and he was
tortured to death."

To go back to central Europe was out of the question.
She learnt from Alan that Meidling was in a fearful state. In
the park were graves of German soldiers. Certain trees carried
emotional associations; they had been felled. The house was
badly damaged, and its interior degraded with pictures of
Hitler and photographs from its days as a school for Gauleiters.
In a letter in English, unsigned, therefore probably a translation, an advisor comments in dismay that when he was
admitted to her service, "you could not guess that all the
property in Central Europe was doomed." If Meidling was
not soon sold it might become too expensive a liability and
would have to be given away. The Social Democrats in government were as intransigent as "the worst communists...."

In order to appease the people big conspicuous properties are taxed in a drastic way."

Alan quoted Franz the old butler at Meidling, "Such an end to a beautiful life with the Frau Baronin." Writing for herself, she is restrained, "It does hurt a bit." The Gestapo had stored the Meidling furniture and possessions in numbered containers in the Salzburger salt mines of Altaussee; these were returned to Paris two years later. Alan had seen the Red Army and passed on to Mitzi his fears about Soviet intentions in central Europe. At Lesvár, "commissars have told our people that if they complain to Pokorny or Alan they will be shot. The Russian officer who insisted on riding Trissolin, the 1940 Budapest Derby winner, was thrown, drew his revolver and shot the horse." Pokorny was speaking about an indemnity of six million dollars, but she had no such expectation.

20 November 1945, she writes, was one of the happiest days of her life. Harlé drove her and Max to Maisons-Alfort. "As I walked into the bureau of my beloved factory all the workmen were there to welcome me.... I was given lovely flowers and then the senior workman, my dear old Dubois at 93 still looking 50 read the speech of welcome. Too touching for words. He spoke of poor Pollack and others killed in the war. Only since I was among them did I truly feel at home." At that same moment she learnt that damp had destroyed numerous volumes of her diaries buried for safety at Montreuil. She always felt that masterpieces had been lost. However, "Royaumont seemed more like home to me than ever before." In the visitors' book on 2 December, she wrote a paragraph in French thanking Eduardo and Max, Marcel and Renée and Rimbert for preserving and embellishing everything, ending, "Royaumont made me understand that we are as one in our thankfulness and our

affections." She signed "Mummy" in English. "So happy to be in the family way again," is Frank's contribution.

In post-war letters to Mitzi, Alan describes how he had to go to Sheffield to be demobilised, and the correspondence he was having with the Foreign Office and the Treasury about visas and permissions and finances. In October 1946, about to start at the *Times Literary Supplement*, he tells her rather snarkily about Poppy that "Madame decided to feel better." This allows them to stay put at Castle Hill although, "I suspect there are physical causes which ought to be taken in hand." At that same moment Poppy was telling her mother, "Happily I feel better having come out of a rather bad crisis and I still don't know if physique or morale was the cause of it." Alan, she adds, was well and everyone was enthusiastic about his translation of Hofmannsthal's libretto of *Der Rosen-kavalier*, which he'd just completed. In an undated note in pencil, she says she is haunted by fear of a relapse, "it is so very frightening but I must try to calm myself."

Poppy's letters from that period usually begin with an excuse for not writing often enough. Then in June 1947, "Lots of gossip, we've been rather social." Pearl Diver, Geoffroy and Lulu de Waldner's horse, had just won the Derby, and Poppy had made fifty pounds with the bookies. She and Alan spent one weekend with Eddy Sackville-West at Knole, and another at Buscot with Gavin Faringdon; Alan had given a dinner party for the Romanian Princess Anne-Marie Callimachi; the cocktail party of their friends Honor and Vere Pilkington had been amusing; they had taken Cécile de Rothschild to dine at Somerhill and she had afterwards wondered if she shouldn't regret having refused Harry's hand in marriage.

Granny saw to it that the *vie de château* was restored straightaway at Royaumont. Every morning the household, one by one, paid respects to her, in a personal visit that might last a quarter of an hour or longer. In the second part of the morning's ceremony, I was supposed to go to the Chambre des Fleurs where Frank would be in bed. He'd urge me to sit down next to him but some sixth sense kept me away. A governess gave lessons to Elly, and I might join them in the schoolroom. Raymond the groom came out riding with me along the sandy paths through the woods to the Gros Chêne. We'd go to meets of the local stag hunt, the Rallye Vallière, Max impeccable in its royal-blue colours with gold braid and Lily riding side-saddle. Sometimes at the end of the day the huntsmen assembled on the terrace of the house to sound their horns. Stashed away in the stable block, the Pères, were ancient unmanageable penny-farthings. Magnificent Percheron cart-horses ploughed the fields. When they were let loose to drink in the stream that ran at the edge of the farm, their huge hoofs clattered on the cobbles with a noise like gunshots. In that same stream women washed sheets, scrubbing and slapping the wet linen on a cement incline. One Christmas, everyone from the château and the farm gathered in the yard to take part in the slaughter of a pig. The bladder, a sagging white balloon amid all the blood, was blown up and kicked about like a football.

In the unusually cold winter of 1947 the three lakes froze over so we could walk across them, setting off cracks that thundered through the ice. When I turned back in case the ice gave way, Frank took hold of me, pressing me tightly against him and not letting go until we had reached the far side. One evening we were gathering downstairs for dinner and Frank was missing. He had to be sent for. Entering the drawing room, he fell on the floor, drunk, in front of everyone. Robert helped him back upstairs and a furious Mitzi had his place removed from the dining table.

In the park, a landscaped expanse of water reaches almost up to the side of the house. A small island has a picturesque folly on it, a faux hermit's cave. Staying in the house, Adrian took to the ice one arctic morning on this scenic rink, and gave a championship display of skating, leaping, pirouetting, reversing faster and faster. Double-jointed, he could bend one foot round his neck, and spin on the other foot while lowering himself into a ball like a human hedgehog right down on the ice. By the time he reached this finale, the whole household was leaning out of the windows, cheering and applauding.

The abbey is a couple of minutes away on foot. Its owners Henri and Isabel Gouin had the highest artistic and musical taste. They had an outstanding collection of manuscript scores that had belonged to François Lang, Isabel Gouin's brother and a pianist compared to Dinu Lipatti. Denounced in Vichy France, he had been deported and murdered in Auschwitz. Famous intellectuals and musicians wandered through the immense refectory and other rooms set aside for a cultural foundation with a programme of lectures and concerts. In the part of the abbey reserved for the family were Marie-Christine and Françoise, the Gouin daughters, and the numerous pretty girls they were always inviting. Philip, Elly and I had the run of the place; we used even to roller-skate echoingly round and round the medieval cloister.

For two summers in the aftermath of the war and the heyday of ration-cards, I caught up with Philip and Elly in Switzerland. The Spanish diplomatic service had repaired Eduardo's career by posting him consul in Zurich. The train went straight through, Poppy rubbed it in that I had only to sit tight until Eduardo and Bubbles met me at Interlaken. So at Zurich I stayed alone in an empty carriage reading the Sherlock Holmes stories. Night fell. The train at last crept into a shed, and there the cleaners found me. The stationmaster telephoned a frantic Bubbles and put me on the right train.

The Weisses Kreuz Hotel in Klosters was an escape from

food coupons. Once more, there were as many bananas as could be eaten. Elly and I worked a racket in the best pâtisserie; an attractive little girl, she distracted the men behind the counter while I filled my pockets with sweets. Before dinner one day we made ourselves sick, the truth came out, and Eduardo marched us up to the shop to confess. The Tour de Suisse bicycle race was coming through Klosters and at lunch that day Eduardo and Philip had an argument about the merits of Fausto Coppi, the champion. Suddenly father and son, both so self-contained, were shouting at one another, and the whole dining room fell silent to enjoy it.

Now and again I caught hints that Poppy wanted me to spend as much time as possible with her family in order to get me away from Alan and his habitual indulgence. Rules and discipline were not for him. He seemed to be able effortlessly to remake the world in his own image. Asked to do anything practical, he would say, "Send for a man." In the pantry was a large terracotta bowl of salt water in which eggs could be preserved indefinitely. When a mouse fell in and swam around desperately, Alan took one look and Mr Carter had to be fetched to hoick it out and break its neck.

Conversation was Alan's medium. In a voice beautifully modulated, he made his point indirectly, through anecdote. He would cap and improve other people's stories with an exaggeration that was an art form. "He doesn't dwell in the palace of truth," was the phrase he attached to others though its reference to himself was obvious. His vocabulary had idiosyncracies such as jinken for chicken, barouche or bolide for a car, puddocks or puds for hands, presumably quoting Robert Herrick. An outing or a party was a junket, and either as a verb or a noun smell was "niff." A recurrent simile was, "he ran like a lamplighter." In idioms surviving from the Edwardian era, "dewdrop" was his synonym for compliment,

"the Place" for lavatory, and "conniption" signified an outburst of irritation. "Don't vex me," was how he insisted gen-
erously on stopping someone else picking up the bill in a
restaurant. A few affected pronunciations, for instance "wes-
kit" for waistcoat, "Millen" for Milan, and once something
like "doocut" for dovecote, had a comic effect. "Beim Coquet-
tieren sind die Englishwomen sehr handicappiert," was a sentence he claimed to have heard one Austrian say to another.

To Alan, I was Auguste, pronounced as though French
although it was shorthand from the German nursery song,
"Ach du liebe Augustine, du bist so schön." Schubert was a
favourite composer and in another mode some piece of music
by Scriabin seemed to shake the room. To us he played songs
from a Victorian album, one of which had the title, "The
policeman with the India-rubber boots." Another had a jolly
chorus, "We'll join the glad throng that goes laughing along,
and we'll all go a-hunting today." When the three of us came
home from *Annie Get Your Gun*, he asked what we had liked
about the musical, sat at the piano and played it through.
My admiration for his gifts was boundless.

Another pastime was to scrutinize the houses advertised
for sale in *Country Life* and fantasize about their suitability
for us. Driving anywhere in the country, he and Poppy
might turn in past a lodge that looked like an approach to
grandeur, ring the front doorbell of the house at the end of
the drive and spin some story to justify having a look round.
"Pillars and stucco" was his shorthand for the indispensable
architectural features that he was seeking for himself but
never found. More than once, we climbed into the park of
Finchcocks, the home of Denys Finch-Hatton, immortalized
in *Out of Africa* by Baroness Blixen (writing as Isak Dinesen).
The house was abandoned, ridden with dry rot. As we pic-
nicked in the long grass that grew up to the classical façade,

Alan was already imagining what it would be like to be the owner and how we were to find the money to buy it. "I'll see you a Lady yet," he used to say in make-believe to Poppy. She had a character strong enough to make him do things he didn't want to, for instance to get down to writing. One evening in Castle Hill I suddenly heard him hammering on the door of the dressing room where he was supposed to be working. I'm an adult, he began shouting, let me out, you can't lock me in. "I will unlock," Poppy answered, "but only when you've finished your article and slipped it under the door so I can see it."

By the time I passed Common Entrance and in September 1948 went on from Beachborough to Eton, Alan had become editor of the *Times Literary Supplement.* A journal of reviews of this kind offers opportunities for the ambitious and unscrupulous to make or break reputations. An article by F. R. Leavis in the June 1951 issue of his journal *Scrutiny* has the title "Mr Pryce-Jones, the British Council and British Culture." The parts of this equation are not equal and the charge is false that Alan was promoting "the unanimities of the *New Statesman*, the Sunday papers and the BBC." In his rather cumbersome wording, Leavis was accusing those in charge of these outlets of running a racket promoting each other. Alan's literary tastes were too wide for that, and savoir-vivre usually saved him from literary quarrelling. Looking out of the window of the office in Printing House Square, however, he noticed a lorry off-loading packing cases containing the many volumes of the Maoist *New China Encyclopedia.* He had them re-addressed to Dr Leavis at Downing College, Cambridge, and sent a letter asking Leavis for ten thousand words by the following Thursday. That was the story he told, at any rate, and Edith Sitwell, at daggers drawn with Leavis, took great pleasure in it. (It says something about Poppy that Edith Sitwell kept inviting her to lunch and gave her a volume of her poems with a particularly warm inscription.)

To avoid commuting from Tonbridge, Alan rented a pied-à-terre on the top floor of the house in Little Venice of the composer Lennox Berkeley and his wife Freda. Patrick Kinross lived in the same street. Alan fitted Poppy into a social life of people with much the same invitations as themselves to dinners and dances, and much the same attendance at the theatre and the opera. They sailed on the *Queen Mary* to the United States and returned talking about Edmund Wilson and Louis Auchincloss. "You do know, don't you, that your father is the fourth most intelligent man in England," Tony Quinton, the philosopher and future President of Trinity College, Oxford, was to say to me before I knew that this was how he liked to talk. I believed it.

Away either at school or at Royaumont, I was unaware of the life of Castle Hill ebbing. In the period of transition from one house to another Mitzi's diaries fill with complaints. "Poppy took it out of me on Sunday morning," she wrote. "Poppy says Alan is killing himself because they need lots of money to live the right way among the people he needs to meet." Much as she would like to help, "Alas! I cannot do it, my head is no more up to it, nor are my nerves and nor is my cheque book."

In the Easter holidays of 1951, Poppy came to Royaumont. She stood in the doorway of my room and held on to me, to say that she had had a miscarriage. I would have had a brother. In her papers is a page with the heading "A Letter to a miscarried child."

My little one, why have you left me? Where is your soul? Oh! The years of longing and strange solitude before you came! Sometimes, as now, I feel like breaking, my body is useless, my mind weak, my courage nil, my heart torn to shreds. I would like to protect you always, that my heart and soul are also with you and that all that is in me (alas so little) of good is yours to surround and shield you for ever. Darling, if perfect love can be given, or could be measured by the degree of sorrow that is now mine, then you have all which I am able to give.

Another page runs:

> How can I escape? Why do I hate? Why can I not think of anything except myself, my feelings and my sorrow. Please take away this hate which is insupportable. Why is it that because I am in pain I need to inflict it on others? I fear the present and I *dread* the future and the immediate past haunts me like an unending nightmare, visions pass in my mind at a terrific speed, and all alas the same. What is it that I am seeking which I have not learnt to understand? No experience seems to improve me, I am worthless and long to disappear.

The final word of this cry from the heart is in French, "*Pitié*."

Afterwards Camille Dreyfus and other of Poppy's doctors were to tell me that her cancer was the result of the miscarriage; others say this is medically unsound. At any rate in that same year she found and arranged the house we were to move into, 27 Cavendish Close, the end one of five freestanding in a secluded cul-de-sac in St John's Wood. Three houses away was Dame Myra Hess whose piano-playing we could sometimes overhear. Monty Woodhouse, once the youngest colonel in the army and then a Conservative M.P., was four houses away. Poppy had the large house with lots of servants that had once been her fantasy. The chef came from Lord Mountbatten. Doris Gibbins had risen from housemaid to housekeeper for Lord and Lady Carnarvon at Highclere; her divorced husband had been King George's chauffeur in the war. Arthur Briggs, the butler, also came from Highclere. A quiet humorous man, he could be persuaded to do a turn imitating Lord Galloway putting on his overcoat. Arriving from Eton to the new house for the first time, I found we had a servants' hall. "The servants seem excellent, really excellent. Hard-working, nice, competent and out to economise," Alan wrote to Mitzi on Christmas Eve 1951. He is also soothing, "I find Thérèse as well as could be hoped – not tired or shaken or gloomy – and all her doctors are pleased. I shall try to see Mayer later in the week. Of course she has her moments of Angst, but nothing to what they are when she is quite well!" A month later, about to leave Castle Hill finally, he tells Mitzi that Poppy is showing "an unwillingness to come back into ordinary life. I think she feels, as she felt in 1936, that to be ill is a kind of haven, and that to be well demands too much of one … it is perfectly normal to be rather low after a ray treatment – but there it is, she feels that everything is pointless and impossible." After which he gave a spirited account of the lying-in-state of King George VI at Windsor, complete with gossip about the Dukes of Kent, Norfolk and Marlborough on this occasion. And he lets drop that he had seen me at Eton and found me busy and cheerful. "Van Oss was delighted with him and the day passed off very well indeed."

Jessie had been let into the secret that Poppy had cancer and was feeling sick from the radiation she had to undergo in the American Hospital in Paris. Jessie wrote to her from Castle Hill on 7 January 1952, "I'm hoping and praying that every day and in every way you are better, and am pleased to know you have spent a happy Christmas in your family. Here it was awfully dull, I put a little holly in the vases for luck but everything seemed to say 'Where is she?' Yes! Where is she and how is she?" Jessie goes on, "You must feel fed up with all this treatment." Next week they are taking up the carpets: "I'm getting on with it, Hickmott helping, a little every day. In a way I'm glad you are not here for you would insist on doing it all yourself." In a subsequent letter she writes, "it worries me to know when you are 'down and out' and I'm not there to look after your small wants, although I suppose you are better off without me bossing round with hot water bottles and powder." Then leaving Castle Hill for the last time, "The strife is o'er, the battle won, as they sang at the King's funeral, which means we have cleared out of the farm. It was not so terrible. Alan's attitude seems to say 'Hands off Cavendish Close,' so I did not even suggest it." But she finishes, "All these changes make my old heart cry." Quite right in her perception of Alan, she could not have imagined that he was writing to Mitzi at the moment of moving house, "Please God Jess will move too, and in the direction of Royaumont. That noble woman has become as high a test of my character as I could conceive and it is only my love of you all that has kept me from murder and suicide every day."

Back at Royaumont, Jessie tells Poppy "I had a very nice letter from David, said he was well and was writing a story for a book, so I hope as it is his first he will be successful but if not, then he must try again. I often wonder what he will do in life." And then this – surely evidence of greatness of soul after a lifetime of sacrifice on our behalf was being brought to an end with such little consideration: "Please don't send me any more thank yous. I know I've done my best for you, and my biggest worry now is that you find someone sympathetic who will take an interest in their work and look after your small wants which are so much more necessary to you than the big ones. I'm also grateful to you and Alan for putting up with an old frump for so long. So we're even, shake hands and say no more about it – either way."

No expense was spared in doing up Cavendish Close. Poppy employed Ernst Freud, father of the painter Lucian, as her architect. When Edmund Wilson dined there, he recorded in his diary *The Fifties* that "the large house and the splendour" puzzled him until he heard that Poppy was "some sort of Rothschild" – which was wrong. He went on to note that Alan obviously "loves living in this way" – and this was right. It wasn't long before Alan was writing to tell Mitzi that he was at the top of the social scale. Princess Margaret and the Edens were coming to dinner, "Rather a bore, because of police and extras," adding a telling throwaway, "it is *so* expensive living at no. 27."

In the few months that Poppy lived in Cavendish Close, she was too unwell to enjoy it. Suffering constant pain, she spent much of the time in bed. A ball was due to be held at Hever, the home of Lord Astor, owner of *The Times* and therefore ultimately Alan's employer and also a relation through Violet Astor. George Dix, an art dealer from New York with feline if not feminine manners, had invited himself to stay. That evening, Poppy had still not got up, and I was sitting on the edge of her bed when these two men came into the room to say that they were off to Hever. It was a white-tie occasion and they had dressed up for it. Poppy implored Alan to stay with her but the two waved themselves away and hurried down the staircase. Then she sobbed her heart out. Later that same evening she told Doris Gibbins (who repeated it ever afterwards) that she had not long to live, and made her promise to look after Alan and me.

Around that time, she put down on paper for Alan the position she found herself in.

> I am deeply grateful for your great kindness, your patience and especially your wish to try and make things right again

but it just does not work, I fear. I am better when away from you and quite alone. This trying to pretend is hopeless and a strain and impossible and it is just wearing you down and does me no good at all. I know I am unreasonable, that I am ill etc, but this crisis has not been brought on by the recent events but as you know has been brewing for some time. All this comes from me. You have nothing to reproach yourself with, I have always interpreted life the wrong way and when events have been against me thought it was a personal offence. David's unwished for birth was the first terrible crisis and my love for him has been never what I had hoped to feel for my children because of it (I know that my nervous breakdown was due to that.) The only moment when you did misunderstand me was during the war when I wanted another child, that might have brought my complete balance back and fulfilled what now never will be. I am bored by my life. I pretended at "playing houses," I pretended that my home my garden etc filled my life but they did not and my loneliness grew and grew until it was unbearable. Your life, your friends, your interests don't (it is my fault) give me that steady feeling which I search for – and now I realise that I had hoped that the baby would give all this to me and of course it was not so. I was selfish and was not thinking of it but of me and now that I have lost it I realise that it would not help and that something somewhere is broken and wrong. I can't start life again with you. I am deeply unhappy and don't wish to ruin your life and make you miserable too ... for the time being everything you say is wrong and jars on my nerves. My trust and confidence in you is now different, perhaps that is the reason why your help means so little to me. I can't remain trapped and pinned down nor even to start again. I just want to be alone.

That evening in her room, I had wondered whether she was making a scene, crying because she was feeling left out of the ball at Hever. I had no idea what she was really going through. No idea either that she was about to leave for Paris to be with her family and might never return. No idea that she was weighing her despair in these letters to Alan: "You seem like a dummy. Your life is filled by your work, David is independent. I feel intensely lonely, exiled here or in England, bored by your friends." No idea that she would be dreading seeing Dreyfus because there was no escaping what he would say. No idea that in the American Hospital at half past seven in the morning on 1 October 1952 she was writing to her mother, "I have passed my crisis and greatly regret that you were not only the witness but to some extent a victim. Sometimes things seem too much for one but I suppose that resignation comes in the end. In any case I have no fear of operations which is a great blessing." No idea that in spite of her clarity about Alan and his friends she had one last plea for him on the eve of the operation, "Please be there when I open an eye, I shall then feel life is still worth trying to keep a while longer though alas I have no more hope for the future." And she tacks completely, to make her peace. "But we must never mind as our existence has not only been wonderful but so exceptional in every way that we can't feel too bitter or reproachful of our fate." She signs, "thank you for your immense kindness, your sad old Pigling."

Sixteen

One's Rothschild Cousins

Who knows what goes on in the head of a Rothschild in Paris?
SHOLEM ALEICHEM

COAL WAS RATIONED in September 1948 when I went to Eton and each boy could light the fire in his room only once a week. Ice formed on the water in the hand basin and I had chilblains on my hands and feet. Soon after arriving, I came shivering into my room to find a note on my desk: "Your mother is a dirty Jewess." The boy in the room next door came from a well-known banking family, I recognised his handwriting and went to find the housemaster. Reading the note, Oliver Van Oss gave one of his deep chuckles, then sent for the culprit and said, quite possibly improvising, that there were now three people of Jewish origins in the room.

Known by his initials as OVO, Oliver was an exceptional schoolmaster, genuinely interested in bringing out the potential of the boys in his care. Open-minded and generous, widely read and an artist at heart, he was ready to break the rules in a good cause. In the Easter holidays of 1949 Alan had received a proof copy of George Orwell's *1984* for the *Times Literary Supplement* to review. The excitement in the house prompted me to start reading it but I had time only for the astonishing opening pages. Returning to Eton, I went to the school library to ask Mr Cattley, the librarian, for the book. He was a bald stooping crotchety old man straight out of Dotheboys Hall. "I shall report you for asking for filth," was his response. That evening, OVO came to find me in my room to say, "You must forgive Mr Cattley, he is a very simple soul."

I was familiar with the old Eton Calendar that printed the list of Alan's prizes and I thought the right thing was to earn a longer list. At the end of every term, my parents would ask how I had done and their faces would fall when I told them about winning this, that and the other prize, not just for English or French but for neglected subjects like divinity. As an antidote, they arranged social occasions for me until after a teenage dance for no discernable reason I was sick all over the floor in Lennox Berkeley's house and Poppy in her nightdress had to clean up. OVO told them that in time I would put this mark-grubbing to adult purposes and make a fortune as a banker. He nicknamed me Monsieur le Maire. One term, I wrote a short story in French for him, and his comment in red ink, "This is the real thing," encouraged me to see myself as a writer. Others in the school at the time who were to become writers included the prolific Andrew Sinclair, Bamber Gascoigne, the mastermind of a television game that popularised a repeated phrase "Your Starter for Ten," sociologists Garry Runciman and Benedict Anderson, the underrated novelist and travel writer Philip Glazebrook, Duff Hart-Davis, John Hemming explorer and historian of Latin America, Michael Holroyd, who by himself banged a little black rubber ball up and down in the squash courts and has brought out massive biographies researched and written with the same solitary engagement – industrious but hardly a match for the Orwell and Connolly generation. At the moment when I must have bettered Alan's list of prizes, the Calendar decided to save money by no longer printing the footnotes that recorded this voluntary competition.

The Eton Society, colloquially known as Pop, gave boys at the top of the school the freedom to select themselves as what in effect were prefects. It was a sort of club in embryo, with a room of its own. The twenty or so members had the power to fine and even cane boys for minor offences, and they were allowed the privilege of wearing clothes that dis- tinguished their status, most visibly a fancy waistcoat when everybody else had to make do with a black one. Since then, authority everywhere has been busy centralising power in all manifestations for fear that it might fall into uncontrollable hands, and even Pop has long since been reformed to exclude anyone who might get in just because he was popular. Election in my day meant the approval of my peers, and suddenly, badly, I wanted it. Everyone at Royaumont became anxious on my behalf. If I got in, Elie de Rothschild promised to give me a waistcoat the like of which nobody else would have. I got in, and a waistcoat with show-off patterns of gold, green and purple duly arrived, chosen and made by Dior. Uncle Elie had entered my life.

In spite of the breach in the generation of their fathers, Rothschild and Fould-Springer children had been at the same dancing classes in Paris. In a perfect metaphor for the disruption he was to cause, the young Elie rolled marbles across the floor there. It was said in his favour that he never had the chance to come to terms as an adult with the way of life he could expect. His early twenties were spent as a prisoner of war either in a camp in Lübeck or in Colditz and then he returned to an essentially dynastic marriage that had been celebrated *in absentia*. He and Liliane had hardly had time for any courtship.

"Elie came to see me," in November 1945 Mitzi recorded the first of innumerable mutual testings of their intentions, "and for one hour we talked business, the [illegible word] account, the factory, Czechoslovakia, Export and Import came to be spoken about, each question one after another. He said, 'I see that your adoring children are afraid of you with reason, you are the only one with whom one can talk business. The others never have the time for it.' How true! He is the first member of my family with whom it is a rest and a comfort to talk business. What a help! Elie, the son of Robert, has very quickly got into my and my angel's hearts. He is sweet and capable and too adorable with Lily." From beginning to end, he played her with a rather perfect pitch of humour and intimacy. For instance he addresses a letter of 26 April 1946 concerning some equipment for the factory to "My very dear, very worthy and very respected Mother-in-law." The opening sentence is, "Your least desires are orders for me," and he closes using the second person singular, "*Ton gendre préféré*," your favourite son-in-law. All her children stuck to the more impersonal form of the second person plural.

A year or so after the end of the war Elie invited Alan and Poppy for a cruise on a yacht in Danish waters. Separated for so long, Poppy and Lily had to renew what had been their close relationship, with their husbands to be taken into account. Alan's personality was so different that he and Elie were never likely to be close. Realistic though Alan was, at the same time he took snobbish pleasure in the association with that family and the material that it provided for gossip, so much so that years later Brian Urquhart, a friend who was the deputy of Dag Hammarskjöld at the United Nations, proposed that Alan ought to give his memoirs the title *One's Rothschild Cousins*.

Few people were in a position to speak to Elie as an equal, but Poppy was one of them. To her, he was the naughty boy she had known in childhood. Liliane was the little sister whom she had in tow. At school, I used to receive letters from her in Paris full of detail about the doings of Liliane and Elie, the state of their marriage and the birth of their children Natty and Nelly. When she fell ill, she suspected she had cancer but the doctors, her mother and her sisters thought it kinder not to spell it out to her. The one person she asked to tell her if her illness was fatal was Elie. On the advice of the doctors and the family, he too concealed the truth. It was to his house that she went to die. Had she lived, he used to say, everything would have been different. What he meant was that he had very mixed feelings towards the Fould-Springer family into which he had married, and Poppy might have been the ideal go-between.

Good-looking and fit, Elie had panache. His clothes were hand-made; it was immediately clear that nothing but the best would do for him. You could also sense whether or not he was in the house, and you could further tell his mood by the shouting and swearing and the dirty talk, or alternatively a menacing drop in the voice. The impulse to be generous might suddenly break through. My parents had never thought to give me pocket money. Elie had in his pocket a gold clip containing a wad of French franc notes whose denomination had many zeroes at that inflationary time. Obviously having thought about it, he'd peel a few of them off for me on the understanding that I'd be going to the Place Pigalle and we would then discuss the women available there. Bought as investments, modern paintings were stored on racks in the attic of his Paris house. In the course of looking at this proto-museum one day, he suddenly pulled out a small but valuable abstract painting by Fautrier and gave it to Alan who passed it on to me.

Money was the source of Elie's power, and he knew it. My father was very rich, he said to me one day, repeating that "very" half a dozen times with rising emphasis. The knowledge that he could pay for anything governed everyone's responses to him. The whole carry-on was a function of his surname and his fortune. Writing from Royaumont on Christmas Eve 1951, Alan gave Mitzi a picture of things. Max was "in excellent form: he gets on very well with David, who answers him. The exact contrary is true with Elie, who is at his most insufferable when David is about, though well-meaning to David. But the noise, the curses, the horse-play, depress David beyond all expression, *et alors la chose risque de se gâter* [and then there's a risk of things going wrong]. One has to be fully grown in order to take the Rothschild family in one's stride."

At the time when Elie was keeping the secret of Poppy's cancer, he put himself out to be helpful. He had a Bentley, and drove me in it through Germany. He took the trouble to show me Ulm and Augsburg and finally Hitler's Eagle's Nest at Berchtesgaden. The chalet he had rented high above Scharnitz in the Tyrol had the rare quality of being simple and luxurious. In my turn, I acquired the Austrian fancy dress of lederhosen and a green felt hat adorned with a *gamsbart*. Out stalking, Albert Ragg, the head keeper's eldest son, led the way up the mountains and I shot a chamois and a roebuck. Their horns were duly mounted as trophies.

Had Poppy been in good health I would surely not have been dispatched to sink or swim in this setting. I spent a couple of summers at Deauville with Elie's elder sister Diane, her husband Anatol Mühlstein and their three daughters, Natalie, Anka and Tototte. In the afternoon we took our place in stands to applaud Elie playing matches of polo that he was almost sure to win thanks to the Argentine professionals on his team. (He was playing some years later when a ball hit his eye. The courage and humour with which he accepted the loss of sight was certainly a facet of his complicated character. On occasions he took out his glass eye for the effect that had on those watching.) Another summer I stayed in the south of France in a house near Saint-Raphaël belonging to Elie's other sister Cécile. Victor Rothschild, head of the English branch of the family, was there with his wife Tess and his son Jacob, an Eton friend and contemporary, also destined to come up to Oxford on the same day as me. Victor, a Cambridge scientist then investigating the reproduction of sea urchins, suggested as though it was harmless that Jacob scrape some specimens off the rock from which we used to swim. He appeared unmoved when the luckless Jacob surfaced with so many prickles all over him that he finished in hospital. "We Rothschilds," as one of Victor's memorable generalisations has it, "are quick to give and take offense."

One winter on my way to ski with other Eton friends, I stayed with my grandmother in her Paris flat. In her archive, a typical memorandum from Mr Hickman notes that in his pre-war style Alan was asking him to forward to me five hundred Swiss francs. Hearing that I had no anorak, Cécile had lent me hers. In due course I came back to the Paris flat and returned the anorak. That same evening, my grandmother's butler Robert informed me that Elie had telephoned, and I was to be at his house in the Avenue Marigny at seven o'clock the following morning. The walk from door to door took perhaps ten minutes. Nobody was about in the winter dark. With ceremony, Monsieur Henri, the concierge, opened the main door and handed me to some other retainer, who with equal ceremony escorted me upstairs into a drawing room with an inlaid cabinet along one wall. The curtains were still closed. Elie came in with his dressing gown flapping around him. You borrowed my sister's anorak, he said. Yes. And you returned it without having it dry-cleaned. Yes, there wasn't time, I have to go back to Eton today. Whereupon he landed me a punch in the face so unexpected that it knocked me to the ground as he left the room with his dressing-gown still flapping.

Laversine is to the French Rothschilds what Waddesdon is to the English Rothschilds, a proclamation in the form of architecture. In the days of his parents Elie had lived there, but after the war the house became a police college. Laversine is a short drive from Royaumont, and Elie took me there to join three or four other guns to shoot rabbits of which there were a great many. I made a clean kill in front of me with no beater anywhere near. Standing to one side, Elie was not in a position to see my shot but began to shout that one of the beaters had been in the line of fire. I protested. He ordered me to go and sit in the car. In front of everyone he came for me, but this time I ducked and he caught my neck. He had an American station wagon, with a section at the back for his labrador. We drove away in silence. On the way home, as luck would have it, the dog was sick. Elie stopped the car and said, "Clean it up." There wasn't a cloth, I had to use my hands.

Poppy's coffin was removed from the Jewish section of Père Lachaise and reburied in the Catholic cemetery at Viarmes. At the best of times, that cemetery's carefully sanded paths, inscriptions and commemorative photographs set in granite or marble, have a lugubrious piety. A religious ceremony was out of the question. While we were standing around the grave, Elie behind me suddenly barked, "Stop snivelling!" and gave me a push. I slipped. It had been raining, and now wet sand was streaky on the overcoat I had to wear at school.

What was up with him? It is possible that he saw himself in the role of the father I ought to have but didn't. He perceived Alan as an intellectual, mostly contemptible, sexually suspect, spending money but incapable of earning it, and I had to be stopped from developing along that track. Psychotherapist that she is, Elly has a theory that he was hitting me to repress homosexual feelings to which he could never admit and may even not have known about. Baby Winston Churchill (as he was known to distinguish him from his grandfather) had the simpler view that Elie was a bully for whom the humiliation of the young was natural. His mother Pamela, by then the wife of Averell Harriman, was a *grande horizontale* of her day, and sometime mistress of Elie. Baby Winston could not forget Elie's various devices for getting him out of the way so that he could be alone with Pamela. Particularly patronising was the gift one day of a very expensive camera that he was supposed to go out of doors with and photograph the streets.

After Laversine it was a comedown for Elie to be living in the Faisanderie at Royaumont, even though it had been done up as if it were a luxurious country house rather than a cottage. Inside the entrance is a small space, too small to be a lobby let alone a hall, and on the wall there is a rack with an array of riding crops and whips. In a recurrent dream I used to see myself grabbing one of these whips and slashing at Elie, consciously turning his possessions against him. Over time, contradictions piled up so you never could guess quite where you stood with him. In the course of having a summer job in Paris, Candida rang up and Elie happened to answer, saying, "What do you want? Money, a car?" No, she said, just to talk to my aunt. (Yet he was generous to servants, and they and sometimes their children were employed year in, year out, with almost tribal fidelity. Doucet, the butler, had been with him since the war, first in the Avenue Marigny, and afterwards in the almost equally grandiose house Elie bought in the rue Masseran, not far from the Invalides. In the 1968 upheavals, Doucet made an entry into the drawing room with the words, "Monsieur le Baron aura besoin de son revolver," and there the requisite weapon lay shiny on a silver tray.)

Violence, verbal or physical, was certainly close to the surface. He genuinely liked animals and handled them expertly, but one day at the Faisanderie a dog of his, a huge and fierce Bouvier de Flandres, jumped up towards Elly. The dog was on a chain and couldn't do harm. She has never forgotten how he thrashed it to within an inch of its life. When she was sixteen or so, she tells me, he said to her, "*Je sais que tu sais que je suis fou*," I know that you know I am mad. Had he not been who he was, she thinks, he would never have gotten away with his behaviour.

Elie held his drink pretty well but vodka before the meal was liable to fire up his loud, coarse and insulting language. At a lunch in the Faisanderie, he jeered at Max as a homosexual. As though he wasn't hearing, Max went on chewing his food in his usual methodical manner. By then, Max had made his share of Royaumont over to Natty, and given Elie power of attorney over his accounts, presumably hoping that this abdication of independence would bring him a quiet life. At the table were Philip, Elly and I, and it was evidence of Elie's projection of power that we too said nothing, allowing ourselves to be humiliated.

The worst mistake of his life, he'd repeat when the spirit moved him, had been to come to Royaumont and be mixed up with the precious Fould-Springers. Rude to Liliane sometimes to her face, sometimes behind her back, he could be scornful of her taste, her friends, her appearance and her family. Elie's attitude to *boiseries*, pictures and furniture that any museum would have been glad to acquire, was at times proudly possessive and at other times careless and even contemptuous as though Liliane was obliging him to show off. Where she was the butt, Liliane's tactic was to remain passive. Where others were under attack, she found some way to associate with him. In a core conspiracy they override their disunity by uniting against others. Stories nevertheless came back about how she had stood into the small hours feverish with jealousy outside the house of Pamela Harriman or some other woman whom Elie had taken up. Her sorrows were wrapped in secrecy but she did once let drop to Elly, "You

have never been humiliated in public by your husband."
A maxim of hers was, "Money doesn't bring happiness, but
it allows you to cry more comfortably." Wondering why she
put up with it rather than setting up on her own, people easily felt affection for her, and then pity.

A forceful, lawless and very rich man was on the loose.

SEVENTEEN

Radio Toscane

AT THE BEGINNING of November 1952 Grandpa Harry, Mister Colonel, had pneumonia and died as dutifully as he had lived. Mitzi came to his funeral. A few days later, on November 13, Vere replied to condolences from Liliane: "Of course we are all *one* family. We could not possibly have loved you all more. We adore you all, and your precious mother was quite wonderful last Sunday, and I thank God with my whole soul that Beloved Little Poppy is really better from her gland troubles. She has been so *tremendously* gallant, and Alan is so lucky to have such an adorable wife. Unluckily I am frozen, and can neither see, hear, read a letter, write, sleep or rest. And I am so slow and inadequate. I have had about 500 letters and telegrams, but although I write the *whole* of every day not even stopping for a cup of tea, I have only answered about 30." She and Harry, she wrote, had had "47 years of *Perfect* Happiness. I don't think we ever had a disagreement." A fortnight later she was writing to Poppy, "How *blessed* it is that *at last* your Gland Trouble is better, and that you will probably be coming home to your own lovely house." She talked at this emotional pitch, as if underlining and capitalizing her speech. But she had been misled. Poppy had only a few weeks of life left.

Vere's will to live weakened fast. At intervals, she would stay in Cavendish Close where Doris could look after her. Adrian was often at Windsor Castle while Alan pleaded that he had the *Times Literary Supplement* to bring out every week. What was to be done about me in the holidays gave Alan a good deal of trouble. His pursuit of a social life consigned me to a series of suppers alone with Doris. A secondary social life was organised for me. On one occasion, Ivy Compton-Burnett invited me to a meal, and quizzed me for material to put into a novel. Lord Radcliffe, the lawyer who had drawn the partition line between India and Pakistan, also invited me. Lord Birkenhead took me to listen to William Plomer reading his poems.

As soon as he could after the deaths of his father and Poppy, Alan embarked with me on a series of restless trips abroad. First came Mitzi. By a process of eliminating Austria, France and England on political or fiscal grounds, she had settled on Florence. In 1947, in the lobby of the Excelsior Hotel she overheard conversation about a house for sale at Arcetri, a little cluster of unspoilt buildings including Galileo's villa on the hills overlooking the city from the south. On impulse, she bought this house. Communists then painted a hammer and sickle on the main door. They're taking over the country and they'll come to cut your throat, Poppy and Lily both told her, to which she is supposed to have replied, I'd like to see them try.

At this point Alan owned a Bentley, which gave him as much satisfaction as the pre-war Tatra, and as much trouble and expense. Historic monuments could always be visited, he said, but on the way to Mitzi we could tour human monuments who'd soon be disappearing. Douglas Cooper qualified as an art critic and collector rather than a human monument. He was then living in a château difficult to find on little roads halfway down France. His exaggerated manner and mincing voice made him seem to be acting in a pantomime. Reviews in the *TLS* were then unsigned, and under cover of anonymity he pursued vendettas against colleagues and rivals, leaving Alan to smooth things over. John Richardson, his boyfriend, was conventionally dressed except that he was wearing red shoes with high heels.

Next stop was the Villa Mauresque, where Somerset
Maugham and his secretary Alan Searle lived together in
style. With his wrinkled features and speech impediment
that broke up communication, Maugham seemed to be an
antediluvian species. After dinner, he could hardly wait to
play cards. I was in bed when he came into the room as
Bobby Pratt-Barlow had done, to present me with a book, not
Krafft-Ebing but *Don Fernando*, about his travels in Spain.
Maugham made it clear that his admiration of Max Beerbohm, our next human monument, was mixed with envy
because the Incomparable Max had far lower sales but a more
selective reputation. Beerbohm lived modestly in Rapallo,
in a back street out of the way. His companion, Elisabeth
Jungmann, had prepared something to eat, all of which,
Beerbohm said gravely, was home-grown. Still the Edwardian dandy, he was beautifully turned out in an old-fashioned
suit. He led me across a small terrace to his workroom,
opened a cupboard and showed me what he called the false
title pages he had drawn in a number of books to make fun
of them or their authors. Take one, he said. Such was the
care that had gone into these cartoons and the amusement
he derived from them that I felt I couldn't take advantage of
him. I see you don't like them, he said. (I regretted my inhi-
bition all the more when these books were sold off at auction
after his death.) Then we drove on to Lerici to call on Percy
Lubbock, retracing Alan and Poppy's visit there before the
war. Blind, Lubbock had to employ someone to read to him,
and at the time this was Quentin Crewe, himself already suffering from the degenerative condition that cost him his life.

Over the Futa pass as it zigzags from Bologna to Florence, Alan almost crashed the unsuitable Bentley a number
of times. Mitzi had done little to San Martino, a villa in brick
and stone whose jumble testifies to a past that goes back
centuries. Roofs are at several different levels. A fortified

wall encloses a courtyard where the lemon trees blossom in terracotta pots. Externally, huge buttresses against the wall support a squat tower. Indoors, the staircase, lintels and a fireplace are in pietra serena. All that is left of a former farm is a garden and a dozen olive trees. Two gnarled contadini turned up one day to say that as boys they'd driven the cows from here down to the Arno to water.

The last of our human monuments was Bernard Berenson, then the world authority on the high art of Italy. He and Mitzi had a similar psychological evolution. Both wanted to believe they had adopted a new identity so that other people no longer thought of them as Jews but they couldn't be completely sure of success. At Settignano on the far side of Florence, I Tatti housed his library and his pictures. Admirers, acolytes, scholars swarmed around him. With a cashmere shawl around his shoulders and a hat to keep off the sun, Berenson was in a wheelchair in the garden, a great man and conscious of it. At lunch, he sat me next to him, and asked humdrum questions about school. I told him that the Eton Essay Society met in the rooms of the headmaster Robert Birley, and my turn had come to write and read an essay to the members. And what about? The Dreyfus Affair. Berenson raised his voice. Conversation stopped. As a Jew, he said, he had lived and suffered the scandal, and it wasn't a subject for schoolboys. What did I know about it? All I had read was a pot-boiler by some unknown author. Further down the table, someone who could have been Hugh Trevor-Roper sidetracked Berenson with an interjection. Nevertheless the date April 11 1953 is under Berenson's signature on the flyleaf of the copy of *The Italian Painters of the Renaissance* which he presented to me. Alan recommended that instead of the Dreyfus Affair I write up an account of the human monuments. Birley had an immense range of knowledge and enjoyed imparting it, however abstruse. I could see that this first attempt of mine at the higher journalism seemed to him light-weight, snobbish.

At San Martino, Mitzi and Frank had rooms at opposite ends of a corridor. What Alan and I did not know was that they were getting on badly. As from about October 1952 Mitzi's diaries become more and more critical of him. This is unprecedented. Frank, she writes while still in her Paris flat, "made me sit on his knees and pressed me to his heart, [saying] 'you must come and rest with me at San Martino. All will be peace there now as I have finished with that awful drinking.' Frank went ahead there by himself. The day after his return, "He was drunk and fell in the garden. Then quite sober for three days, later going at it hard." Mitzi comes to conclusions: "I suppose now I *have* finished being a fool. I don't go back to live at San Martino alone with him.... If he drinks again now his liver is in this state I suppose it will be the end. An end would be better than the sort of life he is going to have.... When I think of the misery he knows I have, to go and add to it by drinking simply disgusts me." Rejoining Frank in San Martino, she repeats that she would rather return on her own to Paris than stay with him. "This time Frank Wooster has I believe properly finished me off. *Il m'a sûrement coupé bras et jambes.* [He's surely cut off my arms and legs.]... I will not return before he begs my pardon, before I see a small hope that life with him will not kill me." Day after day the tone rises: "So angry at Frank I could not face the thought to see him again ... he'll have all he needs but not me to be unkind to.... I must keep myself fit for more important work." Years were to pass before I heard Harold Acton's story of meeting Frank in the Via Tornabuoni at this point. He was so down in the mouth that I bought him a cocktail at Doney's, Harold said, and he gave me the advice, "Never get married."

It was spring, and we sat out on the terrace at the back of San Martino. At midday, the butler, Giovanni, overweight but always jolly, wheeled drinks out on a trolley. Frank took exception to the jug of tomato juice, saying that "everyone knows" tomato juice is served in bottles. "Are you telling me how to run my house?" Mitzi bridled, whereupon the two of them started shouting. Alan led the way to a bench at the bottom of the garden, where we could hear the noise but not make out the words. Within hours Frank had left for London. In their old stamping ground of the Connaught Hotel, he fell ill. Although only 63, Frank had bronchitis and was dying. The doctor, an old friend of theirs, sent for Mitzi. Now she reproached herself in her diary for having made things worse. For example, "If only I could stop thinking of when I was unkind to him." After his death, she was to have a breakdown and a spell of three weeks under the care of nuns in a *casa di cura* in Florence.

In his lifetime Frank had paid lip-service to religion, but was no church-goer. Worship and theology were not for him, and penitence even less. In the manner of a novelist putting real experience into imaginative form, Mitzi had created a fictional version of herself as someone giving but never receiving love, and now she created a fictional version of Frank. On occasion, often in resorts like Venice or Salzburg, he had given her trinkets, it might be a ring or a brooch, it might be a stone, a medallion, a flower or a leaf, even a letter or photograph. Sixteen in number, these were what she called "Proofs" of divine blessing. She had two handsome and sizable boxes made of dark green leather with an inscription in gilt lettering, "Supernatural Realities As Experienced By Frank And Mary Wooster." Ungrammatical and strictly meaningless phrases of the sort became sacralized. The materialistic, happy-go-lucky Frank was compared to his near namesake Saint Francis of Assisi.

Montesoni is a hilltop a few miles south from San Martino, up an unmade track that leads to a church. Since the war, Harlé the chauffeur had driven Mitzi and Frank between

France and Italy in an Armstrong Siddeley. To preserve the car's sacred association with Frank, she had it buried and immured under the church. A hundred yards away stands a shrine that she had erected to commemorate him. At its centre is a structure in brick, the shape of an altar. She had set into it a safe in white marble about eighteen inches high. On the door of the safe, another example of the linguistics inspired by Frank was incised in large black lettering, "He made souls shine out." Her diaries often record what she took to be illumination, for instance, "To my horror and misery as I returned to my seat I felt a stream of light inside me and it took me above my angel."

A great deal of her time was spent on a high mission that she called, "Unite The Impossible." According to this oxymoron, religions had a common divinity, and once this was acknowledged diversity of belief and worship would be fulfilled in ecumenical harmony. As a promotion, she had the three words printed on Christmas cards and brochures. She pointed to the weather, to vapour trails of aircraft, the flight of birds and many a small coincidence as evidence that Frank was influencing the details of her life as well as the course of world events. Things might appear to be going badly, but that was because human beings were unable to see higher purposes at work. The phrase she invented to register evidently predetermined advances or retreats was "Pushed And Blocked." Every morning, she would mark up articles in the newspapers to be clipped and filed in order to demonstrate that politics and history itself were moving in the approved direction.

At one level she remained her former self, up to date with exchange rates, say, the virtues and vices of statesmen and the publication of new books in at least four languages. She let you know that she was reading Teilhard de Chardin, Simone Weil and Thomas Merton, and corresponding with Roger Schultz, the well-respected Prior of the Protestant seminary of Taizé. Her nose twitched at any conversation bordering on her preoccupations, however, and she would say, almost sing, Ha, H'm, implying that she had insights that you were too blinkered to appreciate. Your eyes will be opened one day, the knowing look on her face indicated. Not knowing where to put this or how to respond, you kept silent and behind her back passed it all off as her signature tune. The grandchildren had a joke that she was broadcasting on Radio Toscane, a very private station.

The emaciated figure of Don Fosco Martinelli, the parish priest, was often in San Martino. He wrote and published little devotional stories for children. While Mitzi was in the *casa di cura* she sent him a blank cheque. Astute enough to post it back to Max with a covering letter, he could be sure that his bona fides was assured and specific requests were granted. Mitzi paid for a *campo*, a playground for the parish children, and she took on the expenses of a young Florentine woman paralysed from polio and hitherto supported by the church. In England, she paid for restoration work on the west wing of Peterborough Cathedral because Frank had been confirmed there. She paid for the Wooster room at Canterbury Cathedral.

The clergy homed in. To my knowledge, she was on terms of friendship with Cardinals König, Willebrands and Dalla Costa. I can put a name but not a face to a whole crew open to the accusation of taking advantage of an elderly lady forging a fictional identity to free herself from guilt and Judaism. Pater Hildebrand, the priest of a modernist church built in the park at Meidling, Dean Riddell, the Reverend Howard Root, a Vatican insider by the name of Father Pierre Deprey (who "borrowed" her books about Proust) were among others in constant touch, careful to hit the exact note of admiration and humility. For years, Father John Livingstone of the Anglican Church in Paris was pre-occupied with her diaries. Writing to his superiors long after her death, he could speak of the fanciful nature of her wishes yet thought the diaries would interest researchers into religious or sexual psychology. Inexplicably he recommended that the family ought not to be allowed to lay hands on them. In a letter in September 1972, Father T. M. Hesburgh of Notre Dame University, Indiana, wrote in his capacity as head of the Ecumenical Institute at Tantur near Jerusalem to thank her for what he called the immensely interesting portfolios and documents she had presented. "Generations of scholars," he assured her, "would find this gift a source of new insight into spiritual matters."

A competition opened up over the future of her house between Monsignor Agresti, Bishop of Lucca, on behalf of the Catholics and Harold Isherwood, Bishop of Gibraltar, on behalf of the Protestants. A letter of 25 March 1976 with the signature of John Fulham and Gibraltar laments the legal and financial difficulties the church would face if Mrs Wooster made a gift to it of San Martino. All clerics were ready to turn the property into a religious institute on her terms, but she was offended when they asked for higher endowments than she was prepared to pay. Robert Stopford, Bishop of London, and his wife invited themselves regularly for holidays at San Martino, and in return they entertained her at Fulham Palace. How much of her diaries, if any, the Bishop had actually read is not clear, but he flattered her that they were of the greatest importance as the testimony of a genuine mystic in modern times. He arranged for photocopies to be lodged in the library of Lambeth Palace. Hints that the family might contest her gift of the house skilfully drove a wedge between her and her rightful heirs. This particular Bishop appeared to be the one who finally had got his hands on San Martino.

"I see him married to Elizabeth Cavendish before long,"

Mitzi wrote about Alan in her diary just before her big and final scene on the terrace with Frank. Alan had evidently confided in her, but not to me. The stay in Florence, I thought, had been an obligation, the subsequent visit to Ireland a junket. First stop was Birr, belonging to Lord and Lady Rosse. Tony Armstrong-Jones, her son by a previous marriage, was there. Moving on, we lost the way and stopped to ask where our next host, the Duke of St Albans, lived. "His Grace is round the bend," was the answer. Across the threshold of this mad Duke, I spotted just in time a trip wire at ankle height. In fact, Alan had the serious purpose of getting me together with prospective in-laws. The Duke and Duchess of Devonshire had a house party at Lismore, their rambling castle. There was nobody my age. The Duke's sister, Lady Elizabeth Cavendish, was ten years older than me. After dinner the Duchess made everyone play a game that involved writing a line of poetry and passing the paper on to the neighbour who composed a rhyming line and then the first line of the next couplet, and so on round the room until everyone had a complete doggerel. The aristocratic in-jokes were above my head. That was awkward enough, but the day we left Lismore, Alan told me that he would like to marry Elizabeth. I understood that I had been brought to Ireland so that she and I could have a look at one another. I couldn't help seeing this as a betrayal of Poppy, in her grave only a matter of weeks, and said so. Alan never mentioned it again, but unwittingly I had closed off what might have been a much happier outcome to his life. She devoted herself to John Betjeman and on the occasions when I met them I regretted my uprush of emotion on that Irish visit.

A week at Bayreuth with Alan after I had left Eton really was a junket. In the pension was an upright piano, and in the morning he would sit at it and take me through the leitmotivs of the Ring cycle. Jane Panza, an American lady with

245

a large car and a chauffeur organised afternoon sightseeing. She already had in tow Cyril Connolly and George Weidenfeld, his newest publisher. On good terms, the two were not yet entangled in the rivalry over Barbara Skelton that made them the talk of literary London and put them at odds. The dining room in the magnificent Schönborn castle at Pommersfelden had rows of silver double eggcups, and Cyril did a sudden extended turn about the cooking and eating of eggs, three at any one time being too many. We trooped into Haus Wahnfried, more a shrine to Wagner and his descendants than a home. Alan played the Welsh card with Frau Winifred Wagner who came originally from the next-door valley to Dolerw. Marrying Siegfried, Wagner's son, she had worked the composer's mystique into an essential component of Nazism. On her desk were signed portraits of Hitler and Goebbels. What would your reaction be if Hitler were now to enter the room? Alan asked. I should be thrilled, she answered. In the midst of her raptures about these former patrons and her regret that they could no longer help, I caught George Weidenfeld's eye and we have been the best of friends ever since.

After my eighteenth birthday, Mitzi began pressing Alan to make over to me shares that she had given Poppy but which for fiscal reasons had been held in his name. At the moment of signing the relevant papers in Lloyds Bank, Alan asked if I knew that I would be well-off with an income of thirty pounds a month. He had a friend, Richard Howden, whom he thought I ought to meet. Once or twice, not more, I dined with Mr Howden in his club in Pall Mall. A pot-belly pushed out the waistcoat of his three-piece suit. I thought him a crotchety old buffer and rather a bore. Another secret: he was a psychiatrist and Alan had commissioned him to write a report about me. Whether by accident or design, Alan left lying about a longish letter from him where I was bound to find it and pick it up to read. According to Mr Howden, the ideal for a young man was the old Roman one of *mens sana in corpore sano*, and it was a sorry state of affairs that I did not correspond to it. In this view I didn't love Alan, and the reason was very simple: he wasn't rich enough. I would always turn to Granny Wooster, Mr Howden concluded, because my one true love was for her money.

EIGHTEEN

Second to None

IN THE YEARS of the Cold War, it was possible to enlist in the navy for national service and learn Russian in Cambridge on behalf of naval intelligence. I sat for a scholarship to Magdalen College in Oxford, which if I passed was credential enough for the naval course. Several dons sat in on my oral examination. One of them, a small man with a slightly nasal waspish accent, opened proceedings by asking, "Why are you wearing a tie?" I thought it the right thing to do, I replied. Upon which he said, "What a boring boy you must be." He was himself wearing a bow tie, so my comeback should have been, "For the same reason as you." At the porter's lodge in Magdalen, a note was waiting. John Sparrow, Warden of All Souls, somehow had found out where I was and he had invited me to lunch in his college. Another guest was Somerset Maugham. Back at Eton, at about the same time that I heard I had won the scholarship, out of the blue a letter arrived to inform me that the military college at Sandhurst was about to call me up. Keeping the secret to himself, Grandpa Harry had put me down at birth for a regular commission in the Coldstream Guards and was no longer here to help me back-pedal. At an appointment with General George Burns, the officer responsible for the regiment, I had to agree to drop the navy and serve two years with the Coldstream on the understanding that afterwards I'd give up Oxford and sign on for longer.

On a beautiful September day, I reported to Caterham, the Brigade of Guards training depot. The barrier at the entrance opened to what might have been a foreign country.

Everything was done at the double amid a lot of shouting. Those who aspired to become commissioned officers had been enrolled in the so-called Brigade Squad, perhaps half of whom in this intake were Eton friends. An hour or so of haircutting, the issuing of kit, the foul-mouth talk of an old sweat of a Grenadier sergeant about sexual activity, began the transformation into soldiers of public schoolboys like me, hitherto sheltered from experience of the world at large. The day's routine of inspection, marching and drilling, the process known as spit-and-polish for bringing kit up to standard, instilled instinctive obedience to orders and a sense that whatever has to be done must be done as well as possible. Perfectionism connects to artistry. The national servicemen in the Brigade Squad as a rule endured this shaping more easily and with better humour than the much tougher regular guardsmen in other squads.

Alan had written the libretto for *Nelson*, Lennox Berkeley's opera that was to have its opening night at Covent Garden a few days after my arrival at Caterham. Ian Erskine, a sleek Grenadier captain, was in charge of the Brigade Squad, and it was foolhardy to ask him for a twenty-fours hours leave. Opera? Covent Garden? He grimaced as if he'd bitten into something vile and the duty sergeant hurried me out of the office. I couldn't persuade the others in the hut to listen to the BBC broadcast of the performance.

Army boots were blistering my feet, the blisters were turning septic, but it was perhaps even more foolhardy to report sick. Malingering, pronounced the Caterham doctor without bothering to have a look. By the time the thirteen weeks of basic training were over and we had leave, I was hobbling. The moment I was home, Alan announced that he had arranged to have me invited with him that same night to a ball given by Chips Channon at Kelvedon, his country house. Chips, properly Henry Channon M. P. shared his life with Peter Coats, improperly known as Petticoats. Chips's son Paul was my exact Eton contemporary and had often asked me to a meal in the Channon house in Belgrave Square, a decorator's extravaganza worthy of Chips's hero, mad King Ludwig of Bavaria. My feet were not up for dancing. Now it was my turn to be left alone at home in the company of Doris waiting for the doctor while Alan drove out into the night in a white tie.

Officer cadets went on a course at Eaton Hall, the immense Victorian house built by Alfred Waterhouse for the Duke of Westminster. Duly commissioned, I spent my first few days as a second lieutenant in Chelsea Barracks. Grandpa Harry had marched out of these barracks in August 1914 for France, and just half a century later I set out from the same barracks for Germany. The Coldstream Second Battalion was stationed in Krefeld in the Rhineland. Rubble from wartime bombing was still piled throughout the British zone. In nearby Düsseldorf, the Park Hotel was intact, but its street, the central Königsallee, had shop fronts with nothing behind them. The damage in Cologne was even more extensive.

The battalion occupied an impressive barracks built in Hitler's day. A great deal of planning and a great deal of expenditure had gone into it. The buildings were in solid brick. Framed in the middle of the main block was a huge panel, also in brick, of Nazi insignia. Bullets had been able only to chip away at this indestructible relic. The officers' mess was in the main block and their rooms were up above it. The first level below was a garage. The second level below had gun mountings and holes in the wall that could only have made it an execution chamber.

Rehearsals for the annual ceremony of Trooping the Colour were in progress. The occasion is a display of turnout and drill at the highest standard possible, and so an assertion of regimental pride. There was also an element of competition with the Scots Guards and Grenadiers in Fourth Guards Brigade. On the morning of the event, about 1,500 guardsmen mustered early and anxiously. General Sir Charles Loyd, a distinguished old soldier, was to take the parade. I had hardly had time to get to know the men in my platoon. Standing still while waiting for the ceremony to begin we were inconspicuous somewhere far down the parade ground. Suddenly I heard my name called out over the loudspeaker. Drill-sergeants are the impresarios of such an occasion, and the next thing I knew was that I had to fall in with one of them on either side. We marched at the drill-sergeants' pace right across the parade ground in full view of the entire Brigade. The only question was what could I have done to be disgraced so publicly? I was brought to a halt in front of General Loyd. My heart pumping, I took in his bright blue eyes and white moustache. I'm so glad you're here with us, he said as he leant forward confidentially, your grandfather Harry was one of my best friends, we were at Modder River together, he was such a fine soldier, he'd be so proud to know you are here today.

Senior officers and NCOs were more of the men who had won the war, and out of admiration for them and their *esprit de corps* I did consider for a while signing on as Harry had hoped. One of the junior officers happened to be Lord Lucan, later believed to have mistaken the nanny of his children for his wife and murdered her, then vanishing without trace. With his heavy moustache and deliberate manner, seemingly he intended to be taken for an aristocrat from another age, accustomed to have his way and keeping to himself. One way or another, there was a great deal of acting up, surely a component of bravery in combat. On NATO exercises, we were dug into a wood. The absurdly exaggerated up-and-down voice of a colonel (who had won a Military Cross in Italy, incidentally) came over the microphone in an exchange with the quartermaster, beginning, "What's for supper?" Mushroom soup. "How delicious!" For several days discipline was suspended as the men went about repeating and mimicking, "How delicious!"

Contact with the Germans proved a strain. Shopkeepers, policemen, hausfraus, were overly deferential, as though expecting the worst. There was the occasional drunken brawl. Fraternisation was discouraged. The day the British ceased to be occupiers and became allies by treaty, as at the touch of a switch the German police were on the lookout for traffic infringements, shopkeepers turned their backs, waiters made a point of not serving. The obverse of former deference was open resentment. Encountering people of a certain age, it became impossible not to wonder what they had done in the war.

While I was away, Alan moved out of Cavendish Close and into a set of chambers in Albany, the supposedly exclusive but slightly austere building in Piccadilly with tablets on walls here and there recording the poets and prime ministers who once had lived in these pseudo-collegiate surroundings. Just as Jessie had organised the departure from Castle Hill, so Doris now decided what to keep and what to be rid of. His chambers, numbered A10, had a large drawing room, a small dining room, a bedroom for him and another up a flight of stairs for Doris. By chance, the adjoining A9 was available, and Alan set me up there, with Briggs the butler upstairs in my spare room – Noël Coward might well have built a play around a father and twenty-year-old son living next to one another like this.

On leave, I went to Vienna. Meidling by then had been sold for two hundred thousand dollars. All I remember of my first years there is splashing about in a tin tub put out somewhere in the park. To revisit the house was, and still is, to be caught in the pervasive melancholia and sense of loss that is an aftershock of Nazism. I wrote a letter postmarked

18 April 1957 to Max to describe the sadness "because it was easy to see what it must have been like."

In Paris on another leave, Cécile de Rothschild invited me to her apartment in the Faubourg Saint-Honoré. Classical features, an easy manner, a fortune, wonderful possessions, she had everything life has to offer, except that she couldn't shake off feelings of ambivalence towards her brother Elie and by extension other men in her life. In Cécile's drawing-room there was Greta Garbo. A uniquely celebrated film star, she too appeared to have, but not to enjoy, everything life has to offer, instead enclosing herself in a veil of mystery. People who had never seen her roles as Anna Karenina or Queen Christina of Sweden were familiar with her keynote abdication, "I want to be alone." A soldier! Garbo exclaimed when I was introduced. And what do soldiers do? She insisted that I show her how we drilled on the barrack square, so I found myself demonstrating stand-at-ease and about-turn, stamping my feet in front of Cécile's well-known Goya and early Picasso. My next encounter with Garbo was at Royaumont. Cécile had driven her over from her own house in the nearby village of Noisy. Garbo and I knocked up on the tennis court. The day was so hot that she took off her shirt and played topless, so flat-chested that she looked more masculine than ever.

Towards the end of my two years of national service, I was transferred to Pirbright, another Brigade of Guards depot. In July 1956, Gamal Abdul Nasser nationalised the Suez Canal. On stand-by to retake the Canal, we blancoed our webbing a desert colour instead of khaki, and painted vehicles yellow. In the final years of the British presence in Egypt, the Coldstream had been stationed there, and some remembered Fayyum and Lake Deversoir. Former national service officers were recalled. One of them, Angus Macintyre, already an Oxford undergraduate, was so annoyed that he came into the officers' mess in nothing but a buttoned-up greatcoat and boots without laces. I wrote to my grandmother, "Preparations for war are very exciting here. We sail for Cyprus next Thursday week, and then on to Tripoli and the Egypt approaches via Tobruk. Everybody is hankering for a fight but sadly it won't affect me as I leave the army on 24 August." Tales of incompetence came later. It was as if the British army had never undertaken operations abroad. Brigade headquarters and front-line soldiers had apparently crossed in opposite directions. On 25 August, the day after demob, I arrived at Royaumont. Also released from national service, Jacob Rothschild was driving me in an Aston Martin lent to him by his father. We were to spend a fortnight with Antoinette de Gunzbourg in a villa she'd rented at Estartit, a village on the Costa Brava. On the way home, the Aston Martin broke down and, incongruously roped on to a bullock cart, had to be hauled off to a garage.

A day or two after I was installed in Magdalen, Cécile and Garbo were my first visitors. We walked through the Cloisters out on to the lawn in front of the New Building where I had my rooms. As luck would have it, a hundred yards away were Tom Boase, the college President, and with him Peggy Ashcroft, almost as famous an actress at least in this country. They hurried over. Agitated, Garbo ran off much faster and was gone. "Was that Garbo? I've always wanted to meet her, you have to fetch her back," Tom Boase pleaded, to which I could only say, "I'm afraid she doesn't want to meet you." Feline and manipulative, he had the manner and fixed smile of the *faux bonhomme* he was. I didn't improve things later with a parody of Goethe's poem, "Boaselein, Boaselein, Boaselein rot, Boaselein auf den Heiden."

After the freedom of the army, Oxford was a stultifying return to school. Girls had to be out of your college by a certain time, undergraduates had to be in their college by a certain time. Breaking these rules condemned you to climb

ABOVE: Jessie Wheeler and David in the last summer before the war in the garden at Montreuil, the house Mitzi and Frank built close to Le Touquet.

RIGHT: Even retired, Jessie still looked as if she were gathering us together from the four corners of the earth.

Refugees on the sea front at Cannes in 1940. LEFT TO RIGHT: Jessie, six-year-old Elly Propper, Aunty Lily just married by procuration to Elie de Rothschild, David, and Marian Stainer, Elly's nanny.

After their London house was destroyed in an air raid, Alan and Poppy and David lived at Castle Hill Farm, a couple of miles from Tonbridge.

Max and his three sisters celebrated their survival and reunion at Royaumont at the end of the war.

At Seefeld, then an undeveloped resort in the Tyrol, Poppy made the effort late in January 1953 to ski with David. Three weeks later she was dead.

LEFT: Mitzi outside the ancient church of St. Mauritius, Alltmawr, in the Wye Valley for the wedding of Clarissa and David in 1959.

BELOW: Mitzi's 80th birthday with family and staff on the terrace at Royaumont. On her right Max, on her left Bubbles, behind her Eduardo looking sideways. To his left David, then Clarissa.

Long since sold, the Royal Welsh Warehouse acknowledges its origins.

Clarissa in front of the Gros Chêne, an oak of immemorial age in the woods of Royaumont.

in, which in Magdalen's case involved hauling oneself up a lamp post fitted with discouraging spikes. Since I failed the obligatory means test, my scholarship was taken away but I still had to wear a gown. Now married to Isaiah Berlin, Aline de Gunzbourg lived in a beautiful house in Headington. I knew that for Poppy's sake she would be in loco parentis and I went to tell her that I had outgrown Oxford and proposed to leave.

Aline and Isaiah persuaded me to hang on. She was a study in elegance, and he looked like one of the preoccupied, benevolent and humorous figures H. M. Bateman drew in his cartoons. A three-piece suit and a battered felt hat completed the picture, even in summer. His rapid and bubbling way of speaking conveyed genuine interest in the human race and its doings. Whoever had something new, especially gossip, to recount could be sure of a hearing. Under the liveliness was a determination to play the game, and the expectation that you too would do so. Isaiah was central to the only intellectual activity that mattered in the university, namely disputing which elements of Left-wing doctrine were essential to Utopia. Education was a process of indoctrination. Openly to oppose Communists like Christopher Hill, Master of Balliol, and the large numbers of fellow-travelling dons spell-bound by Stalinism, required courage, and the few who wore cavalry twill trousers and a tweed jacket were written off as conservatives to be ridiculed. Isaiah had personal experience of the Soviet Union far more meaningful than a fortnight in the country under the control of Intourist or the group-think of the Left. Heart-to-heart meetings with Akhmatova and Pasternak in their homes gave him unique moral authority. Several times I was to hear him say that Stalin was worse than Hitler. Nonetheless he held the progressive views of equality and liberty that had become standardised in the 1930s and had not evolved since then. Liliane was unkind but not wrong to sum him up as "un vieux Juif gauchiste de Russie" – an old Leftist Russian Jew.

Thousands were demonstrating in the street against British participation with France and Israel in the Suez campaign but not against the Soviet invasion of Hungary. The juxtaposition of these crises put Isaiah to the test. Commitment to Israel was a defining part of his identity. For fear of being labelled a Conservative, he could not bring himself to adopt a public position in favour of Prime Minister Anthony Eden and the military operation. Instead he wrote privately to Eden's wife, Clarissa, to offer admiration and sympathy. I had been determined to join volunteers from Balliol taking medical supplies to Budapest. Isaiah discouraged it on the grounds that such a risk offered no useful gain. For reasons that must have been deep in his personality, he wanted influence without the attendant publicity. In the absence of civil courage, that necessary virtue, he perfected a strategy of backing into the limelight. Mitzi congratulated him on his knighthood in July 1957, and what he wrote by way of thanking her catches exactly his ambiguous attitudinizing: "I do not see myself on a noble charger – still, what must be must be; and if the Queen says 'arise Sir Isaiah' – not easy to say – I shall try at least to avoid *fou rire* – to which I am sadly and dangerously liable at critical moments." (Lady Berlin, said Liliane, sounded like the title of an operetta.)

Against Isaiah's advice, I returned to Vienna, to stay with Dr Pokorny. Also in the apartment was a young relation of his who had horrifying stories of the Communism he had just escaped. I hitched a ride on a vehicle delivering medical supplies to Budapest. Fresh bullet-holes pockmarked the streets. Russian soldiers patrolled. Either then or in the course of a later visit I interviewed György Lukács, the Marxist critic whose books were much respected at Oxford. A veteran of Red Terror after the First War, and then an émigré in Moscow, he was one of the many who narrowly escaped execution at the hands of those he had done his best to promote.

The academy and reality seemed disconnected. I spent my first year escaping. John Betjeman's wife Penelope took me for rides on the Berkshire downs in her pony trap. I was almost as often in the house of Roy and Billa Harrod as in Headington with the Berlins. Billa had seen me at Meidling when I was a few days old. As though in a reconstruction of the Thirties, Brian Howard was at one party of hers, and at another she went round the room introducing her guest with the words, "This, I regret to say, is Sir Oswald Mosley." Dominique de Grunne also kept open house. Belgian, he was a Dominican monk researching for a doctorate. Writing to Berenson in February 1953, Hugh Trevor-Roper rather sourly marks him down as "obviously the real, handsome, intellectual, social, aristocratic *abbé*" and a first-rate cook into the bargain. A family friend, he officiated at the wedding of my cousin Elly and Raymond Bonham Carter at Royaumont in the summer of 1958 in the local church where her parents had married. His film-star good looks and his red and gold vestments stole the show. When he subsequently left holy orders, Elly and Raymond wondered what the status of their marriage was. The following year, my cousin Philip married Renata Goldschmidt in Austria. (How did we survive our upbringing? is a question Philip and Elly periodically discuss with me. Spouses who were foreigners had been the means of escape for Bubbles and Poppy, and it was the same for us.)

In a postscript to his novel *The Rock Pool*, Cyril Connolly was appalled to note that the originals from whom his characters were drawn had died, but he, the author with his "cautious reptilian tenacity of life" remained – so it is with me. Alasdair Clayre had a masterful intellect and a laugh so comprehensive that it was a shout. As junior officers we had met in the army one snowy night at Pickering, the Yorkshire training ground for fire and movement with live ammunition. I heard music coming from one of the huts, and there was Alasdair, a Grenadier, playing Schubert on the flute and reading Kant. After a starred first and a fellowship at All Souls, he roared through the profession of architecture, published a novel, some poems and songs and a big book about China. My life's mission, he once said to me, is to reconcile Christianity and Wittgenstein. Out walking in the Oxford Meadows, he suddenly turned and sang Heine's words set to music by Schubert, "Ich grolle nicht, und wenn das Herz auch bricht" – I don't complain even though my heart is breaking. That, he said, was his secret. Too brilliant for his own good, he threw himself under a train at the age of forty-nine.

An Eton scholar, Francis Hope made sure we all knew he was an agnostic intellectual by reading a book disguised as a prayer book throughout the daily compulsory services in chapel. Also a fellow of All Souls, and a columnist for the *New Statesman*, he published a volume of poems that could hardly have been slimmer. He introduced me to John Fuller, the poet of a generation as W. H. Auden once was. Had Francis not been killed prematurely in a plane crash, he might have become a successor to Malcolm Muggeridge, that is to say an oracle of the media. Angus Macintyre, the Pirbright rebel in 1956, taught history at Oxford, a natural scholar who also happened to be a wit. Clarissa and I and the children spent holidays in Scotland with him, his wife Joanna and their children. Elected Principal of Hertford College, he died in a car crash on his way to Scotland before he could take up the position.

At Easter 1958, I walked round Mount Athos with David Winn, a farceur able to turn anything and everything into a joke. Unaccustomed exercise made him long for Michael

Astor's Bentley to come round the corner. At the monastery of Vatopedi we shared a guest room. Entering in the half-light, an elderly monk had to be fought off while he made advances saying, "Do you understand me, boys?" – a sentence that David quoted at monks in other monasteries. In the library there he came across a specialist paper written by Professor L. R. Palmer on some incunabula in the library, which he annotated, "Entirely disagree with Palmer. David Winn, Student, Christ Church." Next term David came to find me because Professor Palmer had written to ask him what these objections were and was inviting him to All Souls for a learned discussion. The professor took it all in good heart. David had a walkout with my childhood friend Sarah d'Avigdor-Goldsmid, and both were drowned in the Channel when Paddy Pakenham took them out in his boat and it capsized in stormy weather. John Calmann, an heir to the high German-Jewish culture, was murdered by a hitch-hiker he picked up in France. Jeremy Wolfenden, an old Etonian in the Guy Burgess mould and the capo of a Magdalen left-wing mafia, had written an essay for his All Souls fellowship that Isaiah Berlin said was unmatched in his experience and could go straight into print. Correspondent for the *Daily Telegraph*, perhaps a secret service agent or even double agent, Jeremy was found dead in Moscow in mysterious circumstances.

Peter Levi, poet and classicist, Jesuit of Baghdadi Jewish origins, took me to listen to Allen Ginsburg and Gregory Corso glorifying the atom bomb to an audience all of whom far preferred to be red than dead. (Next day, the pair stormed into the town hall where Edith Sitwell was giving a recital of *Façade*. "Oh you are dear boys," was her winning response.) In the hall at Heythrop, the college for training Jesuits, he said loudly that it had been a great relief to discover that theology was a real subject after all – other Jesuits within earshot looked as if they had received an electric shock. In the Vatican he was given a chastity stick to push his shirt down into his trousers in the bathroom avoiding the risk of touching untoward parts of his anatomy. In the unlikely role of scoutmaster at Stonyhurst public school, he took a party of boys to France and had them leaning out of the train at stations singing the old favourite, *Il est cocu, le chef de gare.* His imagination ranged from Serbian epic poetry, schemes against the colonels in power in Greece, travels with Bruce Chatwin, to theories about Shakespeare. When Yaakov and Felice Malkin, lifelong friends of mine from Jerusalem, visited him in Oxford, he told them that Israel was the only place where he could be happy. When Cyril Connolly found out that his wife Deirdre had fallen in love with Peter, he coined the multiple pun, "What does she see in this Peter Rabbi?" Leaving the Jesuits to marry, Peter was happy to be living in the English countryside, too happy to bother about his fatal diabetes. One evening Deirdre telephoned with the news that Peter had died, and next morning the post contained a letter from him.

Contemporaries such as Julian Mitchell and Ved Mehta were already in touch with editors and publishers, and well on their way to becoming successful writers. Another poet, Quentin Stevenson, was praised by Edith Sitwell. Dom Moraes, the Indian Rimbaud, was also very young to have published. His big brown eyes gave him a lifelong childish appearance, but he was soon married to Henrietta Bowler. The friend of Francis Bacon and Lucian Freud, she recruited the willing to wild bohemian London. Invited to a black tie dinner, I found myself sitting next to John Caute, and learnt that under the name David Caute he was the first person of my own age to be publishing a novel. *At Fever Pitch* was impressive. A Marxist who told me he intended becoming an English-language Sartre, John exposed my ignorance of praxis, Chernychevsky, Frantz Fanon and the rest of the obligatory apparatus. Under peer review, so to speak, I took on the protective colouring of the infantile Leftism that was the key to peaceful tutorials and a decent degree.

261

Of course I recognized that the man who had thought it boring of me to wear a tie for my scholarship interview was A. J. P. Taylor. He had become a household name through television broadcasts on recent history timed to last exactly an hour and spoken without a script as though impromptu rather than carefully prepared. A way of walking brusquely through the college signified that he had better things to do than waste his time on undergraduates. His rooms were near mine in the New Buildings, and one night he came to my room without warning on some pretext of playing Stravinsky's *Histoire du Soldat*. It was long past the time when girls had to be out of the college, and he had caught me with one who was evidently going to spend the night there. He overstayed his welcome but at least he did not have me sent down as he might have done.

A messenger interrupted one of my tutorials with him to deliver his freelance earnings from the Beaverbrook newspapers. Cash, a bundle of notes that Taylor held on to, fondling and counting, while at the same time he was muttering to me, "This is what it's all about." Discussing the French revolution, he said, "I'll show you what the Jacobins were about," seized a poker and swung it at me, hitting the chair I had just jumped out of. And in yet another tutorial he suddenly asserted that there was no such thing as Gulag in the Soviet Union, it was horror-propaganda put about by White Russian exiles in Riga. But survivors have left testimonies, I answered. And you believe them? he sneered. Actually he had spoken out against Communism when it mattered at

Congress for Cultural Freedom conferences, and I can only suppose he was putting me through some obscure test of his own devising.

At the end of term, college fellows sit at the high table in the hall, and undergraduates come up one by one to hear in no more than a couple of minutes what their tutor has to say about their work. Taylor said of me, "It would do this young man good to go hungry and have to steal his food." I started shouting in anger that while Taylor was safe in England giving vent to his spleen about the course of German history I was stealing food in Vichy France. Presiding, all silky smile, Tom Boase broke in, "We are not responsible if you take Mr Taylor's advice." I refused to have anything more to do with Taylor and might have been sent down for that too.

By chance, I encountered Taylor in the London Library just after the publication of *The Origins of the Second World War*, his partial exoneration of Hitler that was raising a storm. "This time I've trod on their toes," he said with very revealing satisfaction. I was researching my biography of Unity Mitford. Taylor had a dinner date in the Ritz in the near future with Sir Oswald Mosley, Unity's one-time brother-in-law, and proposed that I join in and have a lesson from one who had made history. Eyes bulging as he spoke, Mosley was even more conceited and unrepentant than Taylor. The more Mosley defended his Hitlerite past, the more Taylor fawned on him. So frustrated was his love of power that if Mosley in 1940 had become Hitler's British Gauleiter, Taylor would have been a natural collaborator.

Raymond Carr of New College, a man with a more open mind and a wider range of interests, was prepared to give me tutorials. He also persuaded New College to permit the staging of a play, *Down You Mad Creature*, a skit of sorts on the *Odyssey* that I had written with Peter Levi. John Cox, later of Covent Garden, was our producer, and Dudley Moore, later of Hollywood, wrote the music. Dmitri Shostakovich happened to be in Oxford to receive an honorary degree, and he came to the party after the performance. So many went up to him speaking the Russian they had learnt in the navy that the KGB minders became suspicious and frog-marched him off.

Whenever I was in Albany during vacations, Alan incorporated me into his literary life. I was present in A10 when Alan played the song from *West Side Story*, "Gee, Officer Krupke" to T. S. Eliot, with the intended compliment, "it might have been written by you." Wincing as he listened, Eliot said he was sorry to see that Alan thought so little of his work. Also Alan's guests in A10 were Sir Lewis Namier and his Russian-born wife Julia de Beausobre. When I let drop a typical Oxford apologia that Stalin at least had industrialised Russia, the Namiers bombarded me for the rest of the afternoon with statistics to the effect that the Romanovs had done better and, if allowed to, would have done better still. A disturbed Eugène Ionesco asked me to believe that a ghost was chasing him out of the house he had rented in Maidenhead to finish writing a play. I accompanied Alan to a cultural conference in Geneva, where the main Soviet speaker was Ilya Ehrenburg. He launched into a diatribe against Western intellectuals one and all, only to lunch at the same table as Alan and Stephen Spender, putting himself out to flatter and charm two men in a position to promote his career.

In the summer of 1958 Francis Hope and I travelled together on the continent. He was pursuing Carol Gaynor, an undergraduate, and I was pursuing Clarissa Caccia, whom I had met at a ball and fallen in love with at first sight. Reaching Salzburg ahead of us, Alan obtained scalper's tickets for us at the opera and introduced Francis and me to Sam Barber and Gian Carlo Menotti. Clarissa and her cousin Phyllida Barstow then arrived. What further determined my future was a visit to the so-called World's Fair in Brussels. I wrote it up in an article for *Isis*, an Oxford student magazine. Soon afterwards, a letter arrived from John Guest, editorial director at Longmans, to say that he could tell from this article that I was a novelist and would I be sure to send him my first finished work of fiction.

Clarissa also lived on fault lines of nationality and identity. Harold Caccia, her Anglo-Tuscan father, had been personal assistant to the Foreign Secretary Lord Halifax, and then to Anthony Eden. He did not subscribe to the policy of appeasing Hitler. He and like-minded colleagues in the Foreign Office, he used to say, never thought we might lose the war but couldn't see how we would win it. Posted to the embassy in Athens, he had his wife and two young children with him in April 1941 when the Germans invaded Greece. Leaving by boat from the Piraeus with a party of commandos led by Peter Fleming, they put in to an uninhabited island by day. Clarissa was in a cave onshore when German dive-bombers sank the boat, killing several commandos including her uncle Oliver Barstow. Crete, Egypt, South Africa, the West Indies, were staging posts in a roundabout and dangerous journey that brought her to Liverpool. By coincidence, we both returned to England from our experiences of war in September 1941. We had still more in common: Clarissa had been educated in Vienna because after the war her father had been appointed British High Commissioner in the occupied zone. Her Austrian accent was raw, she used special dialect words, for instance *hopatachik*, meaning stuck-up (derived from the French *de haut en bas*) and sang songs with funny words, "*Wer hat so viel binki-binki? Wer hat so viel Geld?*" We had both been brought up with such nursery jingles as "*Halli hallo, wer sitzt am Klo? Der Krampus und der Niccolo,*" and we had similar responses to such music as the lyrical aria "Aber der Richtige, wenn's einen gibt" in Richard Strauss's opera *Arabella*. At Eton, her brother David had become a close friend, and we used to break the rules by slinking away on bicycles to the cinema in Slough. It took him by surprise that his little sister might want to marry me. (An amusing and gifted man, he was to die young of a brain tumour.) When Clarissa came to Royaumont to meet my relations, Jessie patrolled the corridor and at two in the morning suddenly entered my room on the pretext of asking if I was sure that Clarissa's blond hair was not dyed. The silver pepper pot she gave us as a wedding present was, she said, "To grind away your troubles,"

By my final year at Oxford, Clarissa was in Washington and had a job under Johnny Walker at the National Gallery. As British ambassador, Harold had weathered the Suez crisis. Engaged to Clarissa, I was staying in the embassy in April 1959 when they rang up from Royaumont with the news that Jessie had suffered a stroke. Her handwriting is completely uncontrolled in a letter she wrote on her deathbed to Mitzi, but the spirit is constant: "My dear Madame, thank you for all your goodness and kindness to me. I have not been perfect by a long way but I have done my best for all of you big and little. Bless you all, Jess." I could not be there when she was buried next to Nanny Stainer, both of them close to Poppy in the Viarmes cemetery. "Well done thou good and faithful servant" is the inscription chosen by Max on the tombstone.

Under some impression that I could combine a literary life and a diplomatic job, I sat the Foreign Office entrance examination. Those who then interviewed me were sure that with my background I would insist on postings in France and Germany and they were unconvinced when I said I rather fancied Mogadishu. At another interview a lady psychologist asked me what had been the happiest day of my life. My answer was that sunshine and clouds went together.

And what, she went on, had been the unhappiest day? I had already answered that. Quite soon, I received a handwritten letter to say that out of a total of 150 marks, the minimum acceptable was 50, and I had scored 35. In a sorrowing tone, the letter informed me that I would not be able to cope with life, and advised that I go for professional treatment. This was not good news for my future father-in-law, soon to be Permanent Under-Secretary of the Foreign Office. Looking into it, he discovered that according to the psychologist, failure to provide specific incidents of happiness and unhappiness were grounds for absolute and permanent disqualification from any responsible job. At that time, furthermore, the Foreign Office could not countenance anyone with a French and Jewish mother. Luckily, Harold had a sense of the ironic and the ridiculous, and never held it against me that becoming a journalist I had enrolled in what the Foreign Office like to consider the Opposition.

I wrote finals and married six weeks later in the twelfth-century chapel next to the house of Clarissa's Barstow grandparents. I was twenty-three, Clarissa just twenty. Everybody encouraged us. Those who thought us too young kept their counsel. The gathering in the churchyard of Mitzi, the assembled Fould-Springers and Rothschilds, prompted Aunt Marjorie, widow of a Caccia uncle in Florence and in her day a steadfast fascist and anti-Semite, to jot down in her diary, "All the noses were there." At the reception that afternoon, Alan whispered in my ear that Bobby Pratt-Barlow had died, leaving me the capital of half a million dollars with the life interest to him.

Always generous, Cécile de Rothschild gave us the wedding present of a week on a yacht with a crew of a captain and a mate that we picked up on the Greek island of Hydra. In Austria on the way home, we visited the monastery of Stams. I was wandering by myself in the sacristy when a priest came in, advanced towards me and without a word started hitting my head. I put my arms up to ward him off, and he knocked my watch to the ground. Outside the monastery was a police station. The priest charged me with breaking off the diamond pendulum of the clock in the sacristy. At which point, a busload of German tourists entered the police station to testify that they had witnessed me doing it. The police sergeant on duty duly wrote down the particulars. If I had stolen the pendulum, it had to be on me. While I was trying to get him to search me, he asked why Clarissa spoke German like a native. Because her father had been the British High Commissioner in Vienna and she'd been at school there. And where were we driving to now? To Baron Elie de Rothschild at Scharnitz. The policeman stood up, saying that everyone knew the pendulum had been missing for at least ten years. Ordering the priest and false witnesses to leave, he begged us to take the matter no further. Apparently the priest had suffered a breakdown, we were to make allowances, but anyone who did not have the right credentials might very well have been framed. The false witnesses drove away before I could have it out with them, but they had given me a feel for the malice and lies of the Hitler period.

Every inch an earl, Lord Drogheda, the managing director of the *Financial Times*, had offered me a job on the paper as a feature writer. The features' editor, Nigel Lawson, gave the impression that he was bound for the top and had the generosity to be taking you with him – Roy Harrod, the economist and a fellow of Christ Church, Oxford, said he had never taught a better pupil. Gordon Newton, the paper's experienced editor, gave me an early lesson in the way of the world when he called me in to listen to R. A. Butler on the telephone briefing against colleagues by leaking what they had just said in cabinet. After a while I was writing a daily column with William Rees-Mogg, who had the air of the editor of a great paper long before he actually was one. In a short space of time, then, I had acquired a wife, a house in Knightsbridge, the prospect of money one day in the future, and a career.

Time and Tide was a rundown weekly magazine that the rich and idiosyncratic Tim Beaumont – a priest into the bargain – had bought in order to revitalize. It was something of a gamble to accept its literary editorship. The foreign editor Mark Frankland and the home affairs editor Richard West both wrote books as well as articles. Among contemporaries whom I was the first to put into print were Martin Gilbert and Francis Hope, the novelists Margaret Drabble and Susan Hill, and Tony Tanner, Cambridge's specialist on American literature. Every Wednesday, Burgo Partridge, Julian Jebb and other regular critics brought in their copy and we'd have lunch. Burgo was almost sure to talk about his parents Ralph and Frances Partridge. He hated their Bloomsbury values of anything-goes so passionately that he had always wanted to murder them. As a little boy, he had shown his mother the grave he had dug for her in the garden. In a case of mistaken identity, the police did arrest him for murder. Assuming that the trauma had wiped out the memory of his deed, he made a false confession and wept when his father came to fetch him from the cells. This made such an impression that I was to take it for the *donnée* of my novel *Safe Houses*.

In the first interview I did, Aldous Huxley described how his house in California had caught fire. Almost blind as he was, he had risked his life to save the manuscript of *Island*, his last novel. To have lost his library with its archive including letters from D. H. Lawrence was a foretaste of death, he said with impressive lack of self-pity. One occasional contributor was David Jones, the poet and painter, for whom art had to be a genuine spiritual experience. Arthur Koestler never kept his promise to write for the magazine. His circle of friends included Paul Ignotus, who looked too frail to survive the persecution by Hungarian Communists that he recounts in *Political Prisoner*, a book that ought to be better known. They would gather in his house for a drink before lunch on Sunday, and on one of these occasions around 1963 I heard Goronwy Rees tell the assembled company that Anthony Blunt had tried to recruit him into the KGB. Didn't you know, said John Mander, then on the staff of *Encounter*, standing next to me, it's Goronwy's party piece. The security services needed years to catch up with common knowledge in this room.

In any spare time, I finished *Owls and Satyrs*, my first novel, and sent it to John Guest. Clarissa and I had a summer holiday in Turkey. We had an introduction to a surviving Ottoman grandee who asked if Clarissa was really my wife. What a catastrophe, he went on, you have married a woman of the world, she'll want clothes and jewellery; you should have done like me, married a peasant woman and kept her in the fields. While we were there, tanks came out into the street, the army staged a coup to depose Prime Minister Adnan Menderes and finally to hang him. By chance, we met Patrick Kinross, my parents' best man and a Turkophile. By an even greater chance, he had in his pocket an advertisement of a book by Dom Moraes with a flippant quote from a review of it I had written. We were alone in the Mena Yacht Club as his guests; its members were under arrest as Menderes's cronies, and we could hear them howling in the prison across the water on the island of Prinkipo. On our return to London, a letter from John Guest was waiting to say he was delighted to be publishing the novel. The copy editor was Elisabeth King, sister of the novelist Francis King, and a letter from her just picked out turns of phrase she particularly liked. In this comedy of manners the main character is Alan, represented as a woman too preoccupied with herself to pay attention to others. I did not want to hurt his feelings, and

this fiction was the way to come to terms. He never mentioned the novel, which I take as evidence that he must have
read it and was determined to avoid any discussion that
might arise. That was his way of coming to terms with me.

NINETEEN

Midnight Mollie

AT DAWN ONE DAY while we were still at Cavendish Close, I was woken up by footsteps and the noise of a car starting. Peering out of the window, I saw a woman leaving the house in a dishevelled evening dress. A day or two later, I was to meet Alan for dinner in a restaurant. Plans had changed, he had this woman with him, and he handed me some money for a taxi home. The woman was Mollie Duchess of Buccleuch, known to all as Midnight Mollie.

The snobbish side of Alan was flattered to have a duchess running after him. As though they were in the same social set, he used to refer to her as a cousin whom he had known since childhood. It looks as if Midnight Mollie took up with Alan while Poppy was still alive, but I cannot be certain about that. A rather withered beauty by then, she had evidently had a past from which her nickname derived. She and her husband Walter, the Duke of Buccleuch, were on distant terms, each going their own way. Rumour had it that the Duke was not the father of all his children. His mistress was a rich South American lady.

From my perspective, Mollie had her claws into Alan and would not let go. Possessive, she was also supercilious, drawing attention to herself with a mincing way of speaking unlike anyone else's. She simpered. The staple subjects of her conversation were the Royal family, her own family, and problems with domestic servants. She expected Alan to entertain her as though he had a fortune as large as the duke's, no expense spared. Over the years he was to pay for their flights on public and private aircraft, for safaris and hotels and five-star meals that he could not afford but which the rapacious Mollie took for granted. Invitations to stay in the duke's great houses of Boughton and Drumlanrig were what she could offer, and it was enough to tether him. A letter to me has no date, but since it is written on Cavendish Close writing paper it has to be early in their relationship: "Boughton was very pleasant – no other guests: the children enchanting. We fished for tadpoles, collected cowslips, went for long walks, did a little local sight-seeing, including a very unsuccessful visit to Burghley, which was shut when we got there (just Mollie and I)." Telling my daughters Jessica and Candida to call her Granny, she was too obtuse emotionally to work out that this was bound to miscarry. Indignant at the implied claim, they hit instead on "Mollie Duchess," which says all that there was to say.

Poppy's death was a blow to Alan as a man and a writer from which there was no recovering. His diaries record a social life as hectic as ever, but this was a front for loneliness and mourning. Already in September 1955 he is contemplating how "to wind up my intricacies with Mollie." The same diary paragraph elaborates, "Castle Hill keeps coming back and I wonder how I can go on living without my darling. . . . I can't go on getting tangled up with people and then explaining to them that I am only looking, like Orpheus, for my lost Eurydice." His papers contain a good few letters from Mollie that he never opened. There are also a good few self-analyses, one of which has the date of June 1956, about the same time that he was painting the idealised picture just quoted of those tadpoles and cowslips. "I have smashed my link with Mollie and caused her a misery which I can't assess because I can't bring myself to open her letters. Why? Conscience? Boredom? Claustrophobia? I don't really know. It is all bound up with a shirking of the act of love, yet that too may be no more than an equal horror of nympholepsis and impotence."

Up from Oxford, one evening as usual I went from A9 into A10, never imagining the discovery I was about to have. The place seemed empty. I opened the drawing room door, turned on the lights and there on the sofa was Alan with a rent boy. Surprise turned immediately into a feeling of guilt that I was in the wrong. I backed out, closed the door and stood in the narrow entrance wondering what to do. Pretty soon hurrying past me on the way out to the landing, the rent boy in his embarrassment made sure not to catch my eye. Instead of speaking about this incident, Alan and I behaved as though it had never occurred.

The hero-worship I had felt for my father was beginning to transform into questions. I was obliged to ask myself what Poppy had known about the man she had married. Had she been aware of rent boys? What had she made of the fact that by and large his friends were homosexuals? Where did the rent boy leave Midnight Mollie? I was often hearing that she hoped to marry Alan. Was she better informed than Poppy had been, perhaps indifferent, or maybe supremely self-confident?

Doris was the only person I could turn to. White-haired with a slight blue rinse in it and careful to dress for the West End, she had once been approached in Bond Street by an Austrian who kissed her hand and spoke under the misapprehension that she was Princess Lobkowitz. Like Jessie, she had worked so hard that her legs had swollen. Like Jessie too, she was possessed by the sense of duty, which meant keeping oneself to oneself. A Dorset farmer's daughter, she took the realistic view that people do what they do, and it is nobody's business to be censorious. Midnight Mollie might pester Alan and propose this and that, but she'd never leave the Duke, she enjoyed being a duchess far too much to become plain Mrs Pryce-Jones. Doris had some phrase about the boss liking his oats. What she minded about the rent boys was that one of them had stolen a Cartier bedside clock given to Poppy as a wedding present from Lulu de Waldner, with the lettering Love From Lulu replacing the clock-face numerals.

On 19 May 1960, Alan notes in his autobiography, he flew to New York and his life up to that point "closed abruptly." The Ford Foundation had taken him on for six months as a cultural advisor. On the last day of November that year he was writing to Mitzi on paper from the Shamrock Hotel in Houston that he was dashing from San Francisco to a university in New Orleans. Even if the Ford Foundation did not extend his contract, "I shall be very tempted to stay on here for a few years (in New York, I mean) and just write, coming back to Europe in the summer.... I love it so in the U.S. One can escape, and I perceive that in London I never can."

A9 was given up, and A10 let to Lord Gladwyn, the former British ambassador to the United Nations. (His wife Cynthia had such an artificial air that many years previously Poppy had joked that she looked like a broken porcelain figurine badly glued together, nicknaming her Lady Seccotine.) "I shall never willingly again make my home in London, nor (if I am honest with myself) in Europe again," Alan was opening his heart to Mitzi in a letter of 6 August 1960. "For the first time since I tried to make a life by myself I find that I can relax, work, avoid bores, make a little money, feel well, feel simple – and it's a magical sensation.... I see myself very well spending the last years of my life with extreme contentment writing away in Boston or New York – or anywhere in the clearer, fresher air of the New World. I feel like Florestan climbing up out of the dungeon."

The job at the Ford Foundation put a gloss on the reality that actually he was escaping from Midnight Mollie and from me. He could leave her letters unopened if he felt like it, and I wouldn't be bursting in unawares at the wrong moment.

Doris retained her upstairs room in Albany but would go over to America in the summer to keep house for Alan. Calling on her for a cup of tea on two or perhaps three occasions, I found a youngish American by the name of Tex Barker. His friend Alan had insisted that on a visit to London he was to be sure to contact Doris. Tex was so silent that it was hard to attribute any character to him. When I asked Doris about him, she just laughed saying, We know the boss. But did we? In his papers are a number of letters that are unattributed but he thought worth preserving. Someone signing Andrew wrote from Malta, "Hallo, my dear old fruit." Someone else wrote from H. M. S. *Excellent*, and Chuck wrote from the U. S. S. *Chas. S. Sperry*, "I don't know how I will ever repay you for what you have done for me." Graeme in Sunderland asked, "Can you tell me how to cope with repressed homosexuality?"

A letter of mine dated in December 1962 to my grandmother says that Alan has been in London as the librettist of *Vanity Fair*, for which Julian Slade composed the music. Unlike *Salad Days*, the previous musical that made Slade's reputation, this one ran for a few days only. I go on, "He has decided to go to America for good. He will have no job and will rely on Pratt-Barlow money for his main financial support." That money was in a trust. At a joint meeting, Roger de Candolle, the Swiss banker in charge of administration, told us that Bobby's purpose had been to prevent Alan from spending the capital. Roger de Candolle had spoken very bluntly, "and made my father blush."

In fact, the Ford Foundation renewed Alan's contract, and he became an alternate book reviewer for the *New York Herald Tribune*, then still an independent newspaper. Doris's real worry was that Alan was living beyond his means. She saw him paying for Midnight Mollie and Tex, for an apartment in Manhattan and his house in Newport; she knew the costs that his social successes were incurring. The diaries he kept from then on consist mostly of names of people and the invitations that he gave or received. He seems to have found his place in a circle of people like the Parisians he had known as a young man, with a taste for the arts and the means to indulgence in whatever they liked. One such was Robert Rushmore, who published two works of fiction that are not much good but have elements of his demonic character. A kind friend, John Richardson, he of the red high-heeled shoes and biographer of Picasso, saw fit to tell me that in the matter of sex Robert was afraid that he was going to split the Pryce from the Jones. Another kind friend was Clarice Rothschild who lived in a very grand Park Avenue apartment. She let drop to me that Alan had complained, "What did I do to David that he dislikes me so much?"

Twenty

Middle East and Middle West

Owls and Satyrs made almost a thousand pounds, enough money for John Guest to invite me to meet colleagues of his and ask what I would like to write next. A book about Israel, I said. Longmans initially offered an advance of one hundred pounds, but the very next morning I received a letter to the effect that they had to consider their Arab markets and when they proposed a hundred pounds they had meant fifty. Taking me on without demur, George Weidenfeld became my publisher of choice. *Qui plume a guerre a*, to have a pen is to have a war, so Voltaire thought, and George Weidenfeld has backed my pen and its wars through thick and thin. Once again, Isaiah Berlin advised me against embarking on something with much to lose and little to gain. Eton, Oxford and the Guards, he surmised, was a combination virtually certain to dispose me against the noisy egalitarianism of Israel.

Poppy had never practised any Jewish ritual, nor taught me anything about Judaism. On Sundays, she would accompany Alan and me to Pembury church next to Kent College for Girls. I had no inkling of a scene that had taken place shortly after the move to London. John Betjeman had rung her up to say that he had seen Alan face-down on the floor of the Catholic cathedral in Westminster in a ceremony of induction. For months he had been taking instruction from the Jesuit Father D'Arcy. Poppy, I was to discover, had given him the choice: either Catholicism or her, not both. Her Jewish identity had been revealed only that once in the tumbledown orchard at the back of Castle Hill, when I had come home bursting to ask questions about Jews wanting world war. Here was a secret of Poppy's heart to explore.

Harry d'Avigdor-Goldsmid had made available the Bothy, a very small cottage in the kitchen garden of Somerhill. Clarissa and I spent occasional weekends there. By way of rent, whoever was in the Bothy had an obligation to add to the party by dining in the big house. Among dozens of familiar guests were Enoch Powell, Cyril Connolly, Sacheverell Sitwell, the virtuoso violinist Jascha Heifitz, Sidney Perelman who wrote scripts for the Marx Brothers, and George Backer publisher of the *New York Post* and a Democratic Party politician. "The trouble with Evie," he said of his pixie-like wife, "is that she's never had an unspoken thought." Gerard Bauer, another star visitor, wrote a column for the *Figaro*, and his friend Madame Naar did not make even a shot at the English language. Handpicking her contemporaries, Sarah gave them the chance to meet the old and the famous.

Harry was parliamentary private secretary to Duncan Sandys, then a cabinet minister. One weekend, Duncan Sandys set about impressing everyone by performing the trick in which the conjuror appears to be sawing someone in half. He made a complete hash of it, not once but twice. I said, that's politicians for you, having made a mistake they make sure to repeat it. Wim and Lia Van Leer overheard me. Even by the standards of Somerhill they were exceptional. Wim's father, Bernard Van Leer, was a successful Dutch industrialist who in 1940 had negotiated his departure to the United States, taking along his private circus in which a hundred Jewish refugees were passed off as circus hands. Wim's adventures included posing as a carpenter to enter the newly built concentration camp of Buchenwald and reporting on it; piloting and crop-dusting; sharing a house for six months in Tel Aviv with Arthur Koestler as Israel was fighting its war of independence; acquiring from his father a factory in Haifa making steel barrels. Playing with words in several European languages, he never learnt Hebrew. To him, any and every orthodox Jew with side-curls was a "Mickey Mouse." Sweltering on a hot and sultry day, he sighed, "Zionism is a winter sport." He emended the words of Tipperary to "It's a long way to Petah Tikvah," a humdrum town in Israel. His documentary film about Israeli experts working on projects in Africa had the title, "Dr Lowenstein, I presume." "Christmas comes but once a year" was his signature tune at Somerhill, "and when it comes it brings Van Leer." Lia kept him in order, just. As a teenager, she had escaped from Moldavia to mandated Palestine. Most of her family had been murdered in the war.

Wim and Lia knew of a flat to rent opposite their house in Panorama Road at the top of Mount Carmel in Haifa. Our eldest daughter Jessica had been born an exact twin of the son of Princess Margaret and Tony Armstrong-Jones. "The Jones baby," was the newspaper headline I read driving home. So I wrote to them that it had been a great day for the hyphenated Joneses, and received a wonderfully stuffy acknowledgement from some equerry. Jessica was four months old in February 1962 when Clarissa and I put her in the back of a Morris Minor and drove off. To help look after her, nineteen-year-old Alice Moorhead came too. On the way through Italy we stopped at San Martino. When we were out of the house, my grandmother saw an opening to advance Unite The Impossible, and summoned Don Fosco, the parish priest, to come round at once. Frank's former room had been preserved as a shrine, and in it, behind our backs, the complaisant Don Fosco and Mitzi improvised some sort of blessing for Jessica.

Israel then was a laboratory in which to observe how Zionism, essentially a nineteenth-century national liberation movement, was transforming Jewish identity. For most

Jews in Europe, Nazi genocide had put an end to the former identity based on religious practice. How to survive now was the question. Was the loyalty demanded by nationhood merely emotional, even tribal? Poppy and her family might think themselves assimilated and secular, but to everybody else they were still primarily Jews. The trial of Adolf Eichmann was under way in Jerusalem. Listening to the evidence of his key role in wiping out Jewish life in Europe, people very often burst into tears. I was in court for the final session when his appeal was rejected. Very soon afterwards the news came through that he had been executed. Outside the courthouse, strangers began talking to each other. In the uncertainty of some and the relief of others, it seemed to me, lay the difference between Jew and Israeli.

The two rooms of the flat were scarcely furnished but had a spectacular view of the bay of Acre and the night-time illuminations of the city and the shore. Three wide balconies provided a Mediterranean touch, and from the one where I sat and worked, I could look down into the barracks next door, more like a cheerfully mixed school than a military installation. A Coldstream drill sergeant would have been horrified by the lack of discipline and the inattention to turnout.

As someone English who had been in Vichy France, I had a curiosity value. Evenings were spent with the Van Leers and their friends; Pinchas Yoeli whose father had been box office manager in Bayreuth and emigrated by himself in 1935 at the age of fifteen to become a professor and cartographer with an international reputation; his wife Agi from Berehovo in Czechoslovakia, an Auschwitz survivor free from self-pity and a ceramicist whose wonderfully imaginative work is exhibited widely; Yaakov Malkin born in Warsaw, a public intellectual, lecturer and at that time director of the Arab-Jewish Cultural Centre at the top of Panorama Road; his wife Felice, an artist, chiefly a portraitist, from Philadelphia. Sometimes

I found myself in the Café Rom amid people speaking their mother tongue of German, and sometimes I sat in cafés on Dizengoff Avenue in Tel Aviv with writers, Amos Elon and his wife Beth, Yoram Kaniuk, Benjamin Tammuz, Herbert and Susie Pundik. For a month or so we were lent a flat on Hayarkon Street, where l could pass Max Brod who had fled from Prague with his friend Kafka's manuscripts in a suitcase, and Marek Hłasko, an early dissident, whose novel *The Eighth Day of the Week* explains why he had fled from Poland.

An old-timer who had held several important posts, David Hacohen had served with the British on sabotage operations in the Middle East during the war and could reminisce about two colleagues of his who had lost their lives, Sir Anthony Palmer and Adrian Bishop, Maurice Bowra's sometime-lover. Expecting me to be as involved in the minutiæ of Israeli politics as he was, he took me to a meeting of the Mapai Party. In the chair, Prime Minister David Ben-Gurion placed me next to him, and out of the side of his mouth kept up a running commentary, most of it derogatory, about the speakers. At one point he gave me a short disquisition to the effect that Germans might appear the worst anti-Semites, but what they'd done under Hitler was an aberration not to be repeated. The worst anti-Semitism was in France, where bigotry was endemic and the French incurable. He insisted that I walk home with him for a cup of tea. I hadn't been with Mrs Ben-Gurion for more than a few minutes before she wanted to know if I was circumcised.

Atallah Mansour, a Christian from Nazareth, was the Galilee correspondent of *Haaretz*, the leading daily paper, and the first Arab to write a novel in Hebrew. His memoir, *Waiting for the Dawn*, makes it plain that he and his family never felt resentful about Israelis but were determined to stand up for Arab rights. That matter-of-fact approach would have questioned the terms on which Jews were to have a state of their own and almost surely have persuaded the Zionist national liberation movement to accommodate the Arabs more easily. Arab culture excluded any such possibility. Rashid Hussein, a Muslim from the village of Musmus in the part of the Galilee known as the Little Triangle, was a close friend of Atallah Mansour's. In the tiny house he shared with his mother, all I saw of her was her bony hand stretching around the door with the food she had cooked for us. His poems are collected in a volume with the title *Sawarik*, rockets. For him, as for other prominent Palestinian writers such as Mahmud Darwish or Ghassan Kanafani, the complete purpose and subject of their work is glorification of their nation, even though it still does not exist as such. In a trajectory that seems symbolic, he joined the Palestine Liberation Organisation in Beirut, worked for it in the United States and died there after accidentally setting fire to his bedroom.

In keeping with the ideology of that moment, the rest of the world mostly approved of the Israeli experiment in self-determination and saw it as the fitting and healthy response to the Holocaust. Europeans shared the country's socialist roots and many of the young from everywhere on the continent volunteered in a spirit of idealism to spend time in a kibbutz, which passed the test because it was a collective. Arab acceptance of what had been essentially a demographic shift would have left Israel as an enlarged Jewish quarter with its distinctive values but still a minority in the end subordinate to the surrounding majority. Historic contempt for Jews, damage to self-esteem and the example of modern totalitarian states instead motivated Arab leaders to politicise and militarise their populations, changing them out of all recognition, prejudicing their future and in the process having the contrary effect of justifying and strengthening Israel.

In Syria and Lebanon I was just in time to catch the last

few effendis who still were wearing a tarboosh and had the gracious manners that had captivated generations of English travellers. Petra was pretty much as Burckhardt had found it over a century earlier. We were alone there, and the only place in which to sleep was the police station. Abandoned, the Wailing Wall in Jerusalem was desolate, even creepy, under Jordanian occupation. Small boys swarmed out of ruined alleys to throw stones at Clarissa and me.

In London, *The Spectator* was looking for a literary editor. An interview with Iain Hamilton and Anthony Hartley, respectively the editor and his deputy, got me the job. The foreign editor was Robert Conquest, whose scrupulous study of Stalin's Great Terror was dismissed as fascist by people I had been at Oxford with. One valued contributor was Evelyn Waugh, whose contributions were in long-hand without a single erasure. A mildly experimental piece by a young writer making his first appearance in print failed to please him, so much so that he wrote to ask me to explain it. I got from Henry Green the last thing he wrote, a paragraph recommending the banning of Nabokov's *Lolita* in order to protect elderly men like him from running into the park and making fools of themselves. Angus Wilson's reviews were ungrammatical and incomplete scrawls in biro. "Do what you like with it, dear boy," he'd say and then put the telephone down. Vidia Naipaul's early books have an astonishingly pure sense of comedy. Hoping to persuade him to write for *The Spectator*, I got to know him and his first wife, Pat, well. We talked about money and markets. On one of our walks in the park, he said that if he had been born into a wealthy family he would never have become a writer.

Hannah Arendt's reportage on the Eichmann trial was published in October 1963, and Iain Hamilton agreed that I should review it. It took a very special type of intellectual to hold that banality was a word applicable to this man's commitment to mass-murder. Cross-questioning had brought out his singular and sinister absence of human feelings. When she blamed Jewish officials for carrying out orders given by Eichmann and his staff, she revealed her inability to imagine the reality of Nazism. She excelled in passing moral judgements about events too frightful to be so simplified, and which in any case she had not lived through herself.

The Spectator's owner, Ian Gilmour, had been in Oliver Van Oss's house at Eton, though he had left before I arrived. A member of Parliament, he was supposed to be an open-minded, progressive Conservative, eventually earning the sobriquet "wet" when he was in Mrs Thatcher's cabinet. His resentment of Jews was obsessive, ignorant and snobbish. I heard him inveighing against the Gaon of Vilna about whom he knew nothing, and he had an obsessive wish to attack the writings of James Parkes, a clergyman with a scholarly interest in Judaism and Israel. Jews, Gilmour believed like any Blackshirt or Islamist, by their nature conspire to do harm to other people, and to Palestinian Arabs in particular. A day was to come when he went bail for two Palestinians who had tried to blow up the Israeli embassy. The strain of talking to me drained the blood from his face, tightening muscular striations and grimaces in his cheeks that became suddenly chalk-white.

Gilmour's wife, Lady Caroline, was Midnight Mollie's youngest daughter and she made a point of gushing over her mother and Alan as though they were a couple of young hotheads who ought to be encouraged to run away together. (She had loved Alan so much, she told me after his death, that she had been unable to write a letter of commiseration.) Likewise, she made no attempt to keep secret her affair with the Labour politician Roy Jenkins. Whenever Alan was in England, he would stay in one or another of the Buccleuch houses as though in an extended family. On one occasion, he and

Mollie drove from Boughton to the cinema in nearby Northampton. Emerging from the film, they found the car park locked. Appealing to a passing policeman to fetch the key, Mollie said, You see, I'm the Duchess of Buccleuch. Before disappearing into the night, the policeman answered, And I'm the fucking King of Romania. Alan also reported breakfast one Sunday morning when Mollie said to her son-in-law Ian, "There's an article in the *Telegraph* written by David about Jerusalem, that'll interest you." "That is something I shall never read," Gilmour replied, then put his newspaper down and stalked out with his breakfast unfinished. It was understandable that on the one and only occasion I was persuaded to go to Boughton, the Duke took care not to speak to me, not even to be in the same room except for meals. Researching in the Public Record Office, I was to find a letter from the Duke to Lord Halifax, then Foreign Secretary, informing him that on behalf of several dukes he would be presenting Hitler with a pair of Sèvres vases on his fiftieth birthday in April 1939. Only Jews could conceivably object, he went on, but they did not count. The permanent undersecretary, Sir Orme Sargent, had minuted tersely that the Duke seemed much too simple to meddle in these matters, and he wished he wouldn't.

Slowly I began to understand that in my upbringing I had enjoyed the advantages of being my father's son, and disadvantages might now outweigh them. I was at the outset of a literary career; he was ending his. Competition and comparison were inevitable. A short story of mine was once printed under his by-line. F. R. Leavis had published his attack on C. P. Snow in *The Spectator*. Given his conviction that Pryce-Jones was the name of a member of a metropolitan clique whose "discovered brilliances burst on us every year," I thought it best to correspond with him under an alias. This introduced farce when this valued contributor set about arranging

a meeting to discuss what he might write next. A knock-
about character, Christopher Logue was one among several
poets who owed their start to Alan. I had met him three or
four times and at some party we were talking when Karl
Miller, a literary editor keen to promote, or more likely demote,
reputations, passed and said loud enough to be overheard,
"Logue and Pryce-Jones, all that's worst in literary London."

Noel Annan, one of Alan's oldest friends, took me on
one side to say, "You do realize, don't you, that your father is
madly jealous of you."

Evelyn Waugh and Alan were not so very different in
their ambitions and aspirations. Editing *Little Innocents*, an
anthology of childhood reminiscences published in 1932,
Alan got a contribution from Waugh. As their lives diverged,
though, Waugh took to referring to Alan as "the man Jones,"
a phrase that hesitates between affection and superiority.
"I used to know your poor dear father," was how he greeted me
at the reception held in the House of Lords after the wedding
of his son Auberon, the name usually shortened to Bron.
(Recovering from the near-fatal accident he had suffered on
military service in Cyprus, Bron spent some time in the
Hospital of St John and St Elizabeth, a short walk from Cavendish Close. Evelyn Waugh had not visited him there. By
chance Alan was in the room when at last he came, and Alan
reported him saying, "It is a soldier's duty to die for his
country.")

Clarissa and I saw a certain amount of Bron and his wife
Teresa. In the *Financial Times* I gave Bron's first novel, *The
Foxglove Saga*, a welcome. Aware that he did not have his
father's natural gift for writing fiction, Bron compensated
by reclaiming for himself as best he could his father's imaginative landscape. From the grave Evelyn directed Bron's
opinions. Without affection, only superiority remained. For
Bron, I was "the boy Jones," regularly fantasized in one or

another of Bron's numerous media outlets as a Welsh-Jewish dwarf with a backlog of unspecified misdemeanours. While he had to earn his living as a hack, independent means allowed me the freedom to write only what I pleased.

Next Generation is a collection of composite sketches of people who seemed to me to represent some aspect of Israel as it was then. Everyone in the country had a story to tell of dispossession and persecution of one sort or another, and another story of recovery. The experiment in nation-building succeeded for the paradoxical reason that Arab and Soviet hostility isolated Israel for the two initial decades of its existence. I had the good fortune to arrive there at a time when these refugees from all over the world were taking advantage of enforced isolation to put in place their very own identity, culture and creativity. Editing *Commentary*, Norman Podhoretz had published an extract of *Next Generation* and Arthur Cohen bought the American rights for Holt, Rinehart & Winston. Reviewing the book for *The Observer*, John Gross saw the point of what I was saying, but in England this was a one-off, so to speak, that set me apart. Terry Kilmartin, that paper's literary editor, did what he could to play my father off against me. Inviting Alan to stand in for Ken Tynan as theatre critic, he ceased asking me to review and let me know there was a political reason for this. Easy-going as he was, he was in the first wave of intellectuals after the Six-Day War to stick the label of fascist onto anyone who failed to condemn Israel. Arthur Crook, succeeding to the editorship of the *Times Literary Supplement*, spoke, dressed and eventually even came to look like Alan. Quite probably thinking that in the absence of Alan, parental responsibility fell to him, Arthur Crook said to me, "Dear boy, you do so many things so well, why don't you give up writing?" With her wits about her, Clarissa then dug out the fact that also rather like Alan he had put away an unfinished novel. (When

I published *Running Away*, he wrote a gracious letter to say that he had enjoyed the novel and Clarissa had been right.) Not long afterwards, Paul Engle invited me to spend a year teaching at the writers' workshop he had founded and was directing at the University of Iowa. Arthur Crook claimed to have recommended me, either to make amends for his put-down or to provide an academic alternative once I'd taken his advice.

Jessica and Candida, our second daughter, were respectively three and one when in August 1964 we caught a Holland America liner to the States. Alice's sister Betty came to help with the girls. In the roughest Atlantic weather the ship pitched and rolled so much that only three passengers were able to stagger to the dining room, Candida, me and an American who said, I sure get a kick out of watching that kid eat. In Newport, Rhode Island, we stayed in a house on John Street that Alan had been persuaded to buy by Nin Ryan, daughter of financier Otto Kahn and a *grande dame* in her own right.

I wondered whether to stay in the United States and settle there. Iowa City had every amenity. The surrounding countryside, especially Lake MacBride and its woods, was attractive. A bygone America could be sensed in farms that sold their unpasteurised milk and fresh eggs. At the same time, the university offered interest and variety: music, a course in photography for Clarissa, the sight of hundreds and perhaps thousands of students swinging golf clubs in unison, not least Professor Bargebuhr whose thesis was that historic Islamic monuments were actually the work of Jewish architects.

In the writers' workshop I learnt more than I taught and in the course of the year I finished *Quondam*, my third novel and a comedy of manners involving the relationship of literature and money, always a vital issue. Paul Engle liked to reminisce about English poets he had known, for instance Edmund Blunden. R. V. Williams, otherwise Bob, was a novelist who spoke about his past more grippingly than he could render it as fiction. The child of a bigamous father, co-opted by an Italian mob, Bob had driven a landing craft in most of the wartime invasions. Living a short walk away, our closest companions were Mark Strand and his first wife Antonia. Throughout the winter we spent our evenings together. His poetry and then his prose poems express a view of the world with a beauty and originality all their own.

A native Iowan novelist at the workshop, Verlin Cassill did what he could to enrol me in his two obsessions, that the Warren Report deliberately obscured the conspiracy behind President Kennedy's assassination, and that only a Jew could be a literary success in America. At a gathering of the English faculty, Cassill approached Renée Hartman, wife of Geoffrey, a foremost authority on Wordsworth, and herself a Holocaust survivor. "Next time we'll get you," Cassill said. The row reverberated round the campus. Cassill's one companion in arms was Richard Yates, author of *Revolutionary Road*, a good writer evidently afraid that his talent was spluttering towards extinction.

To explore the States, Clarissa and I put the girls into the back of our station wagon and drove on and on. Electioneering, Senator Barry Goldwater was staying a couple of floors above us in the Brown Palace Hotel in Denver. I went up unannounced, and he gave me an interview that put paid to a lot of nonsense that Oxford had put into my head. We chased a burglar at two in the morning in Santa Fe and at Taos had lunch with Dorothy Brett, who had come there originally to join D. H. Lawrence's planned collective, and took in the a university football match in New Orleans. We also travelled by train from a halt in Iowa for thirty-six hours to California. "Oh the vice of the English," was the comment of George Cukor the film director, and our host in Los Angeles, when we said that all we wanted to see was Forest Lawn, immortalised by Evelyn Waugh.

In New York on the way back to England I spent a day inquiring into the Black Jews in Harlem, a sect of a few thousand whose belief in their Jewish identity seemed a counterpart to the Black Muslims. John Anstey, editor of the *Telegraph Magazine*, published it. A veteran journalist, he was well known to be difficult, demanding revisions and rewriting even or especially from famous writers unwilling to be edited. George Weidenfeld and his colleague Barley Alison had always accepted what I had written, and so did John Anstey. He communicated by letter, not telephone. Other contributors received two or even three pages of editorial criticism; I received paragraphs of polite thanks. For years I had a contract with him for twelve assignments, or six if I was writing a book and needed the time for it.

Once I wrote a piece in favour of Cardinal Mindszenty, then seeking refuge in the American Embassy in Budapest. Mitzi was furious, she had known the Cardinal since before the war, he had a German name originally and didn't fit her schema of Unite The Impossible. This didn't stop her asking me to travel behind the Iron Curtain on her behalf. She had set up a fund to pay pensions to former employees, nineteen of them, and it fell to me to check whether the Communist authorities were allowing these pensioners to exchange hard currency at a fair rate. In 1966 Clarissa and I first went together to the former Hungarian properties. Carelessly wrecked, Kapuvár and Pokvár were ghost houses, their past irrecoverable. Wherever he lived, Max had planted avenues of chestnut trees but these were now straggly and overgrown, if not uprooted. We took away some conkers as souvenirs. The stabling of the stud at Lesvár was roofless, blackened and burnt out by the Red Army. This was where the Soviet major had shot Trisollin, the Derby winner. To the people in the village inn, my round face and prominent eyes made me recognisable as a Springer descendant. It wasn't much after nine o'clock in the morning when we began toasting each other with firewater of some sort. Don't forget us, the villagers implored, one day you will be back.

(Now forty years later, the town of Kapuvár is much larger and new buildings come close up to Gustav Springer's house. The facades are recognizable, and the wonderful ironwork of the balustrade on the main staircase survives. Otherwise the interior has been converted into municipal offices partitioned with cheap plywood, the rooms containing even cheaper furniture. Nobody has heard of Gustav Springer. Lesvár looks more abandoned than ever. At some point a country hotel, and today the private house of a government minister, the rebuilt Pokvár has the sort of evocative charm of the Turgenev novels Poppy was so fond of. The janitor had never heard of Max, Poppy and Alan and had no idea that he was showing us up the same polished wooden stairs on which they had trod. Partridge shoots are a thing of the past.)

Nagy Istvanne had lived all her life in the same house in the town of Ercsi and remembered the past. She was the widow of Pista, one of the foresters under Rimler Pal and a particular favourite of the family. Conscripted into the army, he had been taken prisoner on the Russian front and returned from captivity having lost his toes from frost-bite. In Communist Hungary he soon died. In Budapest one pensioner produced an album of photographs taken in 1930, and there are snapshots of the sixteen-year-old Poppy and the fourteen-year-old Lily in white linen dresses harvesting in the field with other girls their age. In the background is a fearsome threshing machine, a contraption with driving belts and pistons.

Romanticising Hungary, Mitzi did not have a good word

to say for the Czechs. I never met Countess Otschkoy, a ci-devant aristocratic friend of hers trapped somewhere in Moravia, but she too was on the list for a pension. In Kono-piste, in Slovakia, a former bailiff was one of the few Sudeten Deutsch not expelled from the country. In his house was the life-size portrait of a society lady, probably Mitzi's mother. At Čachtice, a ruined castle where centuries ago Elizabeth Bathory had bathed in the blood of murdered girls, two elderly women were barefoot as they gathered bundles of sticks. Was Mitzi dispossessed for this?

For *The Telegraph*, I specialized in Arab and Israeli subjects. When President Nasser moved troops into Sinai in May 1967, and uttered his menacing "*Ahlan wasahlan*," welcome in Arabic, another Holocaust appeared imminent. The anxiety was global, overwhelming. The Israelis would not sit waiting to submit to extermination, I put it to John Anstey. If you know so much about it, he said, you'd better go out there. On a specially chartered aircraft were men with skills that might be needed, including a team of orthopaedic surgeons. Next to me sat a freelance demolitions expert from Rhodesia, and behind was the actor Topol.

A howling siren broke the country's eerie silence. At the time, there was no way of knowing that the Israeli air force had destroyed the Egyptian air force on the ground, and the war was effectively won. No way of knowing either that the Israeli government had urged King Hussein of Jordan to stay out of the fighting. Shelling West Jerusalem and committing his Arab Legion to war, the king compelled the Israelis to respond, in effect handing them the West Bank and responsibility for the future of its Palestinian inhabitants. This misconceived tactic put in place the Israeli occupation and the cut and thrust it gives rise to. The decisive role of the individual in determining the course of history could hardly be demonstrated more clearly.

In Jerusalem, a colonel drove me out on the Bethlehem road. In the back of the jeep was James Cameron. This most celebrated British war correspondent was holding a bottle of whisky. A few dead Arab Legion soldiers lay where they had fallen. A shell had landed through the roof of the Church of the Holy Nativity in Bethlehem. In the nave, cloudy with smoke and dust, stood an archbishop. By the time I emerged, James Cameron's empty bottle was rolling on the floor and he had passed out. Later in the fog of war somewhere near Nablus, I encountered Martha Gellhorn, instantly recognisable, her hair perfect, and wearing immaculate pressed denims in keeping with a lifetime spent reporting from battlefields. And later still, in the huge refugee camp of Aqabat Jaber thousands of Palestinians were already abandoning their homes, their livestock and in some cases relations too elderly to walk down to the bridge and over to Jordan. They hadn't seen an Israeli, but seemingly the Arab threat to massacre Jews had reversed into fear of being massacred. The panic was collective. All were heading for a worse life but I was unable to persuade a single one of them to stay.

In the small hours I was cabling my copy in the military censors' office in Jerusalem when a white-faced and shaky James Cameron stumbled in. The censor, a studious young lieutenant, did not change expression as he read what was largely make-believe. Passing it, he commented, "Not one of your best pieces, Mr Cameron."

On a calm and beautiful summer afternoon, I drove towards the Syrian front, the obvious next battleground. Kibbutz Gonen was shelled intermittently in the night, and I was pleased to find that I could sleep through it even though not in a shelter. In the morning I passed a grove of eucalyptus trees, and under cover was a battery of heavy artillery. The sight and the sound of the barrage was impressive. The ground shook. Watching spellbound, I could not help thinking that Hélène and Eric Allatini and the boys from the Springer orphanage would not have gone to their deaths if guns like these had been there to defend them. At the foot of the Golan Heights a company of soldiers were praying, swaying as Jews do. In the field the formation on the move looked familiar and I recognised fire and movement, exactly as we had done it at Pickering. At one point, I took shelter in a signals truck. The Major inside had been in the Red Army and was taking down the fire orders spoken in clear and in Russian on the other side. The coordinates gave away the position of the guns, and aircraft then took them out. They were still shelling civilian targets, which could only maximize bad feeling. At the end of the day, I reached the Syrian trenches. A copy of Balzac's *Eugénie Grandet* in Russian lay on the ground. I pocketed it. Appointed for political reasons, the officers had long since fled to Damascus. The men had evidently fought bravely to the end. Wandering by myself in the abandoned town of Quneitra, I came across a brand-new tank with less than ten kilometers on its dial and instructions in Russian. A Paisley scarf was on the seat, and I pocketed that too.

Sinai at all times is a stricken landscape of rock. The Mitla Pass was an enormous junkyard of wrecked Egyptian vehicles. At the Suez Canal I witnessed the Israelis sending the Egyptian army home. An Egyptian doctor was supervising the operation. He entered the name of each man in a large notebook and made him press his thumb on an inkpad and then again next to his name. These were *fellahin*, farm children who had not learnt to write. Fifty at a time, they were conveyed in barges across the canal. On the Egyptian side was a clubhouse protected by high wire fencing. In that arid setting, the watered green grass of this privileged place caught the eye. Half a dozen officers were lounging out there in deckchairs with drinks in their hands, and behind them up against the wire fence were thousands of Egyptian mothers come to search and scream for their sons.

For the Soviet Union, this defeat of their Arab clients was embarrassingly public. Soviet spokesmen and apologists retaliated with a campaign to smear Israel as the aggressor and Arabs as its victims. As a result of this inversion of reality, people who a moment before had been agonizing over the crimes Arabs were about to commit on Jews now agonised over the crimes Jews had no intention of committing on Arabs. The Two Minutes Hate is George Orwell's phrase in *1984* for manipulations of public opinion dependent on politics rather than fact. Staying in the Dan Hotel in Tel Aviv, I happened to witness another guest, the photographer from one of the leading London dailies, taking a young Israeli waiter down to the beach after breakfast and making him kneel on the sand, hands behind his back in the fake posture of an Egyptian prisoner being brutalized. Amos Elon, by now an old friend, told how he had been in a jeep with Avram Joffe, a well-known General. When they came under fire, the General refused to duck and after a bit exclaimed, "Isn't war boring?" Looking to the future, Amos and his wife Beth had already concluded that Israel had to avoid more boredom by handing back the West Bank and Gaza.

Soon returning to London, I was invited to speak to a meeting of Jewish writers. One of them was Harold Pinter, who came up to me in a spirit of wild triumphalism, boasting that the Jews had really shown Arabs what's what. What then changed his mind? On occasions when we met in later years, he couldn't resist coming right up to my face to tell me that Israel was nothing but a pawn of the United States and ought to be dismantled. Triumphalism had reversed into denigration. Who knows how many millions like him did not have the information or the intelligence to realize that they were caught by propaganda, repeating smears that other more artful people wanted them to repeat. A moment was to come when Nadira and Vidia Naipaul were dining with Antonia and Harold Pinter. He asked Nadira if she had made friends since arriving in England. She mentioned my name. Saying that he wouldn't listen to any such thing, he stormed out of the room in a rage, only to pop his head round the door and bark, "Besides, he's a Zionist." Here was another person I could deprive of a meal, and in his own house. (An astonishing life-force, Nadira put an end to Bron Waugh's fantasy about me as an undeserving Welsh-Jewish dwarf. When we met in the Naipaul flat, Bron was embarrassed; he had a way of punctuating his conversation with a laugh more like a cough, with no mirth in it. But he asked me to review a book for his *Literary Review*, and then another, and another, until I was receiving letters from him with the words "gratitude" and "admiration" underlined.)

Granny Wooster summoned me to Paris for a debriefing. We had a couple of sessions in her flat in the Rue de Surène. Unite The Impossible, her doctrine, accorded very well with the wishful view that there was nothing much to choose between the United States and the Soviet Union, superpowers in the process of becoming alike. The doorbell suddenly rang, and Paulette showed in two priests. Mitzi listened to their pitch and wrote them a cheque for a thousand pounds. Bowing low, they backed out like the courtiers they were, whereupon I said that if she was giving money away, the Israeli Air Force could do with it. Her face went black with anger. She shook. Was I telling her how to spend her money? She became almost hoarse. Jewish nerves were driving her rage, as they drove Pinter's, and now drive innumerable Jews and Israelis to seek the integration and acceptance that escapes them, in extreme cases subscribing to Arab and Muslim nationalism directed against themselves.

The contrasted lives of Palestinians under Israeli and under

Arab rule was a worthwhile subject for a book, I thought, and I spent much of the next few years researching in the field what was published as *The Face of Defeat*. My friend from Nazareth, Atallah Mansour, was an indispensible help, introducing me to everyone who was anyone in the West Bank. Another helper was Israel Stockman, who had grown up among Palestinians and spoke Arabic as they did. His special study was the village of Sinjil, a name which he said was a corruption of Saint John. Surely a high-level intelligence agent, he made it his business to intercede with Israeli authorities on behalf of Palestinians. Armed only with a walking stick, he was welcomed everywhere and took me along with him.

The Israelis I knew had no wish to be ruling Palestinians. Unilateral withdrawal from the West Bank and Gaza, however, would signify that Arabs pay no penalty for going to war and so might as well do it again and again in the hope of winning one day. Sure enough, Yasser Arafat, the new leader of the Palestine Liberation Organisation, was sending small numbers of guerrillas, *fedayin* in Arabic, on night operations against Israel. General Uzi Narkiss was prepared to take me over the area along the river Jordan where skirmishing occurred, and I intended then to go on to Amman. Well before dawn on the day we had arranged, I got a telephone call that everything had been called off. All the same, I went down to the Allenby Bridge, where I could hear gunfire at Karameh on the other side. The crossing was closed. One other would-be traveller to Amman arrived, an American in a Brooks Brothers suit and buttoned-down shirt. He produced a laissez-passer signed by President Johnson. When the astonished Jordanian officer let him through – and me with him – this man for the first time revealed that he spoke fluent Arabic. By way of thanks, I invited this probable spy to dinner but he never turned up.

For the first time Palestinians on their own had engaged Israelis in battle, however small the scale. Yasser Arafat, still an unknown quantity, took the credit. On a hillside with olive trees somewhere near Irbid, I heard him address some of his men. Standard mass-produced radicals of that era, other Westerners present were repeating to one another the maxim of Chairman Mao that power came from the barrel of a gun. Put another way, bullies with bouffant hair and designer flak jackets were inciting young Palestinians to march towards gunfire and death in battle, while they themselves were safe in some television studio or the offices of *The Guardian* or *Le Monde*, consciously or unconsciously misrepresenting reality to suit the Soviet political line. I was in Amman in the Black September showdown of 1970 when King Hussein's soldiers shot some 5,000 Palestinians. Women from Baqaa, a sprawling refugee camp outside Amman, set off shouting that they were going to Mousa Dayan, as they arabised his name. Some hundreds of *fedayeen* sought refuge in Israel. In pre-civil war Beirut I interviewed several leading Palestinians, among them Ghassan Kanafani whose writings are variations on the theme of hopelessness.

Again correspondent in the 1973 war, I was back on the Golan Heights when the Iraqi armoured division came into action. The tank commanders put into practice exactly what the Frunze Academy had taught them, their positioning and maneuvering were so predictable that ninety minutes later the tanks were burning hulks. At one point, I came across an Israeli tank whose track had hit a rock and needed repair. The officer was the man lying on his back under the tank at work with the spanners, while the crew stood around smoking. A citizens' army like that tends to win its wars.

I decided to take a day off in the American Colony Hotel in Jerusalem, and there I found that Nick Tomalin reporting for *The Sunday Times* had had the same idea. "You have made the editor laugh," he once commented on a piece I had written when he was editing a glossy magazine. At lunch, he said we would learn more about the war in the capital than by standing in the front line ducking at the sound of explosions. The very next day, he drove with colleagues to the Golan. They got out of the car in a display of the bravado that he thought so little of. Because he remained in his seat, Nick was killed by a Syrian heat-seeking missile.

By sheer luck, I was at the right spot on the Suez Canal when Israeli engineers arrived out of the desert and in a matter of minutes threw across a pontoon bridge. The tanks rumbled over, and leaning out of the turret of one of them was Ariel Sharon. He was not wearing a helmet, and in my memory the combination of his blond hair and a white shirt gave him the look of a man enjoying himself at a sporting occasion.

Walking along the Nile, I had a conversation with a man who was fishing, in which I asked what he thought of Nasser. By way of an answer, the man flicked out his hand, palm down in the habitual gesture of contempt. It's understood, I think, that Nasser had done great harm to his country when he might have done good. It appeared impossible to admit this disaster, indeed parties of schoolchildren are taken round the military museum in Cairo that presents as victory a war that finished with Israeli tanks closing on Cairo. In their culture, the dread of shame is so strong that it enforces denial of reality. Mistakes are inadmissible, and repetition therefore takes the place of correction.

In the 1970s and 1980s I travelled pretty regularly in Arab countries. Whenever Yasser Arafat and the Palestinians were in the news, Marty Peretz of *The New Republic* was liable to ask me for an article about it. Arafat and those around him were practised politicians and the puzzle was that they persisted in taking decisions certain to degrade further those they claimed to be representing. An editor in New York, a stranger, a lady, wrote to point out that I was in the habit of saying in different ways the same thing about the Arabs, namely that they had the kind of society that kept renewing their troubles without ever resolving them. This repetitive process of self-harming keeps Arabs and Muslims from doing justice to themselves. In the Middle East I'd encountered fighting, power plays, leadership, decisions, movements of opinion, that were truly irrational but there had to be a logic to it. After some correspondence, this editor commissioned *The Closed Circle*.

One obstacle to research was the prejudice and ignorance of the British authorities. A first experience of it was discouraging. A hush-hush interview in Athens with Colonel Grivas of EOKA fame led me to believe that this grizzled but theatrical old man was sincere when he talked of invading Cyprus again. I flew to Nicosia to test this out with Archbishop Makarios. This most suave of heads of state was well informed and soon he was explaining how he blocked Communism by sending the children of the rich to Soviet universities and the children of the poor to American universities. I thought I ought to report Grivas's imminent invasion to the British High Commissioner. Caustically this grey eminence opened the conversation with the rebuke that after ten minutes in Cyprus every passing journalist thought he had the key to the troubles. I apologised for wasting his time and left at once. The day my piece appeared in the *Telegraph* Grivas's men did invade, shot down Makarios's helicopter and killed the pilot. For years afterwards, in Greek eyes I was the secret service agent responsible for all this.

Commissioned to write a profile of Mu'ammer Gaddhafi after he had seized power, I was actually in the Libyan Embassy when the Foreign Office rang through with the advice not to give me a visa. The cave paintings of the Tassili plateau in the Sahara close to the Algerian-Libyan border are one of the world's wonders, and in 1983 I arranged with Franz Trost, a desert explorer, to go there. Candida was my travelling companion. Counting duplicates for us both, I had to obtain thirty-six permissions from Algerian ministries. We began in Algiers. My father-in-law Harold, by then retired from the Foreign Office and in a new position as Provost of Eton, provided us with a letter of introduction to the British ambassador. We were invited to dinner in the embassy. Over the first course, the ambassador said that he had previously been stationed in Beirut, where he and his wife had been friends and great admirers of Yasser Arafat. During the Israeli campaign in Lebanon the previous year, he wanted us to know, they had stood on the embassy roof shaking their fists at Israeli aircraft overhead and screaming that they were Nazis. That comparison is the touchstone of prejudice. Abandoning half-full plates, Candida and I asked for a taxi and left. Harold, I can say in his favour, never reproached us.

The silence of the Sahara is pure. We had an Algerian guide (who offered to buy Candida for the right number of camels) but otherwise were alone on the plateau. The night sky is an entertainment of shooting stars. A year later I returned, this time with Jessica. Franz escorted us down the Algerian-Moroccan border to Tamanrasset. On a day in December when it was a freakish fifty degrees in the shade, we were searching for the battlefield where in the fifteenth century a Moroccan army performed the military feat of crossing the desert to surprise and conquer the Songhai Emperor. There were no other vehicles within the hundred or so miles all the way to Gao on the river Niger, when a police car suddenly appeared and gave Franz a parking ticket costing much the same as one in London.

Published in 1989, *The Closed Circle* coincided with the end of the Cold War. Freed from the embrace of the rival super-powers, Arabs and Muslims had the chance to make of this independence whatever they could. Nasser, the Baathists in Syria and Iraq, Haj Amin al-Husseini the Mufti of Jerusalem, their successors and rivals and mimics, had ideological borrowings from Communism or Nazism, sometimes putting in place an amalgam of both. In practice, these turned out to be more pretexts for killing more people. Conducive to authoritarianism, the centuries-old Arab state structure easily absorbed modern features like one-party rule and just as easily stifled civil rights, equality for women and whatever else might induce change.

My sense at the time was that the general public in the Muslim Middle East had expectations of a better future, one with justice instead of enforced obedience to a ruler without mercy. *The Closed Circle* posits that this must happen one day. Saddam Hussein's invasion of Kuwait, Ayatollah Ruhallah Khomeini's seizure of power, the assassination of Anwar Sadat, the whole grisly chain of bloody causes and even bloodier effects means that this time of justice is postponed until reason overcomes superannuated religious and social codes, that is to say indefinitely. Communists tried to destroy Jews; the Nazis then had their turn at it; and now that Arabs and Iranians are operating more or less freely they put themselves next in line for genocide, intent on killing off the Jewish movement of national liberation. The subject of *The Closed Circle* and quite a lot of my writing is what makes people believe the extraordinary, irrational things they do believe and then act upon.

Twenty-One

Influence?

AFTER THE SIX-DAY WAR, John Anstey extended my experience of Communism by commissioning me to write about the Balkans. Admirers in the Foreign Office and the media of Josip Tito and Nicolae Ceauşescu turned a blind eye to the secret police, the only structure that mattered in these dictatorships. At Tulcea on the Danube Delta, a speedboat roared past as the Securitate escorted Chinese officials in their Mao uniforms to see men condemned for years to cut reeds in water up to their waist. A pastor in Sighişoara preached that Communism had been sent to scourge the congregation for their sins. In Zagreb, Vlado Gotovac pointed out the secret police on duty in the street below his apartment; arrested, he received twenty years for nationalism. Entering a Belgrade bookshop, the poet Miodrag Pavlević and I backed out immediately at the sight of Alexander Ranković, the head of the secret police whom Tito had recently demoted.

The name and address of Milovan Djilas was in the Belgrade telephone book. I took a chance, rang him and was invited to his house. Many former Communists like him had broken with the Party, but familiarity with Tito and Stalin gave him special authority. His face, drawn and white as clay, testified to the thirteen years he had just finished serving in prison. The Soviet Union and China, he said, were in the process of dividing the world between them. Small countries like his, and like mine for that matter, would be obliged to take one side or the other unless the United States was a third party. To create this balance and to preserve freedom, he went on, it was imperative that the United States wins the Vietnam war. If you have any influence, he urged me, use it to that end.

At the time, a loophole enabled visiting academics to receive their salaries tax-free on either side of the Atlantic. Bob Williams from the Iowa Writers' Workshop was now teaching at the California State University at Hayward, and he arranged for me to spend a semester there. Staying with Bob and his wife Hatch in 1968, I wrote most of another novel, *Running Away*. A new friend, the novelist Herb Gold, introduced me to nearby San Francisco, his hometown, and through him, I think, I met Mark Schorer, the distinguished critic and a moving spirit on the English faculty at Berkeley. He invited me to give a talk in the university about my encounter with Djilas. The very idea of American victory in Vietnam was quite enough to upset that audience, and its endorsement by Djilas of all people was unanswerable. By the end of that evening, the Schorers were almost alone to be still speaking to me.

That summer there were battles on Telegraph Avenue between the police and blacks and hippies who may or may not have been students. Tear gas was in the air, curfews were imposed and some two hundred demonstrators were arrested. I interviewed a surly Eldridge Cleaver, at that time a rabble-rouser preaching the downfall of the United States. The house was a fortress, its windows blocked, guns were to be seen indoors, and there were men making it plain they were ready to use them. Djilas hadn't foreseen anything like this.

While I was in California, Clarissa and the two girls had spent some time at Deauville as Elie's guests. When I rejoined them at Royaumont and heard that he had tried to go to bed with Clarissa, I insisted on paying for their hotel rooms. He refused to tell me the exact sum, so one morning I walked from the château over to the Faisanderie and shoved a bundle of notes into his hand. This may bear on what happened next. Alan telephoned to say that his house at Newport had been foreclosed and put up for sale. He had a mortgage with Amsterdam Overseas Corporation and by some oversight had not kept up with payments. He was asking for five thousand dollars from the Pratt-Barlow capital. In her boudoir on the top floor, Mitzi was against complying on the grounds that it would only play into his extravagance. If he knew his debts would be paid this way, he'd run up more of them. It turned out that Alan had received the money for the mortgage from Elie. Amsterdam Overseas was an arm of the Rothschilds. Alan, said Elie, hadn't been bothered to respond to requests or letters. They wouldn't sell the house over his head but they would like to hear from him if only for the sake of politeness. Back in London not so many weeks later, I got another telephone call from Alan to say that he didn't need Pratt-Barlow money after all, he wasn't about to jump off a bridge, he was going to marry.

Adrian's crisis was simultaneous. Outwardly his career as film director and then theatrical agent had been successful. Well turned out, usually in a double-breasted, blue pinstripe suit and his hair combed perfectly, he looked as if he was a welcome habitué of the expensive restaurants where he liked to invite us. When he took his nieces Jessica and Candida to an ice rink he could still give an exhibition of figure skating. He dropped the names of Peter Ustinov, Mel Ferrer, Ava Gardner, John Huston and Laurence Olivier. One of his turns was to imitate Marlene Dietrich whom he'd seen in her dressing room, lifting her face by hoicking wrinkled skin up to her ears. We used to think it bad luck that his flat was broken into so often and burglars beat him up so badly. The police had rescued him almost senseless on a train at the end of the line in Southampton and after that he opened his heart. The burglars were rough trade. Terry, a chirpy go-getting Cockney, lived with him in Albany. A few hand-written pages survive in which Adrian gave himself up to some introspection: "I dread the thought of being a queer old bachelor of 70 – even 60." Every so often, he would begin drinking. A small quantity of alcohol was already too much. The bender would last not more than a few days and then I'd get a message to visit him in a clinic, usually the Priory at Roehampton. Dr Conachy, a tough specialist treating alcoholics, kept him on the wagon for quite long spells. When Adrian didn't respond, we'd go round to his flat and let ourselves in. A day will come, Dr Conachy warned, when we'll find him dead. Once, perhaps twice, Adrian went to Newport to recover from a bout. But in *The Bonus of Laughter* Alan from faraway puts the rhetorical question, "What can a brother do?"

Adrian died in a smart hotel in St Moritz, the scene of his skating triumphs. He was only forty-eight. The room had been left untouched but his watch and cufflinks had already gone missing. He was found on the floor, with the telephone upset beside him. He must have realized that the mixture of alcohol and pills was fatal, tried to dial for help, and fallen. I had to identify him in the morgue, his face so twisted with fear and horror that he was almost unrecognizable. It turned out that in his will he had left portraits of his parents, Alan and himself to Terry. These pictures, Terry said, meant everything to him. To recover them, Alan paid five hundred pounds.

Soon I flew to New York for Alan's wedding. Mary Jean Kempner came from Galveston, Texas. She was fifty-seven, six years younger than Alan, svelte, holding herself very well. A journalist and former member of the Office of Strategic Services, she had reported from China during the last war. The marriage was celebrated in January 1969 in her apartment in Beekman Place, one of New York's most exclusive addresses. Standing next to me at the back of the drawing room was Evie Backer, a regular guest at Somerhill. I made some injudicious remark to her, and Evie bolstered her reputation for never having an unspoken thought, saying above a whisper, "Alan, we don't think you ought to get married." If they heard, the bride and bridegroom paid no attention. At the lunch, Brendan Gill of *The New Yorker* gave the witty and affectionate speech that I should have given.

"Have you got a wicked stepmother?" the five-year-old and wide-eyed Candida asked. Unlike Poppy at the time of her marriage, Mary Jean was a woman of the world able to judge for herself what kind of a husband Alan would prove and whether or not she had been married for her money. With unquestioning generosity, she settled the Amsterdam Overseas mortgage and put down a capital sum to pay off Tex Barker. After ten months of marriage, she took Alan to the house she rented in Portugal. There, one morning, she woke up with bruises on her body. The local doctor diagnosed aplastic anaemia, a form of cancer for which no suitable treatment was available in the country. Alan found himself once more with a mortally ill wife in the American Hospital in Paris. Within a matter of days, she was dead. Adding to the sense that he had been through this before, Alan had to give a home to Daniel Thorne, Mary Jean's son by a previous marriage, now at the same age that I had been when my mother died. On a morning with a wintry sun, I sat next to Alan on a low wall outside a church in Paris waiting for the service for Mary Jean to begin. He spoke as usual about this and that while I marvelled at his self-control.

"I ought to be grateful for so much," his diary entry for New Year's Day 1970 opens. "But I feel rather dazed; missing Mary Jean; missing, as I have every day these sixteen years, Rese [shortened from Thérèse]; wanting my parents back, rather as one wants nanny, as a reassurance rather than a pleasure." Stock-taking of the kind had become rare; the diaries of his years in America are really a social register. At the end of June, he flew over for family engagements. Jessica and Candida were to be bridesmaids at the wedding of my cousin Elisabeth de Rothschild at Royaumont. Sonia, our third daughter, had been born that April and she was to be christened at the church in Chantilly the following day. The first weekend in July, he spent with the Buccleuchs at Boughton. "Mollie in a needling mood: repeating that *everyone* had loathed Mary Jean and been distressed by my marriage (not true, of course), that I was volatile to the point of folly and so on. I realised that she had to get this out of her system. . . . Walter was charming: I have 'my' room, with the blue four-poster and the view."

On a tour of the house and its treasures next day, Mollie spoke bitterly again. "Poor defenceless Mary Jean, in the grave. I tried to explain; but brought on a kind of suppressed hysteria. Then all came out well. Just before I left, Mollie took me into the morning room and said that she had prayed and prayed that something would remain of what had been: a love, however disembodied. . . . 'You seem to love people in need,' she said. 'And you cannot imagine how great my need is.' . . . She is impossible; and yet I only do love people in need, I suppose."

Twenty-Two

Sonia

Sonia was two months old when I was invited to teach at Berkeley for a summer semester, and we set off five strong for California. Bob Treuhaft and his wife Jessica Mitford lived in Oakland, and we had exchanged houses with them. Entering the living-room, we could not fail to see their Communist Party cards prominently left on the table. However, we had the use of their brand new Mercedes-Benz while in London they had to make do with our proletarian Morris. On my first appearance in the English faculty office, someone introduced himself as my Vietnam instructor. The class would want to discuss the war, he said, I did not have the requisite knowledge so he would take over. There would be no discussion, I said, because I would send to the South-East Asia faculty anyone sidetracking the class in this way. You won't get away with that, my instructor came back at me, and sure enough, I soon heard that there was a new British fascist on campus. In the beautiful early morning light, I would walk to the classroom past splendid buildings and lawns kept fresh with water sprinklers, enter and invariably come down to earth with a bump at the sight of the boarded-up window with its huge capitalised slogan in black paint, "Go fuck yourself, teacher pig."

One day, Allen Ginsberg and a crowd said to be three thousand strong sat on the grass chanting for hours *Om mani padme hum*, and on another day Ronald Reagan, then governor of the state, had a very different crowd of three thousand faculty members laughing in spite of themselves at his sense of humour.

Everywhere we went, Sonia came too, for instance to the redwoods and Yosemite. Nothing indicated what was to come, and nothing explains it. Back at my desk in London, I would leave open the door to the adjoining room with her cot in it. Whispering, flirting, she would have me spending time with her instead of working. Before she was two, she knew her alphabet fairly well. In the summer of 1972, I had an assignment from John Anstey to drive a big BMW on back roads from Montreuil to Italy. Sonia did not become sunburnt like the others, we noticed, but since she was so fair we thought little of it. Back home in Wales, Clarissa's mother thought Sonia was pale and ought to have a blood test. The Builth doctor very soon telephoned: Sonia had leukaemia and we were to take her to St Bartholomew's hospital in London immediately. We could see our three daughters running in the meadow with ice creams in their hands. Clarissa rang Olivia Stewart-Smith, a cousin who lived nearby, and she came to fetch the two eldest girls. We drove off in two cars, and at a parting of the road waved goodbye. Our London doctor, John Creightmore, was waiting on the doorstep. I telephoned Agi's brother Gabi Izak, a well-known blood specialist in Jerusalem, and whose almost miraculous avoidance of arrest and murder at the hands of Nazis in Hungary had made him fight to save life ever since. But there was nothing to be done. Spending not even a full twenty-four hours in hospital, Sonia died towards midnight. She was two and a half. In the following days Harry d'Avigdor-Goldsmid called unexpectedly at the house. Words didn't come easily to him. His daughter and my childhood friend Sarah had drowned, and it has stayed with me as evidence of a great soul that he was equating our grief with his.

We were at Pentwyn in a snowy February when our son Adam, then four and the last born in the family, suddenly folded up. In spite of the hazard of driving in bad conditions up our steep hill, Dr Davies came from Builth to the house. On his advice, we had to flee once more as fast as possible to London, this time to the children's hospital in Great Ormonde Street. Adam had meningitis. For several days he lay unconscious. On what by a fortunate coincidence was my birthday, he suddenly sat up and said he would like a boiled egg.

Shirley's Guild is the novel in which I sought to come to terms with the death of a child. The doctors have no idea why Sonia succumbed to leukaemia, or why it was fulminating, as they label the form of it that put an end to her life so quickly. We have no clue whether we as parents did something wrong, or on the contrary did not do something we ought to have done. The subject of that novel, then, is destiny.

Twenty-Three

A Burnt-Out Fairground

JESSICA MITFORD, Decca to one and all, had a library of thousands of books, and Clarissa discovered some in which Unity Mitford had written her name and a few marginal comments in a childish hand. Her passionate support for Hitler had been a phenomenon of the Thirties; that much was common knowledge. An essay about her, I thought, might shed light on the irrational mentality of fanaticism. When I mentioned the idea to Decca, she handed me the nine letters from Unity that she had preserved. Unity had been the fifth child of her parents, Lord and Lady Redesdale, and Decca the sixth. I understood that Decca couldn't sort out in her own mind the closeness she felt for her sister and abhorrence for Unity's Nazism.

Many of her age and background had known Unity in England or in Germany. One of them was Mary Wooddisse, originally from Nottingham, who had been with Unity when Hitler first invited her to his table in the Munich restaurant of his choice. Her husband, Klaus Humbach, had been an S. S. doctor holding the rank of Colonel. Captured by the Soviets, he had been reprieved from a death sentence and was among the very last convicted war criminals eventually sent back to Germany. With Dostoevskyian intensity, he wanted me to relieve his conscience. At the outbreak of war, Unity had put a bullet into her brain. Her friend Janos Almásy had taken charge of her papers and in due course he returned them to the Mitford sisters who deposited them in Chatsworth. A Nazi who flew a swastika flag above his castle, he had denounced his conservative sister Mädi to the

Gestapo. What the Mitfords could not have known is that for purposes of revenge, Mädi had had time to appropriate one of Unity's diaries and copy others. Mädi's son, a priest, had inherited these papers and stored them in the attics of the Sacré Cœur in Vienna, the school which once Clarissa had attended. He gave me what he found in a trunk. The projected essay could now enlarge into a book.

Former Nazis remembered Unity. Hitler's military adjutant, Colonel Nicholas von Below, used to find pretexts for entering the room whenever Unity and Hitler were alone, and he could assure me that Hitler had never done more than stroke her hair. Frau Ilse Hess, the wife of Rudolf Hess, and Henriette Hoffmann, the wife of Baldur von Schirach, both confirmed from personal experience that, whatever Unity may have wanted, the relationship with Hitler was platonic. The basis of their mutual attraction was that both loved causes more than they loved people.

A courtier who had fallen out of favour with Hitler, Putzi Hanfstaengl was sure she had denounced him. Enacting the past, he insisted on playing the Liebestod from *Tristan* on the same piano that he had played for Hitler. Rudi Simolin, eighteen at the time and not a Nazi, accompanied Unity inspecting the apartment in Munich Hitler was to give her. In front of the Jewish owners about to be forcibly dispossessed, Unity discussed colour schemes and curtains. Albert Speer was his usual equivocal self. At the end of his prison sentence, he settled in a house in Heidelberg. We sat in a room where the light of day hardly penetrated. My friend Roman Halter, a survivor of the Lodz ghetto, Auschwitz and a death march, had confronted him not long before with the evidence of war crimes. Speer for once admitted responsibility. This shadow of a human being had exact recall of everything to do with Hitler and was evidently still enthralled by him. The sister of Joseph Goebbels had known Unity well, but she was the one and only German who refused to be interviewed out of loyalty to the past. James Lees-Milne, the prolific diarist and in his youth a Mosleyite, was alone in taking the same line in England.

In the haul from the Sacré Cœur was the diary Unity had written in 1933 recording the affair that her elder sister Diana was having at the time with Sir Oswald Mosley of the British Union of Fascists. In a sense, Unity was trying to go one better than Diana. She knew Hitler and Goebbels but could only exclaim that they were "wonderful." When I met Lady Mosley, I had the very different sense that she felt responsible for the fact that she was alive and Unity long since dead by her own hand. I had been born too late to understand Hitler and Goebbels, Lady Mosley thought, but I would live long enough to see statues to them put up in the capitals of Europe.

The Mosleys orchestrated a campaign to stop the biography I was writing. They put pressure on everyone they could think of to withhold their testimony, and then to say I had misrepresented them. The sixth and youngest Mitford sister, the Duchess of Devonshire, surely had forgotten that once she had put me through after-dinner paper games in Lismore. I wrote to inform her about the projected book. Her response was, "Too many people are still alive who might be upset by it." It was open to her to express love for Unity and abhorrence for her politics. Under cover of family solidarity, both these sisters instead chose to apologise for Nazism. In a letter to Alan, the Duchess gave the order "Call your boy off," as though summoning to heel a disobedient dog, and followed up with a similar imperative to Liliane.

(Another of my controversies enveloped her when *The New York Times* commissioned me to investigate the last days of the Duchess of Windsor. Valuable possessions of hers were turning up for sale; nobody knew why or what happened to the large sums of money obtained. The only person in a position to take advantage of the dying Duchess was her lawyer and executor, Maître Suzanne Blum. Liliane invited her and me to lunch and after publication of my article Blum accused her in a series of hostile letters of being my accomplice. Poor Aunty Lily!)

The Duke of Devonshire meanwhile was transmitting messages that I should on no account pay attention to what his wife was saying. At Chatsworth, I was told, argument at dinner became so heated that the Duke had to send the servants out of the room. Unaware of how I knew what I knew, Lady Mosley and the Duchess accused me of twice breaking into the house, the first time to burgle Unity's papers, and the second time to replace them.

After a good deal of research, the thought suddenly hit me that Unity might have been a British agent, in which case she had succeeded in a most successful penetration of the enemy and my account would one day fall apart. Victor Rothschild introduced me to Sir Dick White, former head of MI6. Before the war, he had been stationed in Munich. The secret service archive will never be in the public domain but he was prepared to check it out for me. Unity, he said, would have been a useful liaison between Mosley and Hitler, but since she had no access to British official sources, she was not taken seriously. It was well understood that Hitler was feeding disinformation through her. Today, he concluded wryly, she would have been used without her knowledge to feed disinformation back to him, but the service did not then have the technique for that. Her fanaticism was thought eccentric enough to bring Nazism into disrepute, and so she was left to do her worst.

At the last minute, Mosley tried to bring an injunction. We had sent him an early proof copy, he had three small harmless complaints that were accommodated but reserved his right to take other legal measures. The judge wouldn't have it. When Mosley's lawyers then said that they could not be responsible for the consequences, my lawyer advised me to fetch the girls from school and to ensure that nobody could tamper with the brakes of my car. Here was the authentic whiff of fascism. Invited to confront Mosley on television, I conscripted John Caute to rehearse with me all possible questions and answers that might arise. I was sure that Mosley as usual would deny that he had ever been anti-Semitic so I jotted relevant quotes on index cards, and had them arranged in my pockets. He duly lied and I read out a selection of these cards. "Did you really say that?" Melvyn Bragg the anchorman asked, and Mosley's snarl of an answer, "I suppose so," was a clincher. When finally Mosley left for home, the driver of the taxi took one look and said, "He's not getting into my bleeding cab," and accelerated away.

My book became a nine-day-wonder, I can only suppose, because it brought out into the open collaboration with Hitler and the outlines of a British Vichy regime in the event of a successful Nazi invasion. The British flatter themselves that they had united to defeat a totalitarian enemy, and this was Our Finest Hour. Here I was pointing a finger at people whose beliefs and activities undermined this cosy national myth. I was to hear that I was "a traitor to my class," a charge which concedes that England really did have its Quislings and Vichyites in waiting. Intending to analyse the social significance of my book, Bernard Levin, then the leading columnist on *The Times*, interviewed me over a period of several days. However many drafts he wrote, he finally told me, he couldn't make sense of the storm, and gave up on the idea. It was left to Rebecca West to say what had to be said. She had known Meidling before the war and could remember seeing me there when I was a few days old. She had also studied the subject of treason. In a review she likened the moral atmosphere of my book to that of a burnt-out fairground.

The obvious defender I could call on was Isaiah Berlin. A director of Covent Garden, he quite often invited me to the royal box. Amusingly, we discussed his blind spot about Puccini. I had been his guest in February 1974 when Alexander Solzhenitsyn was expelled from the Soviet Union. A professor published an op-ed piece in *The Times* with the thesis that this was nothing new but a reprise of the historic debate in Russia between Westerners and Slavophiles. Isaiah had read the piece and immediately agreed that this was nonsense. Communism is quite another issue. Nineteenth century Russian political thought was Isaiah's special subject, I said, he should write a response. The professor has his credentials, he demurred – I couldn't get him past this cop-out. A guest once more in the royal box at the height of the Mitford clamour, I suggested that he intervene. You and your book have been shamefully treated, he said as we were taking our seats. Give the word, he went on, and I'll lean out of this box to appeal on your behalf to all the good people down there. Which was his way of saying that he wouldn't lift a finger. On Boxing Day 1976, he signed off with a postcard, "you can well afford to be (not very) bloody and entirely unbowed."

(Coinciding with Isaiah's eightieth birthday in 1989, *The Times* published an article by Roger Scruton to the effect that Isaiah had every quality required to further the cause of freedom, and his reluctance to do so was a flaw in his character. Alas, some kind friend overheard me saying that I tended to agree with Scruton, and denounced me. Isaiah immediately telephoned and wrote to me at full pitch. My reported defence of Scruton's "absolutely odious piece" upset him. He likened Scruton to the Black Hundreds reactionaries in Czarist Russia and to Goebbels, and further to Menachem Begin and Yitzhak Shamir, "horror figures in my life." Among those commiserating, he made sure to let me know, were Lord Carrington, Arthur Schlesinger and Noel Annan.

"Things are what they are, and so are people, and one must get used, particularly at my age, to them." We met regularly but he remained wary. When *The War That Never Was* came out, he said, "Noel Malcolm has reviewed your book, he says you have written a good book, and if Noel Malcolm says so, then you have written a good book. I shall not be reading it.")

Decca thrived on close combat and I had expected that she'd find some reason for turning against me. At her request, I quoted in the epilogue her summing-up of Unity. The epilogue, she wrote to me, "somehow lifts the whole book to a new (and far more desirable) plane." Sure enough, she took umbrage that I had depicted her Communism and Unity's Nazism as two sides of the same coin. Once the book was in the shops, she published some critical comments about it and soon she was no longer in touch. In the literary pages of *The Spectator* which once I had edited, Anthony Lambton dismissed me as "a little white knight in armour, the champion of the Jewish nation," and added an incoherent attack on George Weidenfeld for publishing the book – this from a man with no moral base at all, forced out of public life by his involvement with drugs and prostitutes.

John Gross, now editor of the *Times Literary Supplement*, was a close friend who kept me in touch with news and views of who was in and who was out. He had given my book for review to Alastair Forbes, a writer whose long-winded style was a form of boasting that he had every inside story at his fingertips. His review was nothing but an ad hominem attack and John decided to reject it. Giving it the title "The Piece the Jews Rejected," Forbes made a hundred photocopies and drove round London putting them into letterboxes, including mine. After some revisions had been made to this review, I found myself attacked in the pages that Alan had once edited.

Saul Bellow once suggested that my childhood spell in Vichy France had brought me close-up to the Jewish experience. *Paris in the Third Reich* certainly touched on my background. Tom Wallace, editorial director at Holt, Rinehart & Winston, came to the house with a portfolio of photographs taken by Roger Schall during the German occupation. I was to write the text. Here were the stories and personalities mentioned in everyday conversation at Royaumont. Wartime conduct was as contentious as ever. Passed over in silence for the most part, surviving French fascists and collaborators led a conspiratorial existence in the shadows. Those who apologised were mostly insincere. One of them, Henri Coston, evidently thought he had been right to persecute Freemasons and Jews, and was still doing what he could within the law to carry on where he'd left off. Jean Leguay was the Vichy bureaucrat – the French Eichmann in fact – who had organised the deportation of Jews. He came to London specially and no doubt sincerely to tell me that he'd not done anything wrong. I got to know Ernst Jünger, whose account of occupied Paris is a *tour de force*, at the same time brilliant and inhuman. Arno Breker, the sculptor and doyen of Nazi art, had accompanied Hitler round Paris in June 1940, and the new work in his studio showed that he had learnt and forgotten nothing, Bourbon-style.

At that time, the German occupation was a taboo subject as far as the general public in France was concerned. Pierre Belfond, a go-ahead publisher, had paid quite a bit for the French rights to my book and expected to make a splash. The first translation was so bad that it had to be scrapped and another commissioned. Four weeks before I was to appear with Bernard Pivot on *Cinq colonnes à la une*, the leading literary programme on television, Belfond rang up. Someone at the top of government had objected to my book, his identity could not be revealed, there was no legal recourse, publication now might well lead to the enforced closure of his firm and he wasn't going to risk that. Belfond lost his investment and I was banned yet again. (Lloyd Ultan used the passage I had written about the children's fantasy of Auschwitz as Pitchipoi and set it to music. The cantata was performed in Minneapolis-St Paul with Pinchas Zuckerman as lead soloist. Furthermore, Neil Tennant said that my book had inspired one of the songs of his group, the Pet Shop Boys.)

Fritz Molden, the Austrian publisher and a man larger than life, used to say that the happiest and most carefree time of his life had been as a Wehrmacht soldier in wartime Paris. In fact, he took the immense risk of informing Allen Dulles and American intelligence. Fritz and his brother ran a festival in their Alpine village of Alpbach. I was to read a paper about literature and freedom, a subject about which everything has been said. Marcel Reich-Ranicki, the leading German critic, then followed on by mimicking me in a falsetto voice. Sitting next to me, Zbigniew Herbert, the Polish poet, leant forward and said to Reich-Ranicki in coarse German, "Shut your trap and sit down." In mid-sentence Reich-Ranicki stopped and was back on his chair. I asked Zbigniew to explain the source of his power. In Communist Poland, the censor who had forbidden publication of Zbigniew's poems on class grounds was Reich-Ranicki. A refugee in Germany, Reich-Ranicki had kept this secret, but Zbigniew could ruin him by revealing it.

Up to that point, I had thought of myself primarily as a novelist but now political convictions began to matter more to me. It has been my good fortune to have free-thinking friends. Vidia Naipaul for instance held that every writer should have a public row such as the one I had over Unity

Mitford. Paul Johnson, Frederic Raphael, Noel Malcolm, Tony Daniels and a few others have talents that keep alive the cultural tradition of the country at a time when it seems at a standstill. The wars in the Middle East had revealed Soviet brutality and cynicism, and the invasion of Czechoslovakia in 1968 was another illustration of it. A few courageous Czechs and British sympathizers, with the exceptionally clear-minded Roger Scruton in the lead, launched an underground university to keep alive freedom of speech. On a first visit to Prague I spoke to a small circle of dissidents, and one of them, Michael Žantovský, showed me round the city. Neither of us could have imagined that he would one day be Czech ambassador in Jerusalem and then London. It was already 1989 when I went again, this time to Bratislava. Ján Čarnogurský, a lawyer, had arranged for me to talk about the Middle East to perhaps a dozen of his friends. In the hotel I received a message that the meeting was cancelled. The caller had left the name John, which seemed to me proof of authenticity. Wrong. The secret police had tricked me and now ordered me to catch the first bus out to Vienna: another ban. They arrested Čarnogurský and put him on trial. He served a few weeks, until, thanks to the Velvet Revolution, he was released from prison to become deputy prime minister.

That same year, 1989, I was invited to go with a British delegation to an international conference in Budapest. I accepted partly because Amos Elon, the Pundiks, and Yoram Kaniuk on the Israeli delegation were long-time friends. László Rajk and other prominent Communists executed after the 1956 revolution had just been rehabilitated in the sinister process devised by the Communist Party to apologize for victims of its injustices, up to and including those framed for murder. The Soviet Union was disintegrating. The British delegates at this conference were herd animals, separate in body, that is to say, but instinctively identical in opinion. In a room full of people who had lived through the Soviet or the Nazi experience, and probably both, one of these representative British intellectuals declared that the Soviets may have had Stalin but we have Mrs Thatcher. These Israelis did not have the luxury of posturing like that, and were all the better morally and intellectually for it. The gesture of joining their delegation was a small one, but it gave me a sense of belonging.

I contributed to *Encounter* at the tail-end of its great days as a monthly magazine when its editor Melvin Lasky asked me to write about Elie Kedourie's essays. I admired the intelligence, humanity and unexpected humour that lay behind his austere manner. When he told me that al-Ghazzali was the purest of poets, I learnt Arabic to see if he was right. I also wrote about the week of high jinks I'd spent with Arthur Koestler in Iceland when both of us were reporting on the Spassky-Fischer chess match. Like John Gross, Lasky used to ring up to discuss the latest outrage; it might be the appointment of an unsuitable Leftist, another anti-American outburst by Harold Pinter or Stalinist whitewash from Eric Hobsbawm. Norman Podhoretz and his successor Neal Kozodoy encouraged me to contribute to *Commentary*.

Glasnost and perestroika, I was convinced, were too good to be true. Choosing his moment, Mikhail Gorbachev would surely act as every previous General Secretary of the Soviet Communist Party would have, and order a crackdown. The overthrow of Nazism, the comparable totalitarian system, had required a world war. Unless or until there was another world war the Soviet Union was free to do as it pleased. A few thousand protesters shot dead in the main square of Kiev or Tallinn, let's say, would have shown the danger of trifling with the system. A possible variation was to declare military rule in East Germany, close the frontiers and if need be, stoke the crisis by declaring a nuclear alert. Measures of the kind might have extended Communism and the Soviet bloc indefinitely into the future.

Published in 1995, *The War That Never Was* sought to explain why none of this happened. The former keepers of the Party's ideological flame and those who had replaced them made it clear that violence had only just been contained. Romantics took the view that Gorbachev was a noble character who would not stoop to bloodshed. Cynics preferred to think that he had deceived himself, the victim of an illusion that Marxism-Leninism really held the key to Utopia and he was advancing to it. In either case, history turned once again on the decisions of an individual and not on impersonal forces. Several who had had leading roles in the Gorbachev era requested payment for their interviews. We haggled. When I asked to meet Gorbachev, a member of his staff seemed surprised that I would not pay a fee of twenty-five thousand dollars. Alexander Yakovlev, the advisor who more than anyone justified the rupture with Communism, asked for merely one thousand dollars and accepted one hundred.

In the United States the book was published as *The Strange Death of the Soviet Union*. On the strength of it, Hilton Kramer and Roger Kimball gave me the chance to contribute to *The New Criterion*, the magazine they have edited in order to achieve what Desmond MacCarthy held was the real purpose of all criticism in the arts, namely to build a coral reef against the incoming tide of rubbish. I wasn't to know that all the time I had an attentive reader. When Jay Nordlinger became managing editor of *National Review* in 1999, I began to receive regular invitations to contribute to the magazine. Jay was as welcoming as once John Anstey had been. No editors in England are so congenial, no platform so open to me. I was just in time to become acquainted with Bill Buckley, a man of great gifts and great charm who lived long enough to see this magazine of his celebrate fifty years of publication, a feat almost unheard of in the world of highbrow monthlies. *National Review* has made an American writer of me. Whether I am chasing my father in this respect, fulfilling his literary aspirations or showing them up is something I cannot decide.

Twenty-Four

Grand Guignol

Newport suited Alan. His house on John Street was in the old and attractive part of the town. The porch, clapboarded walls and miniature garden had an air of simplicity. In contrast, he had crammed this bijou residence with furniture, pictures, bits and pieces that he had shipped from England. A few feet to one side stood another period house that he turned into a library. And a few feet to the other side was yet another house in the same style, bought in the first place as a home for Mary Jean's son Dan.

Here Alan's social gifts were at full stretch. In the summer season it was exhilarating but exhausting to stay with him and to drive along Bellevue Avenue for lunches, dinners and cocktail parties in one or another of the great stone mansions that testify to better, richer, times. Alan seemed to know all the families who gathered at Bailey's Beach, an exclusive club with cabins along the sandy shore and a pool in which to swim lengths. Food and gossip were of the highest standards. The *dolce far niente* atmosphere evaporated once when Alan had to write and mail a theatre review. The deadline came and went. I couldn't lock him into his room as Poppy had done. That evening we went to a black tie dance. Around midnight I made him drive me home on the assumption that he would be bound to sit down at his typewriter. Before I feel asleep I heard him driving back to the dance. At breakfast next morning, he hammered out the review in about twenty minutes.

Many who lived in Newport had nothing to do with the

Social Register, never set foot in Bailey's Beach and kept themselves to themselves. Alan was one of the few who managed to overlap two very different sets. Clarissa had accompanied her mother to buy clothes from Hardy Amies, but I met him only when he came to the house with something to confide. One weekend, he had been the guest of Oatsie Charles, a formidable and idiosyncratic lady whose opinion mattered very greatly in Newport. "Oatsie was away but she'd given me the run of her house," as Hardy told it, "and Alan had recommended a gay bar in the town." When he was there, someone came up and asked him to dance. This was Larry Hudson. "Larry liked the older man," Hardy went on regretfully. "Our affair lasted the weekend. Squalid, really, the sort of thing you straights don't know about."

Larry was in his late twenties when Hardy introduced him to Alan. Originally he came from Boston, and his sister and her husband, a master sergeant in the air force, still lived there. Quite tall, trim, he was handsome but his face was expressionless, the gaze hard, his smile an unsmiling brief grimace. His movements were careful, slow, as if something might be wrong. Education after schooling had been out of the question. Literature, classical music, the Newport festival, the arts that had been Alan's lifelong pursuit, were of no interest to him. He sat for hours by himself soaking up television soaps. In an equally solitary pursuit, he spent afternoons going out in one of the kayaks that Alan had been persuaded to buy for him. Ambition began and ended in the search for the older man who could keep him in style and provide a credit card.

To all and sundry, Alan spoke of Larry as his chauffeur, and Larry indeed did drive their expensive Buick. The outward and visible signal that Larry was not a chauffeur was an enamel ring, turquoise in colour. Alan wore this present from Larry on the fourth finger of his left hand between

Poppy's thin gold wedding ring and Mary Jean's thick gold wedding ring. You couldn't fail to goggle at it. Alan had a way of looking at Larry with devotion, but in his eyes was an element of fear. I thought I could detect in Larry a fury that he could neither repress nor express. Staying with Alan, Stephen Spender, a kindred spirit, had come to the same conclusion. Acting on impulse, I asked him if Larry might murder Alan. Yes, Stephen answered after a lengthy pause, he very well might.

The ill-assorted couple arranged to spend their time together in Newport or in Alan's tiny apartment in New York, with trips and river cruises in Europe. What they appeared to have most in common was lunching and dining out in the full range of restaurants and hotels from Dunkin' Donuts to the Ritz. Alan introduced Larry to friends and acquaintances including Midnight Mollie. At Christmas, Larry took Alan to Boston, and described deadpan how Alan regaled his sister and her master sergeant husband with anecdotes about Harold Nicolson at Sissinghurst and Osbert Sitwell at Montegufoni.

One winter, Alan invited Clarissa and me to Barbados. From our hotel room we could look across a loggia to the room whose door Alan and Larry left open so they could be seen in bed together. Working regularly as a tour manager, Clarissa was due to take a group to China. I was going as well and for an eightieth birthday present we invited Alan to travel with us. When he refused, I gave a celebratory dinner for him at the Black Pearl restaurant in Newport. The only woman present among a dozen of Larry's older men, Oatsie was sitting next to me when suddenly she growled, "What the hell are we doing here?" I used to stay in the house bought for Dan. The kitchen was not really used, and Alan's will was left lying openly on the sideboard just as once Mr Howden's psychoanalysis had been left for me to read.

This was his way of communicating that I had been disinherited in favour of Larry.

My diary has accounts of Larry's reaction to my arrival in John Street from London. "Moments later, Larry comes down the stairs, goes out of the door, bangs it to and is gone. No goodbyes. Alan is surprised too. Apparently he's driven off to Florida. This gives Alan some chance to discuss Larry's character. He presents him as moody, no friends, truly content to watch *Top Gun* but also complain of the absence of social life, bored, harassing Alan on the subject." Alan's housekeeper, Mrs Busche, had emigrated after the war from Germany. In staccato English she would reminisce about happy times long ago on parade in her tidy Deutsche Mädchen uniform. She had witnessed Larry building a bonfire in the little yard between the houses, and burning two books I'd written and given to Alan, *Paris in the Third Reich* and *The War That Never Was*. From her and her daughter-in-law Mimi I learnt that Larry was HIV-positive. The doctor had prescribed sixteen pills daily but he had become so unstable that he swallowed them down with vodka.

As he aged, Alan developed diabetes so extreme that he had to take a blood-sugar reading every mealtime. In pain, he began to need nursing. My diary notes a trans-Atlantic call from the head of the nursing agency. "She says that her nurses no longer have access daily to Alan. Larry won't let them in. He is determined to have control. If he were to double the dose of insulin, he could kill Alan and nobody would know ... the nurses hear verbal abuse – 'Get out of bed, you lazy sonofabitch' – and Alan has bruises on or about his face. So she is wondering whether to inform the social services, hesitating only because of Larry's volatility." Alan, she concluded, was showing "the battered wife syndrome."

A distressed Alan discussed coming to live with us in

London. That would have meant abandoning Larry, which ultimately he could not bring himself to do. Larry's immune system had failed – Alan was never able to utter the word AIDS. Confiding, and so to speak making his peace, Larry allowed me to have my one and only glimpse into the real person he buried so carefully within himself. Alone in New York over a period of three weeks, he had been tempted, he told me in detail, he had gone absolutely wild in gay clubs, and was paying the price for it.

At the end of January 1998, Charles Weishar, a friendly and concerned neighbour on the opposite side of the street, rang me. Larry had been ill for about a fortnight, so weak that he could hardly raise his arms. Mimi had brought him some soup but he claimed it was slops and threw it down the sink. Alan seemingly was in bed, waiting for Larry and his insulin injection. Noticing that no lights were on, Charles came over and let himself in with the key he had. Alan was incoherent, almost hallucinating as he verged on the edge of a diabetic coma. Charles arranged for him to be rushed into intensive care in Newport General Hospital. Next morning, Alan's house was again in darkness. Larry had been sleeping in the adjoining house, and Mimi found him dead on the threshold of the ground floor bedroom there. He was wearing nothing but a sweater. Larry's doctor was to say that AIDS ravaged him but the cause of death was hepatitis and a respiratory infection. In the doctor's opinion, "Larry cared for your dad, but no doubt your dad now has better chances of good management care." I couldn't help wondering whether in final despair Larry had kept back Alan's insulin in order to set up a *Grand Guignol* scene when both of them would be discovered dead.

The best part of a day had passed by the time Clarissa and I had flown in and reached the hospital. Alan lay in the fœtal position. My diary entry reads, "Alan cried as we entered, a sort of sobbing without tears. 'These are very miserable times,' he said and hoped that he would die. He had expected Larry to die, and so wasn't surprised in the least. Larry had changed so greatly. Lately he had taken to shouting at him, 'I wish you'd die.' Then five minutes later he became his usual charming self.... I told Alan that it was horrible for him that the three people he'd loved, Poppy, Mary Jean and Larry, had all died young. 'It's no use repining,' a very characteristic word. In another mood he says of Larry, 'There was no emotional attachment but I miss him as a companion. I was with him so constantly.'" Alan's lawyers were to discover the coincidence that Tex Barker had died a few weeks before Larry. The man Tex had been living with had concealed the death in order to continue claiming the $950 Alan had been paying every month.

Thanks to Dan, Alan escaped the East Coast winter as a guest in the Kempner family house in Galveston. Then Dan rang us in London to say that Alan had gone out to dinner in spite of a cold, and returned with pneumonia. It seemed random, disconnected from everything to do with Alan, to find him in the University of Texas Medical Branch. He smiled when we came into his room. Clarissa said that we had talked to the doctors, and he still had the strength to ask, "What are they saying?" And after a pause: "What happens next?" Those were his last words. Eleven days into the new millennium Alan died.

Sloth, he always claimed, was the reason why he had not become the great writer he expected to be. Not in the least slothful, he was tirelessly energetic, always busy. He had real powers of observation, facility, and an individual aptitude for the right word. These gifts were fatally compromised by the fear of giving offense, and this was to be seen in his manner, heard in his voice, and read into his prose.

On his deathbed with nobody to please, his face had set in firm and noble lines. He never passed an opinion on my writing, and so I have no idea whether he took pride in it, as some maintain, or felt challenged, as others tell me. We buried him next to Poppy in the cemetery at Viarmes, a forbidding provincial place for someone so cosmopolitan, but that is what he said he wanted, and it too closes a circle.

Twenty-Five

332 · *The Last Throw*

Mitzi had arranged the three foundation stones of fiscal freedom: British nationality, Italian domicile and Swiss bank accounts. The rhythm of her life was safe and did not vary. You could predict almost to the exact day when she would be at San Martino, Royaumont and Montreuil, and the Connaught Hotel in London. Supervising, Mr Hickman, Georg the son of Dr Pokorny, Giuseppe Badini her administrator in Florence, Paulette and Robert and a dozen more retainers were permanently at action stations. Fuss was exceptional. A Romanian employed in the office turned out to work for the KGB. Somewhere on the journey by sleeper from Florence to Paris her fur coat vanished. She'd had printed a sketch Alan had written of Frank in a few hundred carefully guarded words; he'd promised to do the same for Eugène and for her, but shirked it.

The world in the 1970s nevertheless disobediently refused to fit her directives. After her death, she comforted herself, the heritage of Frank and Mary Wooster would be acknowledged. Time and energy were spent sorting out into carefully inscribed envelopes additional materials for Lambeth Palace, Tantur and Canterbury. "Unite The Impossible" would come into its own. Sure that she was touching on immortality, she looked for a response, for evidence of understanding and submission. No dialogue was possible. It was like being in a courtroom with a judge whose verdict has been reached in advance, and a defendant silent for fear of self-incrimination.

A good deal of her time was spent arranging for her

properties to be perpetual museums to the passage through this world of Frank and Mary Wooster. Reluctantly breaking the century-old link to her father, she had at last made the shares in the factory over to her heirs. Technical and financial skills of a high order were required to manage Maisons-Alfort, and no one in the family had the capability or the wish to do so. Given his career, Elie was the person to negotiate its sale. Mitzi and Max were joint owners of Royaumont. Once the family could no longer count on the factory, it was clear that only the Rothschild branch could afford to live in the château. Mitzi and Max were joint owners. With estate duty in mind, Elie persuaded her to pass her half-share over to his son Natty. From every point of view, this made sense. In return, she made Natty, then in his early thirties, promise that her bedroom on the top floor would be preserved and that he'd never sell the place. Under French law, the Rothschilds were obliged to compensate the other heirs for this gift. How many times did I hear my grandmother telling me that Royaumont had become a white elephant and to receive cash for the share that came to me through Poppy was the better part. "*Toi, tu ne seras pas sur la paille,*" was how she put it, You won't have to sleep on straw.

The Proppers had been due to inherit San Martino. Bubbles and Eduardo had retired to London. For no discernable reason, Mitzi cut them out of her life. Bubbles would send flowers to greet her mother at the Connaught, drop affectionate notes and leave telephone messages, but Mitzi would have nothing to do with her. She forbade me to be present at her arrivals or departures, but burst into tears when I nevertheless turned up. Just in case the worst happened, she travelled with a shroud. Acting as her lady's maid, Doris mistook it for a nightdress and laid it out on the bed.

Montreuil was supposed to come to me. Clarissa and I

had spent holidays in the so-called dream house that had attracted Eugène and Frank. Jessica and Candida and Sonia had swam and played on Paris-Plage at Le Touquet as I once had. Now this house was set to become the Museum of Hope, Le Musée de l'Espoir, the very name suggestive of illusion. The twenty volumes of Proust's correspondence edited by Philip Kolb is the sole putative exhibit that I can identify. She made the house over to the town, and at a reception in the presence of Max and Lily she handed a grateful Mayor a cheque for millions of francs, thirty five million according to Paulette who was also present.

In her late eighties, Mitzi had a heart attack in Paris and was rushed unconscious to the Salpetrière hospital. The fitted pacemaker disturbed her. She complained that she had been robbed of her death. She'd lived in the Rue de Surène for over half a century but never bought the freehold of her apartment. When the landlords began rebuilding, she moved into the Ritz. Almost the last time I was with her, she had become paranoid. Enemies were poisoning her. They had served her with ham prepared to kill her, and she made me flush it down the lavatory.

A matter of days after her death in December 1978, Mr Bill, the librarian at Lambeth Palace, telephoned to arrange a meeting. In an ancient courtyard of that extraordinary building, he helped me load into my car the photocopied volumes of her diary that had been consigned to his library. The material was unsuitable. Shamefaced, he apologised for Bishop Stopford who should never have put us all into this position. A canon from Peterborough Cathedral returned microfiches. The Ecumenical Centre at Tantur could not locate its set, presumed missing. They had had to throw out innumerable folders of press cuttings that ostensibly documented the progress of Unite The Impossible because Mitzi and the servants with scissors had not thought to note their sources and therefore they could not serve for quotation or reference. Formerly incumbent at St George's in Paris but now retired in Biarritz, Father John Livingstone writes that he has appropriated in his house half the volumes deposited in that church, and proposes to destroy them. A disc that he sent me reveals his pre-occupation over the years with Montreuil. He mentions a surreptitious visit to the house, presumably to check out if there was anything in it for the church. Like us, he will have seen encroaching decay, broken shutters, a collapsing door into a yard overgrown with weeds, water stains on crumbling facades. Philip, Elly and I took the municipality to court for failing to spend Mitzi's endowment as intended on the upkeep of the museum. The case was heard in Boulogne. The verdict was that we were right in principle but not in practice. The lawyer who had drawn up Mitzi's deed of gift had omitted to specify that the endowment must be spent on maintaining the museum and its fabric. The mayor was entitled to spend the money on whatever he chose.

The deed of gift for San Martino had not been signed. After all the jostling, the various churchmen and their lawyers came to the conclusion that Mitzi was not giving them enough money to run the place, and they threw in their hand. This tragi-comic sequence of events is the basis of my novel *Inheritance*. One sunny afternoon we sat outside at San Martino with the intention of agreeing to a sale, only to decide to make a go of keeping on a house with so much character. It is better that we and our children and grandchildren own the house rather than church folk, I hear from the locals, "*tutti lo dicono*," everyone says so.

The beautiful leather boxes of "Supernatural Realities As Experienced By Frank And Mary Wooster" contained envelopes and small packages, with accompanying pieces of paper, usually type-written, telling a tale about Frank's Donatello look or some token of the love she had sought so desperately. Nobody consciously throws out these odds and ends but somehow, in the mysterious return to reality, the boxes seem to become empty of their own accord. Don Fosco's campo is so overgrown with weeds that it is hard to locate. At Montesoni, the door of the marble safe had a keyhole, and whoever vandalised and smashed it all up no doubt thought there was something inside to loot. The nearby church is a centre for the rehabilitation of young drug addicts. Nobody has any information how it happened, but Mitzi and Frank's car immured underneath the crypt proved to be a rusty old Fiat. The rising market in vintage Armstrong Siddeleys must be the explanation.

Instead of a will, Mitzi had left a letter of intent, which opens with the sentence, "*Je, soussignée, divise mes biens en quatre*," – I the undersigned divide my goods into four. A day came when all her descendants and their spouses gathered in the Faisanderie. This was Elie's moment. Each of us received a dossier complete with lawyers' pink tape. On the basis put forward in this dossier, he then said, there was no legal obligation on him to compensate Mitzi's other branches. It speaks to the power of Elie's personality that nobody present had a comment. At a silent and humiliating lunch, a jeroboam of Château Lafite from a vintage in the 1920s stood on the table, as much as to state, Swallow that.

Bubbles reminded Elie of conversations in which he had assured her that compensation would be paid. "*Tu rêves, ma pauvre fille*," My poor girl, you're dreaming – the condescension of this answer stuck in her throat. The lawyer whom Bubbles and I consulted was confident that Elie would have to pay us for our share. Gradually his energy faded, however, he answered letters slowly and then not at all, he wouldn't accept telephone calls, he didn't ask to be paid either. We understood that we would have to make our case ourselves. In the Ritz in London of all places, Philip and Elly and I had a confrontation with Elie. You are accusing me of being a crook, said Elie and he got up to leave. If you leave, Philip replied, you are admitting you are a crook. Elie sat down.

The knowledge that Elie had taken advantage of us affected me like an illness. I remembered a pun that he'd referred to himself, one depending on the double meaning of the verb voler, to fly or to steal. "*Quelle est la différence entre un canard et un banquier? Le canard vole de temps en temps.*" What's the difference between a duck and a banker? A duck flies / steals from time to time" (implying that a banker is stealing all the time). At an appointment with him in the Rothschild bank in Paris. I reminded him that Granny Wooster's letter of intent was a moral commitment to fairness and equity. He listened quietly and said, "*Je sais au fin fond de moi-même que tu as raison,*" I know in my innermost self that you are right. We agreed to do a sum. Liliane wished to sell us her share of San Martino, and taking that and other legitimate expenses concerning upkeep at Royaumont into account, he made out that we owed him money. Do the sums again, I said, and the upshot of it was that he paid Bubbles and me twenty five thousand pounds each.

The moment that I knew that he knew he had behaved as he should never have done, I pitied him. Poor fish, he'd have to live with himself. That was already difficult enough, since he had a mistress and an illegitimate daughter. The relationship between these two and Lily and his other children preoccupied him to the end of his life.

Probably he had spotted an opportunity to acquire Royaumont cost-free, and couldn't resist the temptation. Some deeper and darker impulse may have been governing him. Having possession of the château, he never spent a single night in it, nor did Liliane or any of their children. For over thirty years the house remained shut and abandoned just as it was, the contents all in place, mouldering, spoiling, draining the affection that had been put into it and the pleasure it had given. Was this a function of his marriage? You don't love me enough, he might have been trying to tell Liliane, you married me for my money, well, it has the power either to make or to destroy your family, and I've made the choice for you. For a single day in May 1996, the house was opened for a black-tie party celebrating Liliane's eightieth birthday. Jessica and Candida came but Adam had more urgent things to do. In a speech to the guests, Elie said that Liliane had been the love of his life, whereupon he choked. Towards the end of their lives, they invited themselves to dinner in our house. Almost at once Elie began to quarrel with her at the top of his voice over the question whether we would eat in our kitchen or dining-room. In a move that served to symbolise their relationship, she went and sat by herself with the result that they chose to eat their meal separately. I never saw him again.

For several years after both of them were dead and buried in the cemetery at Baillon, a scrubby little village a couple of miles away, Royaumont stayed a sort of shuttered tomb, a Sleeping Beauty taken out of time. A massive catalogue from Christie's arrived in the post. There was to be a three-day sale of the entire contents of the house. Attending the auction in Paris, I was taken aback by how dingy the pictures and furniture looked now that they were out of context. The Thomire table had lost its splendour, the Bosio statue of Cupid was kitsch. These possessions had come Natty's way unbidden and he had no use for them. Long settled in New York, he was making a clean sweep. True to his promise to Granny Wooster, he was not selling the château but emptying it and all the outbuildings prior to converting and then leasing them to a company that manages conference centres. Granny's room is being restored and will eventually be used by guests.

Scaffolding was up on the house the last time we were

there. The past is over and done with. The fault lines have
played out. We went on the usual little pilgrimage past the
lakes to the Gros Chêne. Here Max had scattered Eugène's
ashes, and Elie had scattered Max's ashes. One day the weight
of the immense branches overhead will bring down this historic and magnificent tree.

ACKNOWLEDGEMENTS

I am grateful to my cousins Elly and Philip (more formally   341
Elena Bonham Carter and Felipe Propper de Callejon) for
their willingness to share memories and to encourage without reserve. Dr Lore Mayer's researches into the Springers
in Vienna and E. V. Jones's researches into the Pryce-Joneses
in Newtown, Montgomery, have been invaluable. My father's
papers are in the Beineke Library, Yale University, and every
member of the staff whom I met was truly helpful. Another
debt of gratitude goes to the Huntington Library for allowing
me to quote letters from or about my father catalogued in its
archive, "Patrick Balfour, Kinross Papers, Huntington Library,
San Marino, CA." It has been my great good fortune that
Roger Kimball had confidence in this book from its inception
and carried Rebecca Hecht and the exemplary team at Criterion
Books with him. Beyond and above everyone else, my thanks
are to Clarissa, fellow-traveller for so much of the way.

A Note on the Type

Fault Lines has been set in Kingfisher, a family of types designed by Jeremy Tankard. Frustrated by the paucity of truly well-drawn fonts for book work, Tankard set out to create a series of types that would be suitable for a wide range of text settings. Informed by a number of elegant historical precedents – the highly regarded Doves type, Monotype Barbou, and Ehrhardt among them – yet beholden to no one type in particular, Kingfisher attains a balance of formality, detail, and color that is sometimes lacking in types derived or hybridized from historical forms. The italic, designed intentionally as a complement to the roman, has much in common with earlier explorations in sloped romans like the Perpetua and Joanna italics, yet moderates the awkward elements that mar types like Van Krimpen's Romulus italic. The resulting types, modern, crisp, and handsome, are ideal for the composition of text matter at a variety of sizes, and comfortable for extended reading.

SERIES DESIGN BY CARL W. SCARBROUGH